W9-BZE-941

THE RISE AND GROWTH OF ENGLISH HYMNODY

The Rise and Growth of English Hymnody

By

HARVEY B. MARKS, M.A.

FOREWORD BY

JAMES DEW. PERRY, D.D., LL.D.

Presiding Bishop of the Protestant Episcopal Church, U.S.A.

INTRODUCTION BY

H. AUGUSTINE SMITH, MUS. DOC.

Professor of Church Music and Hymnology in Boston University

NEW YORK

Fleming H. Revell Company

LONDON AND EDINBURGH

REVISED SECOND EDITION

New York: 158 Fifth Avenue
London: 21 Paternoster Square

To

My Alma Mater,

The Western Theological Seminary,

Pittsburgh, Pennsylvania,

and to

The Church Army,

an organization of Lay Evangelists in the Anglican Church in England and America

FOREWORD

AS THE worship of the Church is found in the Book of Common Prayer, so the Hymnal is the Book of Common Praise. The scope of Christian hymnody is known to but a few. (Consequently the choice of hymns for use in public worship is governed by prejudice and sentimental considerations, seldom inspired by educated taste) (The result is that the musical portions of our services fail to express the reverent and intelligent devotion of which our people are capable.) In songs of praise, as well as the spoken word, it is possible to fulfil the commandment, "Thou shall love the Lord . . . with all thy mind."

This volume proceeds from the author's life-long study of hymnology and from practical experience as a parish Priest. It should find its way into libraries of the clergy and of parishes, as a book of reference and of instruction. It will unfold to many congregations the background of our classic hymns: it will uphold standards in the ordering of worship: more particularly it will help to draw many, whose part in church services has been that of silent listeners, into a sympathetic and responsive interest in the language of praise.

James DeWolf Perry,

Presiding Bishop of the
Protestant Episcopal Church, U. S. A.

Providence,
Rhode Island.

INTRODUCTION

IN LOCAL church and church school, in denominational agenda, in books and current publications, in research and committee findings, obvious stress is being placed upon worship, its history and evolution, its nature and acts, and its materials. Out of this revival of worship has sprung a renewed interest in church architecture and the cruciform temple as the home of the Living God. Still another renaissance is following in the wake of the first two, namely choirs; the one, two, three, four and five choir plan and its adoption by all Protestant denominations. It would seem as though vital congregational singing of hymns should follow, but such is not the case. The trend of the aforementioned arts may be away from the assembly and its collective worship and song. Possibly the mystical and solemn nature of worship, the awesome architectural surroundings, the charm and intrigue of quasi-professional singing, may lull a congregation into silence, solemnize into inactivity, degrade to an inferiority singing complex.

Persevering and enlightened pioneering is needed to-day as never before in the leadership and interpretation of hymns. The place to begin is with the hymns themselves, their historical and biographic content, current events as coloured by them, changes in vocabulary, metaphor and pace, more nearly to adapt them to the life of to-day. New hymns are rapidly impinging on worship experience and one must be made ready for them.

Rev. Harvey B. Marks has achieved a most timely book, admirable for fireside reading, rich in values for the pulpit, balanced and accurate for the class-room. Every page has a certain livingness, growing out of the author's preaching and pastoral duties, out of travel and wide acquaintanceship, out of a genuine love for music and poetry, out of a persistent charm in winning folks to the church and to religion.

These pages, first of all, are balanced; the ancient, mediæval, near-modern, and present day lyrics each receiving simple and forceful treatment without undue emphasis anywhere. Again and again practical hymnody and liturgics come to the fore in timely suggestions to clergy and choir on what to do with hymns.

Nineteenth and twentieth century hymns arrest our attention in this book, with their changing verbal expression, their social emphases, their youth pronouncements, their exhilarating translations from ancient sources.

Nowhere has Rev. Mr. Marks lost sight of the fact that, in the last analysis, a hymn book is to *sing from,* by all, through every experience of life, individual and collective, and such a book must therefore be genuine, idealistic, practical, and forward looking.

His intriguing instructions found throughout the book are timely and delightful.

H. AUGUSTINE SMITH.

Boston University.

PREFACE

THE author was led, contrary to his intention, by various friends to write this book at this time. Among these friends, I mention first, three who being dead yet speak, who encouraged such endeavour: Bishop Charles L. Slattery of Boston, Dr. David R. Breed of Pittsburgh, and Bishop J. H. Darlington of Harrisburg, Pennsylvania. Among other friends, President J. A. Kelso of the Western Theological Seminary, Pittsburgh, Miss Mary M. Pillsbury of the General Theological Library, Boston, Rev. Dr. Alfred Poole Grint of Providence, and other friends in different parishes who showed much interest in my frequent talks on famous hymns and their authors.

But most of all I am deeply indebted to Dr. Charles N. Boyd* of the Pittsburgh Musical Institute, who caused me finally to make the decision to write, and to Professor H. Augustine Smith of Boston University, whose sympathetic interest in my decision led me to enter enthusiastically upon the task. To these two scholars and teachers, Professor Smith and Doctor Boyd, I am further indebted for their able assistance, many suggestions, criticisms, reading of manuscripts, various corrections. Without their help this book could not have been produced in its present form. I am grateful for the opportunity of research work at Boston University.

To Carl F. Price I extend thanks for editorial advice on the preparation of the manuscript and for reading the proof.

I wish to express my indebtedness to my wife, Grace C., and sister, Ola M., and to Edith A. Johnson for their patient labours in the mechanical work of my manuscript in preparation for the publisher.

The purpose of the book is to furnish a concise, general survey, and systematic study of the field of English hymnody, for the help of theological students and clergymen; also a readable book for serious readers and musicians, who desire to obtain a general

* Dr. Charles N. Boyd died April 24, 1937.

knowledge of the field of present-day hymnody for their own satisfaction and wider appreciation of hymnic poetry and hymn singing in church worship.

The writer does not pretend to include mention of all worthy hymns of the past and present, nor to give an extended account of the topics treated in the various chapters. But he has endeavoured to include rather the practical thoughts and most useful historic notes on the hymns and authors in the compass of one volume. Despite its limitations, of which the author is conscious, the endeavour has been to make the work thorough, as methodical and comprehensive as possible within the space and time allotted to the preparation of the book.

To keep within the limit of convenient size, it has not been possible to quote hymns in full, except in a few instances. The majority are found in any good modern hymnal and it is not necessary to quote but the first verse, or even a few lines, to introduce these hymns. But the reader might well have at hand three or four of the good new hymnals for reference, especially for the late nineteenth and twentieth century hymns, when it is desired to read through all the verses of a hymn.

Much as the author is interested in music, and the musical side of hymnody, he has only mentioned briefly the musical aspect in accordance with the advice of his two collaborators, Smith and Boyd. The more extensive study and technical usage should be omitted since there are splendid books treating of the musical history and rendering of sacred song.

H. B. M.

ACKNOWLEDGMENTS

THE author wishes to express his deep appreciation of kind offers of permission by publishers and living authors; especially such publishers as Morehouse Publishing Company, Milwaukee, Wisconsin; Charles Scribner's Sons, New York; Longmans, Green & Company, London; Sheldon Press (S.P.C.K.), London; Church of Scotland (Publication Commission), Edinburgh; Fleming H. Revell Company, New York; Macmillan Company, New York; John C. Winston Company, Philadelphia; Presbyterian Board of Christian Education, Philadelphia; Church Pension Fund, New York; Pilgrim Press, Boston; Beacon Press,* Boston; J. Fisher & Bro., New York; D. Appleton-Century Company, New York; Northwestern University Press, Chicago.

The author much appreciates the kindly permission by the various living hymn writers to quote from their hymns.

* Quotation of hymns by Marion Franklin Ham and Frederick Lucian Hosmer used by permission of the Beacon Press.

CONTENTS

Part One

Part Two

Part Three

PART ONE

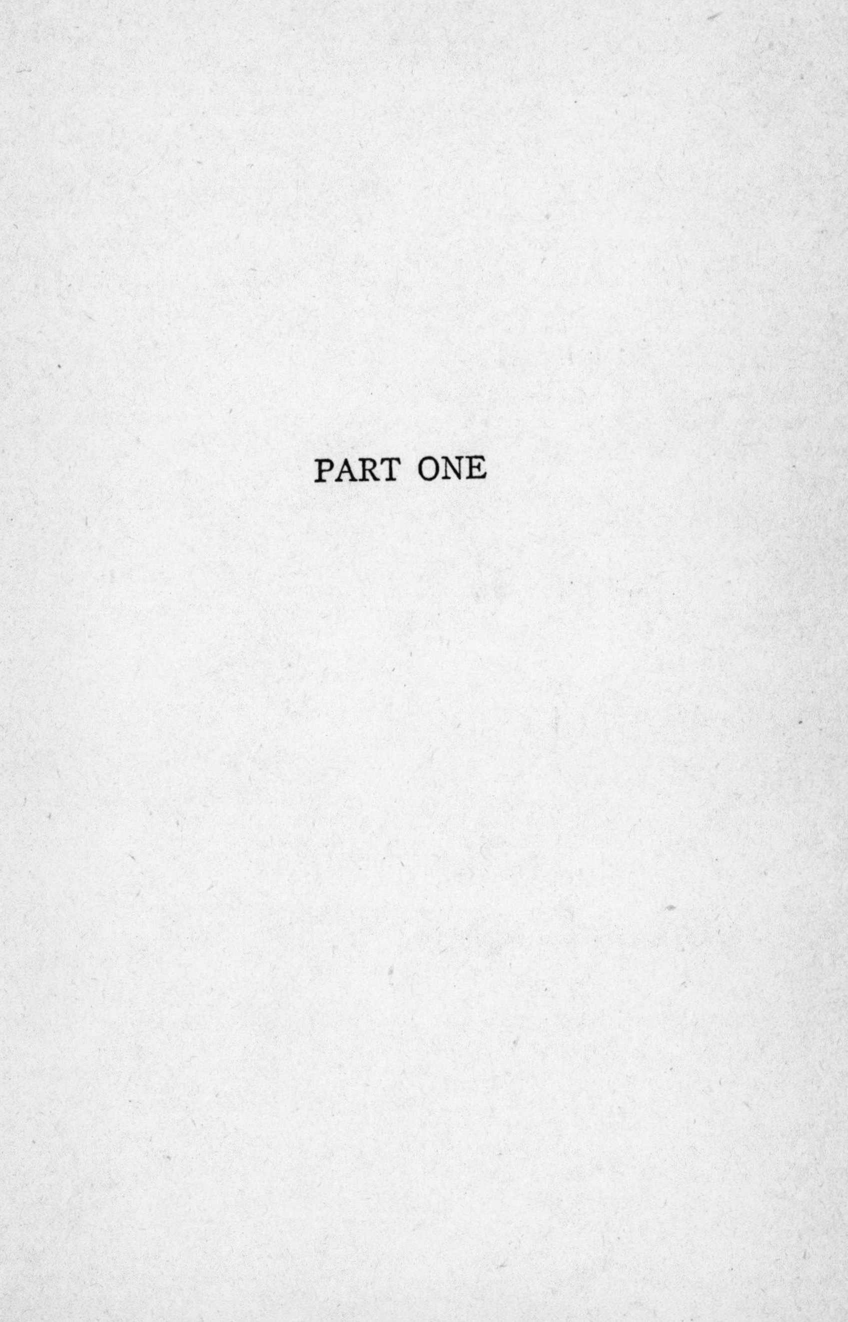

I

WHY STUDY HYMNOLOGY?

ENGLISH HYMNODY may well be called the neglected branch of English literature. In the study of literature in our schools and colleges this special branch of poetry is ordinarily not treated. Yet that portion of religious poetry which has within it the elements of hymnic poetry need not be the less literary because it is lyrical and used for singing. The late Dr. Louis F. Benson, the able American hymnologist, in his last book,[1] and Prof. Jeremiah B. Reeves in his book,[2] have well established the rightful claim of the hymn as literature.

Dr. A. E. Gregory of England has said, "Hymns belong to the belles-lettres of the literature of devotion, and to be familiar with them is itself a liberal education." The acceptance of the hymn as poetic literature is well based upon the following grounds: (1) The hymn has the essential musical and lyric qualities of poetry. (2) The hymn depends upon figures of speech such as the metaphor for simplicity and vividness. (3) The "Who's Who" in more recent hymns has names of poets of unquestionable standing in the literary world. (4) The hymn deals with the emotional side of life, and so is akin to poetry. (5) The realm of subject matter of which the hymn treats is as well-suited to poetry as any other field of thought.

Hymnology may be divided into two main parts: the text or poem, and the tunes to which the words are set. But with many people to-day the interest in hymnody is in the tunes only. Important as this is, the primary stress should be on the words and their significance. (The study of hymnology should be more pursued among users of hymns than it has been in the past.) There is little doubt that much of the confusion arising from the use of hymns comes from the fact that many worshippers are more strongly influenced by the music than by the words. Certainly there should be concern about the music, what the author is pleased to call the second half of hymnology, because the music is so inti-

[1] *The Hymnody of the Christian Church,* Doubleday & Doran, 1927.
[2] *The Hymn in History and Literature,* The Century Company, 1924

mately a part of the words. But why this confusion about the meaning of the term "hymnology" and its uses? The writer has often broached the subject of hymnology to various types of people to see what the word connotes to their minds, and generally it was the hymn-tune. Even various religious educators think only of the subject in terms of music, forgetful of the other part, or what the author is pleased to call the *first half* of hymnology.

Nearly always the words have been written first, and their worth being recognized, a suitable tune has been composed for the hymn, or a tune sought for it from some earlier musical source.

Sometimes a melody, considered suitable as a hymn-tune, has words written for it. Such instances are not very numerous. It will help much to adhere to the usual terminology in speaking about hymns: the words as "the hymn," and the writer of them as "the author," while the music is the "hymn-tune," and its writer "the composer." Fortunately, the hymnals, especially the newer ones, index the two distinctive parts according to this proper terminology; but as usual in conversation to-day this use of terms is carelessly neglected, hence the confusion in people's minds. It is fortunate that our newer church hymnals have the name and date of authorship of the hymns affixed; also the name of the composer and date (when known) of the first appearance of the hymn-tune.

Some systematic or analytical introduction to the period of writing and circumstances which led the authors to pen their noble words, and the biography of their lives, can be very helpful as well as very interesting. Such knowledge, also, enables us when singing to do so more intelligently and with more understanding and appreciation of our great book of praise.

When we read other poetry we welcome some information about the author and his or her biography. Surely such information is as valuable a part of religious education and as much tends toward the development of spirituality in our lives as some other courses of religious education which are regarded as very important.

Prof. Fred Eastman, in "The Christian Century," has forcibly called our attention to the value of biography. Not only does it furnish us anecdote and interesting, even thrilling, experiences but stimulates us as "we see how others have faced experiences of life that are common to us all, and have mastered them or compromised with them." In biographies one will find comfort and consolation from the common experience of trying to face life with handicap: for example, Beethoven, composing his Ninth Symphony, so deaf he heard not a note of it; E. B. Frost, blind for years, but head of Yerkes Observatory, and giving to the world facts about Arcturus lighting the Century of Progress (World's Fair) in Chicago; Michael Pupin, entering America as a foreign, penniless boy; those with poor health as Disraeli, Carlyle, Dickens, Emerson and Florence Nightingale. And so the biographies of our hymn writers furnish us similar and equally interesting lives of achievement. The character and lives of the hymn writers and their work which belong to modern times are as instructive and fully as inspiring as those of the Old Testament characters of ancient times, whose experiences and lives belong to the distant past, whereas the writers of English hymns belong to the comparatively recent past.

The Old Testament characters lived in a very different age under different conditions with different temptations, while our modern hymn writers have lived in times not so unlike our present day, under the influence of the dispensation of the New Testament and more advanced spiritual knowledge, with their teaching more fitted to the needs of our generation. To-day, when the churches and their leaders are advocating personal evangelism, how useful is a knowledge of the circumstances of the writing of the evangelical hymn, "Just As I Am," by Charlotte Elliott, or the circumstances of the conversion of Augustus M. Toplady (author of "Rock of Ages"), so applicable to the present generation of young people. What is more consoling, especially if disappointed in one's achievements or aspirations, than the biography of Henry Francis Lyte, and the occasion of his writing his hymn, "Abide with me"? What more remarkable achievements in the history of hymnology of the Christian Church than the work of Isaac Watts and Charles Wesley? Coming to the later Romantic Period of English Literature, the remarkable lives of James Montgomery, Bishop Reginald Heber, not to mention others of equal fame, are worthy of the study of any Christian. An enquiring father once asked Doctor Russell, famous editor of "The Scotsman," what his son should read to equip himself as writer and reporter. Doctor Russell replied, "Urge the lad to cleave rigorously to three books, and three only, the 'Holy Bible,' 'Pilgrim's Progress,' and 'Isaac Watts's hymns.'" Ramsay MacDonald, the former Prime Minister of Great Britain, upon hearing this story, said, "Upon my soul, I don't think that trilogy could well be improved upon!" So the brief, concise and simple language of the hymns is a valuable help to authors, teachers, and especially clergymen in writing and speaking to the public mind.

Moreover, the use of hymnic poetry far surpasses any other kind of poetry. When one stops to consider the wide usage of English hymns throughout the English-speaking world, we get an impressive glimpse of the vast range of reading or singing of this branch of English poetry. If we count the number of persons in numerous churches in the many denominations of our country alone, we are almost overwhelmed by the great number during any given week. Multiply this number of people by three or four, for this large company of worshippers will have used at least three or four hymns during the week and oftentimes more, then one may get some idea of the millions of people singing hymns, which must surpass the reading of epic and dramatic poetry combined over a period of a year. Consider the large sale of hymn books which runs into the hundreds of thousands in the course of a few years, in any one of the several large communions, as the Methodist, Baptist, Congregational, Presbyterian, Lutheran, Episcopal or Roman Catholic. Also each of these communions has more than one hymn book in use. Besides these there are various hymnals issued by large and small publishing houses which have wide circulation. For example, the hymn books by Prof. H. Augustine Smith total one million and a half, including his "Praise and Service," and "New Hymnal for American Youth." [3] Surely the English hymns hold wide sway in every English-speaking country, as well as in America itself. Our theological students should be taught, and all ordained clergy of whatever name should be awake to the far-reaching influence of the English hymns. It is of importance that the clergy who have charge of services of public worship should know something of the literature of sacred lyric poetry, and it is their duty as well as their great privilege to inform themselves about the value and usage of the hymns of the Church Catholic. They should appreciate also the spiritual force contained in the hymns, and thus realize their opportunity of leading their people to spiritual heights which the hymns are capable of doing. This cannot well be done by indifference to this part of the public service. It requires knowledge of hymns and also thought in their selection: more than five minutes in the hasty selection of hymns, or delegating the responsibility wholly to an organist or choir leader, who is naturally more interested in the hymn-tunes and often indifferent to the words of the hymn which may be selected.

[3] The D. Appleton-Century Company.

Not that the choir leader may not be asked for suggestions in selecting, or even select the hymns occasionally, but the clergyman should not avoid his own responsibility in the matter. He should also have in mind the character of the particular service, and its chief message, and what possible helpfulness can come to the congregation, not simply the music which a choir may prefer to sing. Besides, the message of the hymn may do much to strengthen the message of the sermon, or the occasion for which the service is held, by appropriate selection of suitable hymns. The story of the writing of the hymn or the special circumstances which may directly or indirectly have caused the hymn to be written, an appropriate bit of biography from the life of some author, may enhance the value or spiritual influence of the service of worship. The last time the author visited the late Dr. David R. Breed at his Pittsburgh home, some time before he died, he gave his chief reasons for the study of hymnology, which follow in substance: First, a view of truth through hymns is gotten better than in any other way, so that one cannot easily rid his mind or heart of its teaching by modern anti-scriptural or anti-church influences. The doctrinal teaching of the hymns is so clear and explicit that it commends itself to the minds of people. Second, the literature of the hymns makes for spiritual comfort and help. Third, literary quotations in sermons are the most effective either in the middle or at the end of the sermon. The hymns furnish abundance of appropriate material for such quotations. Fourth, the truth is presented in a way that children can comprehend; and while most simple in words and expression yet at the same time it is profound and deep in meaning.

II

DIFFERENT ASPECTS OF HYMNOLOGY

IN THE preceding chapter reference has been made to those who think of but one aspect of hymnology—the music. Too often the approach to the hymn is along the line of sentimental and inaccurate stories about the hymns. So the first part of hymnology which embraces all phases of it, except the music of the hymns, has various aspects of study which show how broad and extensive the subject of hymnology really is.

A clergyman of more than average education and training remarked sometime ago that the subject of hymnology did not challenge attention since anyone could obtain a book with hymn stories and read them for himself. Is this all there is to the study of the subject? But some systematic or analytical introduction to the times, conditions, circumstances, and influences under which the hymns were written and the religious experiences and spiritual training of the authors, whether in early or later life—all these points of approach furnish various aspects to the wide study of hymnology. Note the following aspects of hymn study. First, the general observation of the sources from which we get our books of praise. The early sources are mostly the Greek and Latin. The early modern sources are the German, and then comes the great source of Anglo-Saxon hymns. Many more of them were produced in Great Britain than in America, although the latter country has produced some of the leading hymns.

It might be noted further that while most of the earlier English hymns were produced by men, yet many a later hymn has been produced by a woman. It is true also that nearly all the best hymns were written by the clergy or members of their families—sons, daughters, wives or grandchildren. The laity has given few hymns to our hymn books as compared to the clergy and their families.

One hymnologist has spoken of James Montgomery and William Cowper as the two laymen who have written hymns of the highest rank; yet Montgomery was the son of a Moravian minister, and Cowper the son of a rector of an Anglican parish in Berkhamstead. So the influence of the rectory or vicarage and the parsonage are well demonstrated by the hymns they have produced.

The second aspect is an examination into the usage of hymns by which we may give them rank. By usage is meant here the inclusion of hymns in various publications of selected hymns, and their comparative popularity gauged by frequent or infrequent use, for the fact of a hymn's insertion in a book does not necessarily mean the hymn is much used. It would be fair to say that many such hymns may be little used for different reasons, yet are worthy of wider use and more frequent singing. Ignorance of them, or lack of appreciation of them, or their setting to an unknown tune, may hinder their rightful employment. Various attempts to rank hymns according to their wide publication have been made. Probably the best efforts made near the close of the nineteenth century were those of James King of London in his "Anglican Hymn Book," and of Dr. Louis F. Benson, of Philadelphia, in his list of "Best Hymns." These give strong support to various hymns of the Church as acquiring rank and recognition. Other attempts since then have been made, but for the most part not so thorough or convincing.

A third aspect of hymnology is the biography and background of the writers, and the history of the different periods of time in which they lived. When we think of the early period of English hymns of original composition (not English translations from earlier sources), we are reminded at once of such outstanding names as Bishop Thomas Ken, Isaac Watts, Philip Doddridge, Charles Wesley, John Cennick, John Newton, William Cowper, Edward Perronet, Augustus M. Toplady, and others.

Then, following the times of these distinguished writers, we have a large list of equally distinguished writers as James Montgomery, Reginald Heber, Robert Grant, John Keble, Henry Francis Lyte, John Ellerton, John Henry Newman and others. Among women writers are Charlotte Elliott, Harriet Auber and Sarah Flower Adams, all these belonging to Great Britain.

Among American writers, Thomas Hastings, William Augustus Muhlenberg, George Washington Doane, Ray Palmer, Samuel F. Smith, Timothy Dwight, William Cullen Bryant, John Greenleaf Whittier, and other able Americans. Then come additional writers who lived in the last half of the nineteenth century and who lived during the memory of our fathers and our young people's grandfathers. First among them should be named Frederick William Faber, the two distinguished translators of early hymns into English, John Mason Neale and Edward Caswall, besides W. W. How and Sabine Baring-Gould. Prominent women authors are Catherine Winkworth, and her sister Sarah Findlater, Cecil Frances Alexander, Frances Ridley Havergal, and other women of letters. In America such men as Whittier, Holmes, Longfellow, Washington Gladden, Frank Mason North and Henry Van Dyke are outstanding. The twentieth century has brought in new hymns and new authors which may yet live and increase in fame. This list of many distinguished authors will naturally call forth an investigation into their best hymns which have given them fame as hymnists, so that we can scarcely think of their names without thinking of their leading poems.

A fourth aspect includes stories of the hymn and influences which produced them. They may be subdivided more specifically: (a) stories of hymns inspired by spiritual experience and personal feelings; (b) hymns occasioned by incidents which moved to their writing; (c) hymns suggested by circumstances or surroundings; (d) stories of striking incidents connected with the usage of the hymns long after they were written, and spiritual blessings resulting therefrom. A book on hymnology written by an American layman, a few years ago, contains little material concerning hymns other than this latter sub-division or method of treatment, strange to say. (e) Another sub-division might well be made of hymns based on the Holy Scriptures that may be paraphrases of the Scriptures, as many of the versions of the psalms are, or some prose story of the Bible rendered into poetry.

To illustrate these different types of hymn writting, (A) consider Frances Ridley Havergal's consecration hymn. She had gone on a visit of five days to Areley House where there were a few people, some unconverted, others converted but not very active Christians, and her inspired prayer was for the welfare of all the souls in the house. One night the governess in the family asked Miss Havergal to come to the room of the two daughters who were crying. From her words of comfort both girls believed and rejoiced. Miss Havergal was even more rejoiced from this experience, and was too happy to sleep, and passed much of the night in praise and renewed consecration, and the following lines formed in her mind, "Take my life and let it be Consecrated, Lord, to Thee."

(B) An illustration of a hymn resulting from striking incidents is the one by George Duffield, Jr., a Presbyterian minister in Philadelphia. The incident and part of the circumstance are as follows.

The Rev. Dudley A. Tyng threw himself energetically into the revival of that city in 1858, and on a Sunday preached in Jaynes' Hall from the text, "Go now ye that are men, and serve the Lord" (Ex. 10:11) to an audience of five thousand men, making a profound impression on them. A few days later, he went into a barn on the outskirts of the city where a mule was working a piece of machinery. Mr. Tyng, with the wide sleeve of his study gown, began to pat the animal, when his sleeve was caught in the cog wheel of the machine and his arm was dragged into it and became severely mangled. After a few hours this resulted in his death. Shortly before he died, he was asked if he desired to send any message to his friends in the revival, and he replied, "Tell them to stand up for Jesus." One of his fellow ministers and fellow workers, Doctor Duffield, learning of this preached a memorial sermon for his friend the following Sunday, and ended his sermon with the original poem, "Stand up, stand up for Jesus." He gave it after the service to his Sunday School superintendent who had it printed on a leaflet and sung by the Sunday School. But Doctor Duffield never thought of its being quoted again. Much less would he have thought it would become one of the leading American hymns. Doctor Duffield wrote six stanzas, but only four of them are commonly sung to-day. So while Doctor Duffield was the author, the life and tragic death of young Tyng were the occasion and inspiration of this well-known hymn.

(C) As an illustration of circumstances or surroundings, the experience of the Baptist minister, Reverend John Fawcett, is a striking proof and a suggestive lesson to young clergy. When a young clergyman and one much beloved by his people at Wainsgate, Yorkshire, he early received and accepted the call to succeed the famous Doctor Gill as minister at Carter's Lane Chapel, London. His farewell sermon was preached, and the vehicles arrived to take the furniture away; but the loudly expressed pleadings of affection of his rural parish gained the day in the heart of Mr. Fawcett, and he decided to cancel his acceptance of the great London parish and remain in his village church for many more years. This touching circumstance inspired him to write the well-known hymn,

Blest be the tie that binds
Our hearts in Christian love,
The fellowship of kindred minds
Is like to that above.

(D) An illustration of the striking incidents, often connected with hymns long after they have been written, is connected with the gospel song by Mr. Palmer, "Yield not to temptation."

In Sing Sing Prison, New York, at a time when women were confined there, as well as men, on one occasion the women were allowed to sit in the corridor to hear an address. The prisoners rebelled against an order of the matron, resulting in a scene of screaming and profanity which filled the place. While the matron went for help, suddenly a voice rose above the tumult singing, "Yield not to temptation, for yielding is sin." It was a favourite hymn of one of the prisoners and as the words pealed out, quiet began to return; then the women joined in the singing of the hymn and finally marched peaceably back to their cells.

(E) The last sub-division is that of verses based on Holy Scriptures and includes versification of the psalms into English poetry by varied writers of which "Tate & Brady's" have been much quoted, as also the original hymn of Sir Henry W. Baker, "The King of Love my Shepherd is," which is based on the Twenty-third Psalm and Bible-time customs. Watts's "O God, our help in ages past" is based on one of the psalms, not to mention others.

Citing one more, a fifth aspect in the study of hymnology is an intensive study of the hymn itself, especially dealing with the characteristics and qualities of a hymn. This is a very wide aspect and may include much, particularly in the examination of the language, the chosen words and phrases which authors have used. So it may also include the ideas, teaching, and manner of presenting the thoughts contained in the hymn, their order and progress; even the choosing of topics presented for singing, their forms of expression and limits to which they are subject, as a hymn lyric is not an extended argument, nor debate, nor merely dictated creed or detailed narrative of a succession of events. The following chapter discusses this phase of hymn study.

III

WHAT IS A HYMN?

IT IS much easier to say what is not a hymn, than what is a hymn.

Many people singing hymns, if asked to do so, could not give much information on what a hymn is, nor give any adequate conception of what constitutes a hymn.

Having made a survey of the field of books on hymnology, the author finds that most of them, despite the interesting and valuable material they contain, give little idea of the necessary elements which enter into a suitable hymn, and many of them give only a meagre indirect answer to this question.

The author recalls as chiefly helpful on this point two chapters by Dr. E. S. Lorenz in his "Practical Church Music"; two chapters of A. E. Gregory (of England) in his "Hymn Book of the Modern Church," and the more recent book of Jeremiah B. Reeves, "The Hymn in History and Literature." The principles explained and taught by these three authors will help largely to answer these important questions. Because of the many limitations and proscribed areas of acceptable usage, the hymn is more difficult to write than any other kind of poetry. Lord Tennyson, although himself a great poet, said, "A good hymn is the most difficult thing in the world to write." This should not be taken as advice for young writers not to undertake writing, even though many people have erroneously thought the hymn was the simplest and easiest thing one could write. Tennyson in old age wrote his swan song, "Crossing the Bar," which is the only hymnic line he ever produced, except one or two lesser poems.

Here is a brief and simple definition: a hymn is an ode of praise to Almighty God. In contrast a gospel song is a religious exhortation to fellow man, and a carol is a simple narrative in verse of some outstanding biblical event. It can be regarded as suggestive so far as it goes, but it does not go far enough.

In a broad sense it may include canticles, chants, carols, spirituals and gospel songs: in a limited sense it includes only religious lyrics in rhyme and metre with other limitations also.

St. Augustine, of old, defines a hymn: "Hymns are praises to God with singing." If there be praise, and not praise of God, it is not a hymn; and if it is not sung, it is not a hymn. So three things are given to begin with. (1) Praise; (2) Praise of God; (3) That praise be sung. But this is inadequate. The third requirement is correct, it must be sung. True, the primary idea of a hymn is that of praise. But our own hymn book, like the Hebrew Psalter, must have not only songs of high thanksgiving, its sacrifice of praise, but also its prayer of the penitent, its sin offering, its intercessions, its meditation, its instructions, and exhortations.

A good definition of a hymn is that "A hymn is a sacred poem expressive of devotion, spiritual experience or religious truth, fitted to be sung by an assembly of people."

Simplicity of style, directness of expression, clearness of thought, absolute sanity of feeling, practicability of metre, and above all, the true lyric spirit must all appear in a sacred poem before it can be called a hymn.

The hymn should be poetry of poetic form with metrical rhyme. This is necessary, of course, for musical setting. Liquid harmony of words should flow through the lines with spiritual thought in graceful expression.

The expressions in good idiomatic English with simple words, monosyllabic or duosyllabic, are best, and words and phrases which are not ambiguous in expression, nor lacking in good discrimination of words, nor crudeness of taste, nor harsh lines. Crudeness of taste and harsh lines were often found in the early English hymns, such as are not acceptable to-day:

A filthy dog I am by sin,
A furious dog, dear Lord, I've been,
A greedy dog in evil ways,
And a dumb dog to all Thy praise.

The above lines may be beautiful humility, but they are crude in taste and over-extravagant in expression and hardly conducive to reverent worship; nor have they any dignity of expression and they lack absolute sanity of feeling, as shown by the phrase, "a filthy dog." How greatly in contrast are Watts's splendid lines of penitence and humility:

When I survey the wondrous cross
On which the Prince of Glory died,
My richest gain I count but loss,
And pour contempt on all my pride

These lines together with all the other verses of this poem are a model of simplicity, clearness of thought, sanity of feeling and poetic form. In fact this is one of the very greatest hymns in the English language.

Then the metrical form is of necessary concern in consideration of what constitutes a hymn as a poem. This again shows the hymn as a distinct and restricted kind of poetry. Its boundaries, both in poetic form and the subject matter contained therein, are clearly marked out. Simply as a lyric it would have the limitations of appropriate words and metre, but as a hymn lyric its boundaries are increased so as to include ideas general in application, not for certain individuals only. It will express social thinking or feeling dealing with moral and religious matters, and in such simple form as to be adaptable for singing by congregations without much musical training and often without previous rehearsal.

The verses must be short enough and exactly regular to fit a simple musical setting. The common metre of four lines, 8.6.8.6., is the most common and easy type of poem to read or sing. In this the second and fourth lines rhyme, and the first and the third lines usually rhyme, yet often they do not.

Next to the common metre is the long metre. It is stately and dignified poetry, the four even lines of eight syllables each, like that of the Long Metre Doxology, and many of the most majestic songs in our hymnals are written in the long metre.

A short metre is of four lines in which the longer third line is found, the 6.6.8.6. lines, where the first and third lines may be in rhyme, and the second and fourth lines must rhyme. Metres as 7s and 7s, and also various others, are found in the modern hymn book which the indices to a hymnal plainly show. The old hymn, "Nearer, my God, to Thee," has a very unusual metre. "From Greenland's icy mountains" was a new metre when written, but new hymn books now have a number of hymns written in the same metre.

Another theory that hymns should not begin verses with the pronouns "I" and "My" is no longer tenable. True, the expression of emotion should be fitted for congregational song, and not be merely personal or individualistic. But often what is personal is also largely general in application, and to fail to adopt the first personal pronoun in hymns (so common in gospel songs) would mean the loss of some valuable hymns.

Miss Elliott's hymn, "Just as I am," while it expresses her own experience in conversion, expresses also the religious condition or experience of many other people. So the old hymn of Horatius Bonar,

I was a wandering sheep,
I did not love the fold,
I did not love my Shepherd's voice,
I would not be controlled,

is most suitable to express the feelings or emotions of many. Dean Alford claimed the first personal pronoun type of hymn the most useful kind, and the above illustration certainly shows his claim is not without foundation. So other hymns employing the first personal pronoun expressed a common feeling in many hearts. The writer may speak not so much of himself, and yet his words may be truer and dearer to the man who repeats or sings them than to the author himself.

Newman's "Lead, kindly Light," one of the most famous hymns, was written as a personal prayer of Newman's, giving expression to temporary experience; yet few hymns better fit the experience of the many. In later years Newman did not explain exactly what he meant by the closing lines, written in "transcient" state of mind while on a Mediterranean journey. But the hymn to-day is sung so often because it expresses the feelings or desire of many hearts.

Other points of criticism are well given, long figures of speech, "strange conceits" and fanciful phrases, long words of prosy nature, and extravagant language and undue familiarity in addressing our Lord, should be largely avoided. Affectionate exclamations, as "Dear Lord," are valuable when used in moderation, but we should never overwork endearing words to the detriment of restrained emotions.

Vague suggestion also is unsuitable: "Beautiful Isle of Somewhere" has no just claim to be a hymn. It is not much better than a song one might write and call "Beautiful Isle of Nowhere." It is a great pity that such a poor excuse for a hymn should become so popular with the unthinking multitude, because of its pleasing and sentimental type of music. It has been condemned alike by Roman Catholics, Episcopalians and Protestant ministers as an unfitting song for the impressive office of the Burial of the Dead. There is no excuse for its singing on such solemn occasions when the hymnals have plenty of noble hymns dealing with earthly death and the future life, and the splendid "All Saints" hymns and the appropriate "Resurrection" hymns. These selections have some excellent tunes in any modern hymn book.

Moreover, hymns of the latter type contain the best Christian teaching which is effective for comfort and strength to the bereaved, instead of being calculated to arouse unduly the sad emotions on funeral or memorial occasions, as does the "Beautiful Isle of Somewhere," and also other similar mawkish sentimentalism.

An illustration of the careful writing of figures of speech, and suitable language, is found in one of the great Latin hymns, translated in our hymnal, "Gloria, Laus, et Honor." This has been abridged in modern hymnals, and an unsuitable verse omitted, although regularly sung in the seventeenth century, as follows:

Be Thou, O Lord, the Rider,
And we the little ass,
That to God's holy city
Together we may pass.

The present generation would likely smile at such words, although the past generations who could sing these words in real reverence possessed a degree of devotion greater than in the present day.

Spiritual force. It is not only important to consider the spiritual force which the hymn may possess or may lack. In general if the hymn is not spiritual it has no great value, no matter how fine its literary quality. On the other hand it is well said by Doctor Lorenz, "Where there is intense religious emotion and spiritual insight, there may be much lack in literary quality, without crippling its temporary usefulness."

It is of striking note, that the hymns of great poets, among the few classic poets, who have written hymnic lines, are mostly lacking in the spiritual force which is found among the writers of hymn poetry.

While Addison, Pope, Milton, William Wordsworth, Bryant, Oliver Wendell Holmes, Whittier and Lowell have contributed to our hymn books, yet none of their verses have the spiritual fervour and influence of many of the hymn poems by some men of less renown.

Spenser, Shakespeare, the two Brownings, Robert Herrick, George Herbert and others have not given us sacred lyrics. Even though Browning, Herrick, George Herbert and the immortal Milton have written sacred poetry, yet they have not given us hymns, except two or three that Milton wrote. William Cowper stands out alone most eminently in both fields of poetry, the classic and the hymnic.

Among the sacred lyrics probably most sung during the past are two poems, Addison's "The spacious firmament on high," and Oliver Wendell Holmes's "Lord of all being, throned afar." These are truly beautiful and majestic lyrics and written by men of world-wide fame. Yet who would compare them for spiritual force and warmth with some of the hymns by Watts, Wesley, Montgomery, Cowper, Heber, Lyte and others of sacred lyric fame. Such has been the consensus of opinion and selection of poems by the generations of the past.

But is the present generation of hymn book compilers going to ignore this recognition of suitable hymns? Certainly there is at present a tendency among some people both in Great Britain and America to do so.

Percy Dearmer of England and a few of his co-workers, as well as some in America, do so, adopting, or trying to adopt, many verses from the classic poets seemingly because they are classic, and written by men of poetic renown, which verses are, of course, religious poetry in rhyme and metre.

But are some of these poems truly hymn poetry as we have judged hymn poetry in the past? Will poetry because it has religious meaning and majestic lines written by men of high recognition in the field of literature be chosen for regular usage in our hymnals regardless of whether such possesses the deep elements of spiritual force? John Wesley and George Rawson tried to make George Herbert's religious poems into hymns, but did not well succeed with their attempt. Even if the present generation does disregard all precedents, as the present generation is conspicuous for doing, what assurance have we that such adaptations for hymns will be recognized by the future generations, especially when we consider the combined consensus of opinion and judgment of the past several generations?

Without naming some other present-day selections adapted as hymn lyrics, the following two recent poems by a friend will illustrate our meaning:

Lord, we offer thanks and praise [1]
For these golden harvest days,
For the fruits and ripened grain
Thou has given to sustain.

[1] Miss Nettie Williams, Pleasantville, N. J.

There is nothing good below
That Thy love didst not bestow;
All the fruits of tree and land
Come from Thy almighty hand.

On this glad Thanksgiving Day
We our grateful tribute pay;
All we give Thee is Thine own,
All has come from Thee alone.

Offered in Thy house of prayer
For Thy love and tender care,
For these golden harvest days,
Lord, accept our thanks and praise.

This poem conforms to the definition of a hymn of praise to God. But on the other hand consider these lines:

The world is full of lovely things,[2]
Of people true and kind;
But we so often see the bad
And to the good are blind.

Tall weeds may in the garden grow,
But if we look we'll see
Fair, fragrant flowers growing there
With honey for the bee.

Within the orchard we may find
A wormy peach or pear,
But that would never make us think
There is no good fruit there.

We read of wrong, and sin, and shame,
In headlines big and bold,
But don't think good deeds are not done
Because they are not told.

There's more of good than bad, I know,
In this great world of ours;
And though the poisoning tares are thick
They're fewer than the flowers.

This is good poetic sentiment, but surely it is not intended for a hymn.

[2] *Ibid.*

Yet this latter caution against some attempted modern adaptations from classic sources is not to be regarded as excluding a certain moderate amount of vivid imagery and colourful description, else Katharine Lee Bates's now popular patriotic hymn would be excluded,

O beautiful for spacious skies,
For amber waves of grain,
For purple mountain majesties
Above the fruited plain!

Here is colourful imagery drawn from nature. Yet the old hymn of Cowper's has an exaggerated figure of speech and bold imagery which will prevent its entrance into some of our new hymnals, "There is a fountain filled with blood." (The Episcopal Church hymnal of 1916 omits it, but the new Presbyterian hymnal of 1933 strangely includes it.)

But we are not to think of hymns as necessarily weak and always mild in expression and lacking in descriptive figures taken from nature, but rather the opposite of these, provided that they do not go to extremes.

There is strength of imagery which may be regarded as permissible in the following from Watts,

Must I be carried to the skies
On flowery beds of ease,
While others fought to win the prize,
And sailed through bloody seas?

or in Sidney Lanier's "Into the woods my Master went," or in Alexander Pope's "Rise, crowned with light, Imperial Salem, rise."

Hymns with imagery and colour seem to be growing in favour rather than diminishing. But in hymnody as in all things, temperance and moderation are greatly to be desired.

IV

EVALUATION OF HYMNS

THAT there is much difference in the quality and influence of hymns is obvious. Some of our English hymns have come down to us from two centuries or more, being sung by each generation since their writing, and have proved to be strong favourites of each generation. Only those of most vitality within them have survived from decade to decade. Most of the hymns written a century or two ago have either never acquired general recognition to begin with, or else have gradually lost their hold until within the hymn books of to-day they fail of inclusion. If they have not been omitted and are still included, that is in itself a large compliment to such hymns. A standard of ranking hymns is difficult because one cannot apply the same standards as to other types of writing. Again, hymns are unique and employed for one great purpose and judged accordingly. While literary style and chaste diction do have proper weight, the chief standard we have is Christian usage and appeal. What the Church most generally recognizes must attain high rank.

Even so, it is important to exercise wise care in choosing. We should seek to find the qualities possessed by hymns which have lived for years, and then determine the degree to which the hymn has these qualities, and so is entitled to high evaluation. We need to consider Christian usage. Mere temporary popularity is not enough. In fact, a hymn of widespread momentary popularity, taken up by the multitude, or even "whistled in the street" because of its melody, is just as apt to be a song of no lasting worth, as one deserving of high recognition. Doctor Breed says that a hymn of rank must conform to at least four conditions: (1) It must obtain hold upon the Christian community, not being partisan or sectional. (2) Its hold must be permanent. If its sentiment suits but one single age, it is not adopted. (3) It must find a place in the stated worship of the great congregation. (4) It must be embodied in some authorized body of sacred song, put forth by some recognized organization of Christians. If it never emerges from the publication of some irresponsible person or firm, it cannot be called adopted.

Even with these standards of measurement and attempts to evaluate hymns by their usage, we do not succeed in enlisting a group of hymns which can be regarded as an infallible guide to highest worth.

Truly speaking, there is no infallible estimate of what are the "best hymns." Various attempts have been made in the past, as also in the present, to estimate the rank of hymns according to well recognized Christian usage and by popular voting of "favourite hymns." The majority of such attempts may not be worth the paper they are written on. But certain faithful efforts made in this direction by competent men or women are at least worthy of serious notice. Besides, we need some guidance in this direction so that we may have whatever value there is in estimating the usage of the many hymns of the Church, and thus be helped to determine what are best hymns for us to preserve in the hymn book, and what we may leave out. We should not trust such weighty decision to the judgment of our own generation only, regardless of other ages.

Our present generation is too much given to ignoring the worthy efforts of the past, and such course, if followed, except in very limited degree, may cause the next generation to lose much of the value of past writings, being unwilling to accept the judgment and work of the present time, thus leaving them to their own efforts, however feeble, or else to search through the old hymnals secluded on dusty library shelves.

Evidently Dr. E. S. Lorenz is unfavourably impressed with Doctor Breed's list of hymns in the latter's book, and he shows that both the lists of James King of London and Doctor Benson's "Best Hymns" are not infallible or entirely trustworthy.

Nevertheless, Doctor Lorenz's opinion of such attempts to evaluate hymns as of no particular value, and "to make any such attempts is nothing more than interesting pastime," is open to as much criticism at least as the lists which Doctor Breed emphasizes. The late Bishop Cortland Whitehead of Pittsburgh, when shown by the writer these two special lists copied from Doctor Breed's book, expressed his deep interest and appreciation of these two investigations. Bishop Whitehead was himself a student of hymnology, and was chairman of the new Episcopal Hymnal Commission, not without good reason because of his knowledge and splendid literary taste.

Among the lists which are not only interesting, but also worthy of attention, are the two lists made near the close of the nineteenth century, previously referred to: James King's Anglican Group, and Doctor Benson's "Best Hymns." The one is a careful examination into the usage of all Anglican hymn books and the latter is the best, so far, of American Protestant attempts at evaluation.

James King in his "Anglican Hymnology" pursued the following method. He collected fifty-two representative hymnals of the Anglican Church both in England and abroad. These fifty-two hymnals were regarded as a committee, each of which could give one vote on any hymn. Two thousand hymns thus tested by this personified committee, being selected and classified as follows: hymns which received thirty votes or more were given first rank; hymns receiving twenty votes and upwards, second rank; hymns receiving fifteen votes and less than twenty, third rank; and hymns which received less than fifteen votes were regarded as not generally approved.

By this examination not a single hymn received the votes of all the hymnals. The compiler also admitted that some hymns failed to receive votes enough to be enrolled in high rank because of too recent date, as it usually takes twenty years and more for a hymn to win general favour.

According to this selection of Mr. King, the first rank hymns are one hundred and five in number. Four of these stand at the head of the list, each obtaining fifty-one votes, only lacking one vote of being unanimous. A strongly supported list, sometimes referred to as "The Great Four," they are as follows:

1. All praise to Thee, my God, this night. Ken.
2. Hark the herald angels sing. C. Wesley.
3. Lo, He comes with clouds descending. Cen.-Wesley.
4. Rock of Ages, cleft for me. Toplady.

Six others obtained forty-nine votes:

5. Abide with me, fast falls the eventide. Lyte.
6. Awake, my soul, and with the sun. Ken.
7. Jerusalem the golden. Bernard-Neale.
8. Jesus, Lover of my soul. C. Wesley.
9. Sun of my soul, Thou Saviour dear. Keble.
10. When I survey the wondrous cross. Watts.

Another method, somewhat different, but even more catholic, was followed in "The Best Church Hymns" by Dr. Louis F. Benson who was an excellent judge of hymn material. Doctor Benson used 107 hymn books including the above mentioned book. He takes eighty per cent of the books as the standard in which a hymn must be found to attain first rank. From these 107 books he obtains thirty-two which he calls his "best church hymns." These make a valuable collection, and the work was done in broadest sympathy, without evidence of sectarianism of any kind.

The compiler expresses the same caution as that of "Anglican Hymnology," that there may be certain hymns not included because they had not yet had time to secure recognition.

These thirty-two lyrics are not easily surpassed.

The list with number of votes given, and also, for comparison, the rank according to the "Anglican Hymnology" placed after the author's name, is as follows:

1. Rock of Ages, cleft for me (106). Toplady. A.H. 4.[1]
2. When I survey the wondrous cross (104). Watts. A.H. 10.
3. Jesus, Lover of my soul (104). Wesley. A.H. 8.
4. All praise to Thee, my God, this night (103). Ken. A.H. 1.
5. Jesus, I my cross have taken (103). Lyte. A.H. 287.
6. Sun of my soul, Thou Saviour dear (103). Keble. A.H. 9.
7. Awake, my soul, and with the sun (101). Ken. A.H. 6.
8. Hark! the herald angels sing (101). Wesley. A.H. 2.
9. Abide with me: fast falls the eventide (101). Lyte. A.H. 5.
10. Jerusalem, my happy home (101). "F.B.P." A.H. 16.
11. How sweet the Name of Jesus sounds (101). Newton. A.H. 15.
12. Nearer, my God, to Thee (100). Adams. A.H. 13.
13. From Greenland's icy mountains (100). Heber. A.H. 17.
14. Our God, our Help in ages past (100). Watts. A.H. 19.
15. Jerusalem the golden (99). Bernard-Neale. A.H. 7.
16. Lo! He comes with clouds descending (94). Cennick-Wesley. A.H. 3.
17. Jesus shall reign where'er the sun (94). Watts. A.H. 40.
18. Glorious things of thee are spoken (93). Newton. A.H. 31.
19. Hark the glad sound! the Saviour comes (92). Doddridge. A.H. 14.
20. Come, let us join our cheerful songs (92). Watts. A.H. 30.
21. All hail the power of Jesus' Name (92). Perronet. A.H. 46.
22. Hail to the Lord's Anointed (91). Montgomery. A.H. 26

[1] Copyright list. Used by permission of Longman's, Green & Co., Ltd., London.

23. O worship the King (91). Grant. A.H. 32.
24. Christ the Lord is risen to-day (90). Wesley. A.H. 37.
25. Guide me, O Thou great Jehovah (90). Williams. A.H. 58.
26. Just as I am, without one plea (90). Elliott. A.H. 64.
27. God moves in a mysterious way (90). Cowper. A.H. 49.
28. Jesus, the very thought of Thee (89). Bernard-Caswell. A.H. 59.
29. Children of the heavenly King (87). Cennick. A.H. 55.
30. There is a land of pure delight (87). Watts. A.H. 70.
31. Thou whose almighty word (86). Marriott. A.H. 29.
32. Brief life is here our portion (86). Bernard-Neale. A.H. 22.

While the numbers do not exactly coincide they show a remarkable degree of correspondence. The only surprising disagreement is with regard to Lyte's hymn, "Jesus, I my cross have taken," which is 5 in Doctor Benson's list, and only 287 in Mr. King's.

It is interesting to note that all of the first ten in James King's list are found in Doctor Benson's first fifteen, except "Lo, He comes with clouds descending" which comes sixteenth in Benson's.

Surely these are good catalogues of the hymns of the past generations of English hymnody up to the twentieth century.

During the first third of the twentieth century we know of but very few convincing attempts to rank hymns. These efforts have had limited results. The *Etude's* attempt to secure popular vote on favourite hymns a few years ago was very meagre, unimpressive and faulty.

A valuable effort was made a few years ago by the General Federation of Women's Clubs, Division of Music. The very able committee of women, with Mrs. Marx E. Obendorfer and Mrs. Frederic Nichols as chairmen, decided to prepare a list of "Best Hymns for American Sunday School Scholars." Miss Anne F. Obendorfer was chief compiler of this selection. The list of fifty selected is worthy of space, with names of authors and composers of tunes given in alphabetical order (but the first hymn is not to be taken as ranking higher than the last one). They are as follows:

Hymn	*Author*	*Composer of Tune*
1. Abide with me [2]	Lyte	Monk
2. Adeste fideles	Latin	Reading
3. All hail the power of Jesus' Name	Perronet	Holden
4. A mighty fortress is our God	Luther	Luther
5. Ancient of days	Doane	Jeffrey
6. Blest be the tie that binds	Fawcett	Nageli

[2] Used by permission of J. Fischer and Brother, New York.

	Hymn	*Author*	*Composer of Tune*
7.	Come, Thou Almighty King	Anon	Giardini
8.	Come, ye disconsolate	Moore	Webbe
9.	Fairest Lord Jesus	Old Crusader	Arr. Willis
10.	Faith of our fathers	Faber	Hemy
11.	From all that dwell below the	Watts	Bourgeois
	skies and Old hundredth	Kethe	Bourgeois
12.	Hark, the herald angels sing	Wesley	Mendelssohn
13.	He leadeth me	Gilmore	Bradbury
14.	Holy, holy, holy	Heber	Dykes
15.	In the cross of Christ I glory	Bowring	Conkey
16.	It came upon the midnight clear	Sears	Willis
17.	Jerusalem, the golden	Cluny-Neale	Ewing
18.	Jesus Christ is risen to-day	Old Latin	Tate and Brady
19.	Jesus, Lover of my soul	Wesley	Marsh
20.	Jesus, tender shepherd	Duncan	Barnard
21.	Joy to the world	Watts	Handel
22.	Just as I am	Elliott	Bradbury
23.	Lead, kindly Light	Newman	Dykes
24.	Love Divine, all loves excelling	Wesley	Zundel
25.	My faith looks up to Thee	Palmer	Mason
26.	Nearer, my God, to Thee	Adams	Mason
27.	Now the day is over	Baring-Gould	Barnby
28.	O God, our help in ages past	Watts	Croft
29.	O Jesus, Thou art standing	Howe	Knecht
30.	O little town of Bethlehem	Brooks	Stevens
31.	O mother dear, Jerusalem	"F. P. B."	Ward
32.	One sweetly solemn thought	Cary	Ambrose
33.	Onward, Christian soldiers	Baring-Gould	Sullivan
34.	O Paradise, O Paradise	Faber	Barnby
35.	Rock of Ages	Toplady	Hastings
36.	Safely through another week	Newton	Mason
37.	Saviour, again to Thy dear Name	Ellerton	Hopkins
38.	Saviour, like a Shepherd lead us	Thrupp	Bradbury
39.	Silent night, holy night	Mohr	Gruber
40.	Softly now the light of day	Doane	Weber
41.	Sun of my soul	Keble	Ritter
42.	The Church's one foundation	Stone	Wesley
43.	The first Nowell	Traditional	Traditional
44.	The King of Love my Shepherd is	Baker	Dykes
45.	The Son of God goes forth to war	Heber	Cutler
46.	Ten thousand times ten thousand	Alford	Dykes
47.	We three kings of Orient are	Hopkins	Hopkins
48.	When I survey the wondrous cross	Watts	Miller
49.	When morning gilds the skies	Caswall	Barnby
50.	While shepherds watched	Tate	Old English

Some denominational hymnals use different tunes but in a few instances only.

It should be observed that all of these are stately hymns and none selected are the so-called "gospel hymns" despite the large number of gospel song books published. It is also a compliment to the last American Episcopal Church hymnal that everyone is included in it. All but five are found in the more recent Presbyterian hymnal. The ones omitted are "One sweetly solemn thought," "O Paradise, O Paradise," "Safely through another week," "Ten thousand times ten thousand," and "We three kings of Orient are." All these hymns are found in the Methodist Episcopal hymnal of 1905, except three. Most of these hymns with stories and their authors are found treated in "Lyric Religion" by Prof. H. Augustine Smith.

It is interesting to compare with the foregoing list the recent wide effort made among nine different denominations which resulted in the publication of "The Inter-Church Hymnal." These are printed in the book in the exact order of their ranking:

	Hymn	*Author*	*Composer of Tune*
1.	Come, Thou Almighty King	Anon.	Giardini
2.	How firm a foundation	"K" in Rippon's	Cantas Diversi
3.	Holy, holy, holy	Heber	Dykes
4.	All hail the power of Jesus' name	Perronet	Holden
5.	In the cross of Christ I glory	Bowring	Conkey
6.	The Church's one foundation	Stone	S. S. Wesley
7.	Love divine, all loves excelling	C. Wesley	Le Jeune
8.	Joy to the world!	Watts	Handel-Mason
9.	My faith looks up to Thee	Palmer	Mason
10.	O Master, let me walk with Thee	Gladden	Percy Smith
11.	Faith of our fathers! living still	Faber	Walton
12.	Stand up, stand up for Jesus	Duffield	Webb
13.	O worship the king, all glorious above	Grant	Haydn
14.	Onward, Christian soldiers	Baring-Gould	Sullivan
15.	My country, 'tis of thee	Smith	Carey
16.	He leadeth me; O blessed thought	Gilmore	Bradbury
17.	O come, all ye faithful	Trans., Oakeley	Cantus Diversi
18.	Jesus shall reign where'er the sun	Watts	Hatton
19.	When I survey the wondrous cross	Watts	Arr. Mason
20.	Rock of Ages, cleft for me	Toplady	Hastings
21.	Blest be the tie that binds	Fawcett	Naegeli
22.	Our God, our help in ages past	Watts	Croft
23.	O little town of Bethlehem	Brooks	Redner
24.	Break Thou the bread of life	Lathbury	Sherwin
25.	Jesus calls us	Alexander	Jude
26.	Dear Lord and Father of mankind	Whittier	Maker
27.	Majestic sweetness sits enthroned	Stennett	Hastings
28.	Day is dying in the west	Lathbury	Sherwin
29.	When morning gilds the skies	Trans., Caswall	Barnby

	Hymn	*Author*	*Composer of Tune*
30.	Jesus, Lover of my soul	Wesley	Dykes
31.	Glorious things of thee are spoken	Newton	Haydn
32.	Safely through another week	Newton	Mason
33.	I love to tell the story	Hankey	Fischer
34.	O Love that wilt not let me go	Matheson	Peace
35.	O beautiful for spacious skies	Bates	Ward
36.	Abide with me	Lyte	Monk
37.	Nearer, my God, to Thee	Adams	Mason
38.	From every stormy wind that blows	Stowell	Hastings
39.	I love Thy kingdom, Lord	Dwight	Williams
40.	I need Thee every hour	Hawks	Lowry
41.	Crown Him with many crowns	Bridges	Elvey
42.	O day of rest and gladness	Wordsworth	Arr. Mason
43.	Lead, kindly Light	Newman	Dykes
44.	What a Friend we have in Jesus	Scriven	Converse
45.	It came upon the midnight clear	Sears	Willis
46.	Hark, the herald angels sing	C. Wesley	Mendelssohn
47.	Lead on, O King Eternal	Shurtleff	Smart
48.	O Jesus, I have promised	Bode	Mann
49.	Jesus, Saviour, pilot me	Hopper	Gould
50.	Christ, the Lord is ris'n to-day	C. Wesley	Arr. Lyra Davidica

A very recent attempt in selecting a highly favoured group of hymns was made in Chicago in 1931 by a prominent Lutheran minister and student of hymnology, who through careful publicity in the bulletins of a number of Christian communions in Chicago, brought some good results. It is said that Pastor Doving's book shelves in his study had hymnals in over three hundred languages, nearly every language in which hymn books have been published. He has translated thirty-two leading Norwegian, Danish and German hymns into English. And we know the kind of stately and worthy hymns the Lutherans are accustomed to singing in their churches.

A recent tabulation by Pastor Doving of the number of languages into which most translated Christian hymns have been rendered, showed the following facts:

HYMNS TRANSLATED

1. A mighty Fortress is our God, into 171 languages.
2. Rock of Ages, 130.
3. Just as I am, 106.
4. Adeste, fideles, 104.
5. Nearer, my God, to Thee, 101.

6. Jesus, still lead on, 93.
7. Holy, holy, holy, 81.
8. O sacred Head, now wounded, 80.
9. Jesus, Lover of my soul, 78.
10. Guide me, O Thou great Jehovah, 75.
11. What a Friend we have in Jesus, 70.
12. All hail the power, 65.
13. Abide with me, 66.
14. Hark, the herald angels sing, 64.
15. I heard the voice of Jesus say, 62.
16. Jesus shall reign, 51.
17. Sun of my soul, 50.
18. When I survey the wondrous cross, 50.
19. Lead, kindly light, 50.
20. I gave my life for Thee, 47. (rev.) Thy life was given for me.

V

ANCIENT AND MEDIÆVAL HYMNODY

THE early Christian Church inherited the Hebrew psalms and adopted the Greek hymnal. What a significant heritage the Jewish Church left the early Christian Church to use!

The early Church was mostly dependent upon this inheritance of song from the Old Testament, and would have been very unappreciative not to have used such a selected group of songs, even though a few of the imprecatory psalms were not according to the teaching of the New Testament dispensation, nor the spirit of the Christ. Still the primitive Christians had no such poets as the Old Testament Hebrews.

According to Jewish tradition, David is the father of Hebrew Psalmody and prepared some settings for the tabernacle worship, as he was an able musician. The Hebrew songs were almost all sung in the worship of their God, Jehovah, while the poetry of other nations is extended to a wide range of topics.

Because of their lofty aim, and aided by divine inspiration, the Hebrew songs were far superior to those of other early races. Hebrew poetry was not metrical, as we understand it to-day, yet it was poetic and adapted to lyrical purposes. When it is translated into modern verse, as the various translators have done, it loses its peculiar literary quality and also is bound up to a musical style to which it is not well suited. But its form is well suited for chanting. The custom of chanting is gaining ground and most churches find use for psalmody, the earliest sacred utterance of the religious Muse. The various branches of the Church have their different hymnals, yet the Book of Psalms, or portions of it, is in universal use throughout Christendom.

Under the reign of David, and by his example also, some impetus was given to the later rendering of temple worship. Subsequently, the service of song was organized on a large scale. The temple choir at Jerusalem with its four thousand musicians and singers assembled and trained together. Large religious musical festivals were given, and much praise became a permanent phase of Hebrew worship.

The musicians were drawn from the Levites. Asaph was their instrumental conductor, and Chemaniah their vocal leader. According to I Chronicles 15 and 16 these musicians were composers as well as performers, and part of the psalms are ascribed to them as composers. Under Solomon's reign the work was enlarged and the worship of the temple and its choral and instrumental music was probably extensively used in the worship of Almighty God.

Sacred music was probably cultivated among the priests and Levites until the exile to Babylon when the choral music of these people became silent. Upon their return from captivity their composition and performance of song were again resumed. The music of the Second Temple, or Temple of Zerubbabel, was even more developed than in the Temple of Solomon. The large choir was now composed of men and boys with at least occasional employment of female voices. The psalms to be sung were assigned for each day of the week, while other special psalms were assigned to special occasions. Such was the worship in the days when Jesus came, and in such songs he joined with his disciples in singing. The "hymn" which was sung at the Pascal Supper was probably a portion of the "Hallel" from Psalm 115 to 118.

While Psalmody was the chief source of their hymn music, yet the early Church was not wholly confined to this. For in the Gospel of St. Luke, in the first two chapters, are recorded four Christian hymns, the Song of Elizabeth, mother of John Baptist, "Blessed art thou among women!"; then the song of the Blessed Virgin Mary, "My soul doth magnify the Lord," called the "Magnificat"; followed by the song of the priest, Zachariah, "Blessed be the Lord God of Israel for he has visited and redeemed his people," called the "Benedictus." Lastly came the song of the aged Simeon, "Lord, now lettest thou thy servant depart in peace according to thy word," called the "Nunc Dimittis."

Such canticles were the divine gift to the young Church about to be promulgated, and to this day are constantly chanted throughout the Church.

After Christ's Ascension the infant Church continued to sing the songs of David and the temple worship, but was destined soon to have new songs added which should be distinctively Christian and be used in the solemn worship of the Christian Church down through the centuries.

There are several more early Christian hymns coming after the ones contained in the gospel record and used in the liturgies of worship. The "Ter Sanctus," the "Gloria in Excelsis," "Gloria Patri," "Te Deum" and "Benedicite."

1. The "Ter Sanctus" ("Holy, holy, holy"), sometimes miscalled the Trisagion, is found in all the liturgies of both the Eastern and Western Churches, and is probably the oldest of these early Christian hymns based on Isaiah's Seraphic Song (Isaiah 6:3 and Rev. 4:8). It joins the Church on earth by anticipation of the perfect adoration of heaven, following the liturgical preface, "Therefore, with angels and archangels, and with all the company of heaven, we laud and magnify Thy glorious name, evermore praising thee and saying,

Holy, holy, holy, Lord God of hosts,
Heaven and earth are full of Thy glory;
Glory be to Thee, O Lord most high. Amen."

2. The "Gloria in Excelsis" ("Glory be to God on high and on earth peace, good will toward men") is sometimes called "The Angelic Hymn," as its opening words are obviously from the Angels' Song at the Bethlehem Nativity. Its early form is apparently of Greek origin. It appears in expanded form in the Apostolic Constitutions of the fourth century, and with additions somewhat like the "Te Deum." Its present form is found in both the Book of Common Prayer and in the hymnals. Its position at the close of the Holy Communion service is peculiar to the Anglican Church, where it may be found.

3. With this hymn we should also notice the "Gloria Patri," sometimes called the "Lesser Doxology," in contrast to the "In Excelsis" or the "Greater Doxology." The first half is distinctive praise of the Holy Trinity, "Glory be to the Father, and to the Son, and to the Holy Ghost." It is clearly traced to the east during the Arian controversy, when in rebuttal of that heresy the second half was added, "As it was in the beginning, is now and ever shall be, world without end. Amen." Thence it made its way into the Western Church and has been used in the present form substantially for over 1300 years.

4. The "Te Deum" or "Te Deum Laudamus" is named after its opening words. The authorship of this sonorous hymn is unknown but it is of eastern origin and has been assigned to Nicetas.

The first authenticated reference to the "Te Deum Laudamus" was in 502, when the Bishop of Arles is said to have ordered it to be used in the Sunday morning service but earlier portions of it are traced to 272 A.D. Possibly, like the Apostles' Creed, it is a growth, rather than a one-time inspiration. This hymn forms a part of the morning service in Anglican churches, although usually omitted during Lent. It does not appear in the Greek service books except in the Russian Church. In addition to its use in the daily service in the west, it is often sung on occasions of victory, or rejoicing on conclusions of peace, coronations and consecrations of bishops. We may truly regard it as a great hymn, a creed and a prayer, or as a creed with lyrical power ascending heavenward.

The English version is familiar to all communions as it is used throughout the world. It need not be set down here, since it is found in all standard hymnals and in the Book of Common Prayer.

5. The "Benedicite": this is called the "Song of the Three Children," and is from the Apocrypha. It seems to be also an expansion of Psalm 148. It is found in the service of Morning Prayer in the Book of Common Prayer, and used as an alternative to the "Te Deum." Many Episcopal churches use it through both Advent and Lent. From ancient times it was used in the Service of Lauds, both in the east and the west. It is worked out in detail, and brings in all The Great Natural Powers and Forces of Creation to sing the Creator's praise, and includes the angels as God's ministering creatures therein.

We come next to early Greek and Latin hymns which were to be used independently if desired outside the old liturgies of worship found in the Eastern and Western Churches.

GREEK HYMNODY

Clement of Alexandria (c. 170-220)—was the earliest writer who has left us a hymn used to this day. He studied in the schools of the east and west. He became the head of a catechetical school in Alexandria where he was distinguished as scholar and teacher, among whose pupils was the famous Origen. It is of interest to note that this man who had studied the various philosophies of his day was not fully satisfied with any of these as a philosophy of life for himself, until he found in Jesus of Nazareth the Water of Life for which he thirsted. He said, "Jesus had made truth simple," and so as a teacher he led his pupils to know Christ. He was an extensive writer on many topics, but we are concerned most with his hymn, "Shepherd of tender youth," our oldest extant hymn, which refers to Jesus as the Master Fisherman. Among different versions Doctor Alexander's is more often quoted, and characteristic verses are as follows:

Shepherd, who dost us keep,
Husbandman, who tillest,
Bit to restrain us, Rudder
To guide us as Thou willest,

Fisher of men, whom Thou to life dost bring
From evil sea of sin
And from the billowy strife,
Gathering pure fishes in,
Caught with the sweet bait of life.

Gregory Nazianzi—It is two centuries later on before we have our next very outstanding writer. Born in Cappadocia, in a town whose name is affixed to his own, he was the son of a bishop and himself became a bishop at Constantinople in 379. He is regarded as one of the leading Greek fathers.

In the fourth century the Arian controversy was raging over the Church and attacked the deity of Christ. The Arians' hymns of propaganda loudly proclaimed their heresy, which were not only amazing to Gregory but soon were likewise amazing to St. Chrysostom when the Arians were holding their meetings and singing insulting hymns outside the walls of the churches. Gregory's last years were spent in retirement when he wrote most of his hymns. Among them is one translated by Chatfield of which we give two verses showing its noble style and devout orthodoxy;

O thou the One supreme o'er all!
For by whatever name
May we upon Thy greatness call
Or celebrate Thy fame?

And lo! all things abide in Thee
And through the complex whole
Thou spreadest Thine own divinity
Thyself of all the goal.

Synesius (c. 414)—Bishop of Ptolamius and contemporaneous with St. Augustine (the first of the two great Augustines), was also like Gregory caught in the net of the Arian heresy. This picturesque figure is more familiar through the portrait in Kingsley's "Hypatia," and better known among English speaking people for accomplishments other than hymn writing. He was soldier, statesman, orator, philosopher, poet and bishop. He attracted not only the attention of Kingsley, but also that of Mrs. Browning who regarded him as the leader of the Greek Christian poets. His last ode is found in hymnals to-day as translated by Chatfield:

Lord Jesus, think on me
And purge away my sin,
From earth-born passion set me free
And make me pure within.

During the next four centuries the poetry of the Greek Church continued and ascended to greater heights, during which time there were writers deserving of special attention because of their hymns we use to-day. We can only give brief space for their mention.

St. Anatolius—together with the following Greek writers, belongs to the eighth century. He is only a few years older than his distinguished contemporaries and of him we know little, except his hymns of which two are in common use to-day:

Fierce was the wild billow
Dark was the night,

and

The day is past and over.

St. Andrew, Archbishop of Crete (660-732)—He, too, had influence upon Greek hymnody. He was author of homilies and a number of canons, and these were based on the canticles of the Greek Church. What we know best to-day is Neale's version of "Christian, dost thou see them?"

St. John of Damascus—who lived till 780, was foster brother of Cosmas, and uncle of Stephen. The latter's name is associated with the hymn, "Art thou weary, art thou languid," according to Neale. John was with his brother Cosmas at the monastery, and they are regarded as the two leading Greek Church poets. Together they wrote their hymns with the aid of each other's criticism.

St. Joseph—called the hymnographer, who was born in Sicily about a century later in 840, wrote more hymns than the other Greek writers. He was for years a slave in Crete, but afterward lived in Constantinople where he founded a monastery. Doctor Neale who claimed the originals were too tedious and verbose, has translated some of his writings. Among the hymns translated are, "Let the Church new anthems raise," and "Star of the morning so gloriously bright." We should not pass by these gifted writers of the Eastern Church without recognizing their work, and particularly our debt to the able translators of these Greek poets, such as Neale, Brownlie, Alexander, Chatfield and Mrs. Browning.

EARLY LATIN HYMNODY

Hilary of Poitiers—died in the fourth century during the period of the troublesome Arian controversy. In this period Christian song began to be recognized in the Latin language, and for a thousand years the Latin tongue was the medium of praise in the Western Church. The Latin hymn not only surpassed the Greek in quantity but also in quality.

The production of Latin hymns was stimulated at first by the same influences which provoked the development of Greek hymns, i.e., the heretical and profuse singing of the Arians which led to production of orthodox hymns for the defence of the true Catholic faith.

Hilary was sometimes called the hammer of the Arians, and his treatise on the doctrine of the Trinity in contrast to Arianism is the first work in Latin on that topic, and he most ably defended Athanasius in his stand against Arianism. Like Ambrose, who soon followed him, he was still a layman (and married) when elected by his fellow-citizens of his native town to the bishopric, receiving ordination as deacon, priest, and consecration as bishop in quick succession.

His learning, sincerity and courage were highly manifest. He publicly rebuked Constantine for which he was banished into exile. But later restored to liberty by Julian, he travelled extensively through Europe in defence of the truth. At last his enemies received sufficient strength to compel his retirement to his own city where his life's work ended.

St. Jerome says he wrote a book of hymns, but only seven or eight have been preserved. A version of one of them by Brownlie is "Gone are the shades of night."

Ambrose (340-397)—born at Treves, was educated for the law, and as a lawyer was appointed consular of Liguria, and in this capacity it became his duty to preside at the election of a bishop for the diocese of Milan. A hard contest ensued. Ambrose then with no ecclesiastical connection was seated in his large chair as civil officer, when at length a child seeing him exclaimed, "Ambrose is bishop!" The excited crowd took up the cry, all parties knowing of his upright character and ability, and forgetting all others, elected Ambrose to the high office. Reluctant to accept the sacred office, he yielded to the people. He proved to be a strong statesmanlike ecclesiastic and did more than any other to quell Arianism; and the Catholic faith in Milan became triumphant.

Ambrose successfully resisted the Emperor Valentinian II who prompted by his Arian mother, Empress Franstina, demanded the principal church in Milan for Arian worship and sent soldiers to force the issue. Ambrose flatly refused, but his supporters fought the soldiers and gained the victory.

Ambrose's strength and courage were further manifested in disciplining his friend, the Emperor Theodosius, in whose face he shut the doors of the church until the latter did penance for his slaughter of the people in Thessalonica. The record of this outstanding man need not be recited further here. Suffice it to say, he did much for the development of music in church worship. He firmly established the custom of hymn singing in his Basilica at Milan to which the Western Church looked for guidance in liturgical matters. He not only adopted the poetry of Hilary but also wrote original hymns of his own. He did much for development of church music also. He taught plain and simple tunes, was called the father of Latin church song, and was the first in the Western Church to encourage congregational praise. Many hymns are attributed to him, but only a few are authoritatively proven as his own original songs. His morning hymn, as rendered by Chandler, begins: "O Jesus, Lord of heavenly grace." A quatrain from his evening hymn is found in Confessions of St. Augustine, his friend and adviser, rendered also by Chandler:

O Blest Creator, God most High,
Great Ruler of the starring sky,
Who robing day with beauteous light
Hast clothed in soft repose the night.

Ambrosiani (Ambrose's hymns) were soon imitated by many authors.

Prudentius (348-413)—He was born in Spain, but was a patriotic Roman who lived to see the imperial influence more taken up with the side of Christianity. In his youth the throne was occupied by Julian, the apostate ruler. Like Ambrose, Prudentius was trained for the bar and acquired high office in the state. But when, in the fifties, he came to feel his past life was not worth while and resolved to change his course, he gave expression to this resolve in fitting lines which begin:

Now then, at last, close on to the very end of life
May yet my sinful soul put off her foolishness,
And if by deeds it cannot, yet at least, by words
Give praise to God.

Many indifferent Christians to-day, both old and young, may well take to heart these lines. Although this poem is not in the present day hymnal, two of his hymns are used to-day by virtue of translation by Henry W. Baker and Edward Caswall as his Christmas hymn, "Of the Father's love begotten," and his Epiphany hymn,

Earth has many a noble city,
Bethlehem, thou dost all excel.

Fortunatus (560-609)—was born in Italy, but spent much of his life in France. In younger years he was the fashionable poet of his day and one of the Latin "troubadours." Later he became chaplain to the convent at Poitiers, founded by the Queen Radegund, who was his friend. When she was to receive a piece of the supposed true cross from the Emperor, the occasion was one for which the Queen wished to have fitting ceremony.

Fortunatus turned from his nature songs and society poems and produced his famous processional hymn, "Vexilla Regis," for the Queen's occasion, which is regarded by Julian as one of the greatest hymns of the Latin Church. In this hymn we find Latin rhyme fully developed for the first time, and in a form not often surpassed afterward. One of the versions of this processional begins:

Abroad the regal banners fly,
Now shines the Cross's mystery;
Upon its Life did death endure,
And yet by death did life procure.

But Doctor Neale's version is the one generally used:

The royal banners forward go,
The Cross shines forth in mystic glow.

The hymnal contains as many as a half dozen or more, contributed by different translators, and they are among the most valuable hymns in use, as his Holy Week hymn, "See the destined day arise," and his Easter hymn, as given us by John Ellerton, "Welcome, happy morning! Age to age shall say," also his "Hail festal Day," with its adaptations for the great feasts of Easter, Ascension Day and Pentecost.

Gregory the Great (540-604)—He was regarded as one of the most famous Popes and one of the four great doctors of the Latin Church, so well known in history that little of his biography need be recited here. The story is well-known of his being so deeply affected, when he saw some Angles sold in the slave market in Rome, that he declared they were not to be regarded as Angles but Angels. He desired soon to go to Brittany as a missionary to give these attractive people the Gospel. He was prevented from going by his official superiors, but his pious wish was partly fulfilled later, when he, as Pope, or rather as Bishop of Rome, consecrated Augustine for the Mission. By his ability, statesmanship, ecclesiastical discipline and high character he did much to extend his influence and with it naturally increased the prestige of his high office.

Gregory is given credit for having done much for the improvement of church music. The exact nature of all he did is now difficult to determine. If he encouraged the use of congregational singing, which Ambrose before him tried to develop, his wisdom on this point may not be challenged. But the Gregorian chants which have been named for him were produced, it is said, so as to displace largely the more melodious style of music, attributed to Ambrose, by the more stately and solemn monotone which is their chief characteristic.

The modification of the scales previously used, and the addition of other "authentic" scales by him have continued in use until the present time. The famous "Veni Creator" ("Come, Holy Ghost, our souls inspire") may be accredited to him incorrectly, but two other good hymns have been generally believed to be his own original songs.

LATER LATIN HYMNODY (MEDIÆVAL)

During the Middle Ages, after Gregory the Great's day, there was witnessed the rising and later the decline of Greek hymnody. The Latin hymnody was developed contemporaneously with that of the Greek, but its fuller development continued till later times and its expansion much surpassed that of the Greek. The Greek hymn was more objective in character, the Latin was more subjective. The Latin hymns were more mystic, more personal, hence more appealing to the heart of succeeding generations. So while the Greek hymns have become less valuable for the present age, the Latin hymns, being restored to the present age by such splendid translators of modern times, have increased in value for our generation. This growth and expansion in Latin hymnody continued until the eleventh and twelfth centuries when the character of a large part of its hymns began to decline, as the Greek had done sometime before. It has been stated that in these two centuries, already mentioned, some of the Latin hymns were addressed to the name of the Virgin Mary and the saints. This type of hymn was of less use and value especially to the Protestant communions. It is noticeable how the improvement in the structure of the verse and its metre and of rhyming increased during the ascendency of Latin hymnody. But they had their use for that middle age. Because of a knowledge or lack of it and a process of reasoning, mediæval hymnists made God the Father seem to be an angry, intolerant, unlovable kind of deity, whom one could not truly worship. On the other hand, the Virgin Mary embodied the kind, humane, sympathetic idealism which could heartily be adored, and so expression was given to worship because of her character and influence. In reviewing the character of the poetry and writers of the mediæval period, we can stop only to mention a few outstanding ones whose names most concern us to-day. Among the first is ***St. Theodolph,*** Bishop of Orleans. He lived in the first half of the ninth century and so was contemporaneous with the last Greek writer mentioned, St. Joseph the Hymnographer. Theodolph was probably born in Italy and became abbot of a monastery in Florence. Brought to France by Charlemagne in 821, he was soon assigned to the bishopric of Orleans. He came into disfavour with the Emperor Louis the Pious, of France, successor to Charlemagne, on suspicion of conspiracy and was imprisoned at Angers. On a Palm Sunday when the procession of the clergy and laity, including the king, on their way to church passed by the window of the cell, according to legend, Theodolph, having already composed his hymn, sang it to the procession. This so impressed the king that he at once ordered his release and restoration to his see. It is the familiar hymn sung to-day on Palm Sunday, "All glory, laud and honour."

From the ninth century we pass to the twelfth century before we take up other names whose words are of practical importance to us to-day. In the twelfth century lived men whose works were of a conspicuous nature, either because of their great character and ability or because of the value of their hymns to us in this twentieth century.

Adam of St. Victor—He was a monk in the Abbey of St. Victor in Paris, who was probably a native of Brittany. The hymnal of to-day does not contain much from his sacred pen. But Trench spoke of him as "the foremost among the sacred Latin poets of the Middle Ages." Doctor Neale apostrophises: "My dear and Reverend Master!" When two such able authorities on hymnology speak so highly of a religious poet, it behooves us at least to notice such a name, even though we have so little of his hymnic poetry in use to-day. He was well learned in the Scriptures, and an able poet, but the metrical construction of his verses and his symbolisms are not easily translated into English poetry. "Hymns Ancient and Modern" contains four of his hymns, a good representation, but the one found in more recent hymnals, and included in the last American Episcopal hymnal, is his "Come, true hearts, in sweetest measure." It is not in the new Presbyterian hymnal.

Abelard (1079-1142)—

O what the joy and the glory must be
Those endless Sabbaths the blessed ones see!

This hymn is contained in a hymn book he wrote for Heloise, a young girl whom he loved, and for the nuns of the Abbey of the Paraclete. It was not known till more recent times since it has been only recently discovered.

Abelard was regarded as the most brilliant theologian of the twelfth century. His career was romantic and his fame as a teacher became established at Paris. He was a pupil of William of Champeaux who presided over the Cathedral School. Abelard disputed his teacher's opinion, and is said to have surpassed him in debate. His career was interrupted by his love for the young woman named Heloise. She was equally devoted by her affection for him, and they were later secretly married. The girl's uncle assisted by others attacked him at night time and brutally injured him. He returned to the Monastery of St. Denis near Paris where he was compelled to spend the last years of his life.

Bernard of Clairvaux—He was one of the two celebrated Bernards whose names stand out more prominently than all others during that part of the Middle Ages in which they lived. Although Bernard of Clairvaux was born near the close of the eleventh century, his works and life continued during the first half of the twelfth century. He died in 1153. A native of Burgundy, born of noble family, he planned to become a soldier but instead became a monk, in accordance with his mother's wish and prayer. His four brothers followed him into the monastery, and he drew so many other young men by his personality and attractiveness, that it was said mothers hid their sons lest they should fall under his resistless influence. He became the head of the Benedictine Monastery of Citeaux. Later, because of his genius and rigid self-sacrificing devotion, he was sent forth with a small band of disciples into an undeveloped region to found another monastery which became the Monastery of Clairvaux. By hard manual labour, the hills surrounding the valley were transformed into a splendid location for monastic life and labours. When Christendom became divided between rival claimants for the papacy, St. Bernard's influence won the throne for Innocent II.

His great influence was further manifested in his controversy with the famous Abelard, much to the discomforture of the latter. He is also well-known as the successful organizer and preacher of the Second Crusade, despite the disappointing results of the First Crusade. The crushing disappointment of this Second Crusade exposed him to the strong criticisms of many. But his lofty and pure motives were never questioned, and he held the continued respect of all who knew him. Luther called him "the best Monk who ever lived"; while Archdeacon Trench truly said of him, "Probably no man during his life-time ever exercised a personal influence in Christendom equal to his; the stayer of popular commotions; the queller of heresies; the umpire between princes and kings; the counsellor of popes." The student of church history should read the fascinating story of his life.

His hymns which we have to-day in our hymnals will be referred to more fully in a subsequent chapter under his able modern translators, as also in the case of the second Bernard who follows.

Bernard of Cluny—He was born of English extraction at Morlas (not Morlaix, as formerly supposed) in or near Brittany. In contrast to the well-known life of the other Bernard, there is unfortunately little known of his biography. But he is second, if second he be, only to the other Bernard, and lived about three years later. He became a monk in the famous Abbey of Cluny, the wealthiest and most influential monastery in France. His greatest poem is called "De Contemptu Mundi," a satire on the world of that day, containing three thousand lines which have been used to comfort the death-beds of many of God's children.

Few dream that these visions of the "sweet and blessed country" are taken from this lengthy satire. It was written in an unusual metre, difficult to reproduce in English. Translators have been obliged to take liberties with it, changing somewhat its expressions, yet preserving its spirit. Three of our great hymns are taken from it; but mention of his poem is reserved for a later chapter, under its best translator.

St. Francis of Assisi (1182-1225)—St. Francis was the world-famous mystic and monk of the early thirteenth century and preached the doctrines of complete self-surrender and poverty. He was also a singer and writer of hymns. He was the founder of the monastic order, the Franciscans. In his early youth he had been worldly and gay, but when he reached the age of twenty-five he was converted during a serious illness. He soon learned the full meaning of the Gospel as self-surrender and absolute trust in the providing care of God, and he and his followers went forth as the Begging Brothers. Because of his great zeal his wealthy father cast him off, and he went out into the snow-covered hills and through woods, a pilgrim bereft of every earthly thing. As he wandered he knew not whither, this formerly gay singer of love songs and romantic ballads now raised his voice to sing of the love of God and the kinship of all nature to mankind. He sang in the language of his hearers, Italian, kindred to the Latin, which others used in his day. His "Canticle of the Sun," or the "Song of the Creatures," is a splendid piece of literature. As a song its rhyme is not exact, and it is curiously irregular in metre, but expresses so forcibly his warmth of love:

Great God of all, omnipotent and high,
To Thee by glory, honour, laud and praise,
And blessing, Lord, we raise.

We are not worthy e'en Thy Name to say,
Praise be to God the Lord,
From creatures one and all,
From Brother Sun, our Lord,
Who lights us by his rays
And radiant makes the days,
All glory to the Lord be given.

Praise be to God my Lord,
From Sister Moon so fair and bright,
And from the stars that make the darkness light.

Praise be to God our Lord,
From Brother Wind, from clouds and air,
From weather dull and fair.

Praise be to God the Lord,
From Sister Weather, chaste and pure,
So precious, useful and demure.

Praise be to God my Lord,
From Brother Fire, gay, robust and strong,
Who sparkles merrily the whole night long.

Praise be to God for our dear mother earth,
In whom all fruits and flowers have their birth.

Thomas of Celano (thirteenth century)—He was a Franciscan monk, biographer of St. Francis of Assisi, and the reputed author of the "Dies Irae." This hymn has commanded more attention even than others of the Latin classics, such as the "De Contemptu Mundi," the "Vexilla Regis," the "Veni Creator Spiritus," "Stabat Mater," and all other famous Latin poems of the Middle Ages. It is used both in the Burial Service of the Roman Church and in Protestant churches as an Advent hymn. Its opening words are based on Zeph. 1:15, and its intention is to awaken the sense of utter helplessness of man to save himself, and then to bring him to trust implicitly in the power of the Lord to raise all from death to life again.

There have been many English versions, among them one by Sir Walter Scott. Doctor Robinson in his "Annotations" says, "It stands pre-eminent not only because of the grandeur of its theme, but also from the perfection of its form and rhythm." Its many merits give it a foremost place in sacred song. Among more than two hundred versions, probably the most used now are Dean Stanley's and that by Dr. W. J. Irons in 1849 of which we give the first half below with its shorter stanzas:

Day of wrath! Oh, day of mourning!
See fulfilled the prophets' warning,
Heaven and earth in ashes burning!

Oh, what fear man's bosom rendeth,
When from heaven the Judge descendeth,
On whose sentence all dependeth.

Wondrous sound the trumpet flingeth;
Through earth's sepulchres it ringeth;
All before the throne it bringeth.

Death is struck, and nature quaking,
All creation is awaking,
To its Judge an answer making.

Lo! the Book exactly worded,
Wherein all hath been recorded:
Thence shall judgment be awarded.

When the Judge His seat attaineth,
And each hidden deed arraigneth,
Nothing unavenged remaineth.

What shall I, frail man, be pleading?
Who for me be interceding,
When the just are mercy needing?

King of majesty tremendous,
Who dost free salvation send us,
Fount of pity, then befriend us!

Think, good Jesu, my salvation
Cost Thy wondrous Incarnation;
Leave me not to reprobation!

Faint and weary Thou hast sought me,
On the cross of suffering bought me.
Shall such grace be vainly brought me?

St. Thomas Aquinas—He has been called by Duncan Campbell the greatest of the mediæval divines and ranking in the Roman

Church next to the four Latin Fathers of earlier period—Jerome, Ambrose, Augustine and Gregory. His theological teaching is still the standard book for Roman Catholic Church students and is held in greatest esteem in the Latin Church.

He was a member of the Dominican Order and greatly esteemed. Duncan Campbell says of him that "great cities and universities and churches contended for his lectures and sermons when he was alive and for his relics when dead." Yet he remained unspoiled and modest and continued to live a devout and simple life, declining high honours. He declined the Patriarchate of Jerusalem, the Archbishopric of Naples and the high office of Cardinal. A legend tells that the Lord appeared to him one day in a vision and said to him, "Thomas, thou hast written well of Me, what reward wouldst thou have for thy labour?" and the reply was, "None other than Thyself; Lord."

The Episcopal Church Hymnal has two Holy Communion hymns from Aquinas, translated by Edward Caswall. The one most extensively used is,

O Saving Victim, opening wide
The gate of heaven to man below,

and

Now my tongue, the mystery telling
Of the glorious Body sing
And the Blood, all price excelling.

Other famous hymns of the Mediæval Church, besides these already named as the "De Contemptu Mundi" and "Dies Irae," are "Veni Creator, Spiritus" ("Come, Holy Ghost, Creator"), whose authorship is unknown, although it has been attributed to various writers. "Veni Sancte Spiritus" ("Come, Thou Holy Paraclete") is often ascribed to King Robert II of France, but Julian holds that it was probably by Pope Innocent III. "Stabat Mater" has also been ascribed to different great men of the Middle Ages, yet its real authorship is as yet unknown. Probably written in the twelfth century, it did not come into general use until the fourteenth century. The favourite modern rendering is by Caswall,

At the cross her station keeping,
Stood the mournful mother weeping,
Where He hung, the dying Lord.

For her soul of joy bereavèd,
Bowed with anguish, deeply grievèd,
Felt the sharp and piercing sword.

SUMMARY

In this chapter we have considered briefly the Hebrew Psalter, the hymns of St. Luke's Gospel, other early Christian hymns, Greek hymnody, Clement of Alexandria, Gregory of Nazianzi, Synesius, St. Anatolius, St. Andrew of Crete, St. John of Damascus, St. Joseph, translators; early Latin hymnody, Hilary of Poitiers, St. Ambrose, Prudentius, Fortunatus, Gregory the Great, mediæval Latin hymnody, St. Theodolph, Adam of St. Victor, Abelard, Bernard of Clairvaux, Bernard of Cluny, St. Francis of Assisi, Thomas of Celano, St. Thomas Aquinas translators.

For Further Reading

The Hymns of the Breviary and Missal, Matthew Britt.
Te Deum Laudamus; Christian Life in Song, Mrs. Rundle Charles.
The Source of "Jerusalem the Golden," Samuel M. Jackson.
Byzantine Music and Hymnography, Tillyard.
Latin Hymnody, Humphrey V. Hughes.
Hymns of the Eastern Church, John M. Neale.
The Hymnody of the Christian Church, Louis F. Benson.
Grove's Dictionary of Music and Musicians.
A History of English Cathedral Music, 1549-1889, John S. Bumpus.
Christian Latin Poetry, F. J. E. Raby.
Early Latin Hymns, A. S. Walpole.
Church Music in History and Practice, Winfred Douglas.

VI

GERMAN HYMNODY

THE English hymn book has been rich in its heritage not only from the ancient Greek and the ancient and mediæval Latin, but also from the rich store-house of German hymnody, not to mention other national sources. The German hymns surpass in number those of any other language, except the English. Philip Schaff said that one hundred thousand constitutes the quantity of them. About ten thousand became classical, and many have been admitted into different hymn books. We may reasonably claim, according to Schaff, that nearly one thousand of these hymns are practical and of permanent value—a large number of worthy hymns to be found in one language.

These German hymns were produced by many men and women from all ranks of life—clergy, princes and princesses, statesmen, generals, physicians, lawyers, merchants, labourers, and private individuals, in contrast to the English hymns which were nearly all produced by the clergy and their families.

The Germans have always been lovers of music and enjoyed their own singing, as well as being listeners. Germany is the home of Protestant church music. From early times the hymn was the usual expression of their religion. Even some in the Latin language were produced by the Germans. They also translated old Latin lines into their vernacular, and to these added their original compositions and sang them heartily at festivals and other occasions. These have not come into our general usage in English for different reasons. Yet there were some early German hymns, still in use, when the German Reformation arrived in this land where the Reformation had its birth.

Many of the succeeding hymns which possessed strength and unction, triumphant faith and deepest consolation, were the outgrowth of the conflicts and storms of the Reformation period, and of the devastation and sufferings of the Thirty Years War. Others belong to the revival period of pietism, and the ardour of the Moravian Brotherhood, and still more sprang up during the unbelieving age of rationalism, "like flowers from dry ground."

All these constitute a book of confessions of faith for German Evangelical Christianity.

As the German hymns chronicle the different periods of German history, we treat them under these heads, with leading writers of each period.

For several centuries preceding, the hymns of Germany were written in Latin and their singing was reserved for the priest and trained singers instead of being sung by the congregations. Luther rescued hymnody from its monastic prison and put it into the hands of the people twelve hundred years after Ambrose of Milan first gave impetus to congregational music.

Whatever may be said of the character of Luther regarding his faults, and he had very definite ones, we must estimate his worth by his important teachings, and his fearless work in making the changes and improvements the world of his day needed so badly. Among his various great accomplishments was his revolution in public worship.

Martin Luther (1483-1546)—The great leader of the Reformation was also the evangelical hymnist of special note. He is rightly credited with giving to the German people in their own tongue the Bible, the catechism and the hymn book, as is truly said, "so that God might speak directly to them in His Word, and that they might speak directly to Him in their songs." He was not only a theologian and teacher, but also a musician as well as an original poet and translator. He was properly regarded as the greatest German hymnist. He also composed tunes to some of his best hymns.[1] He began to write hymns in 1523, only a few years after the posting of his Ninety-five Theses on the gate of Castle Church at Wittenberg in which he denounced the papal teachings, and proclaimed the Bible teaching of forgiveness of sin, in contradiction of Tetzel's offerings of indulgences of penance. Luther continued to write hymns for years with such regard for quality that he is almost equally distinguished for both quality and small quantity, averaging only one a year. He published in all twenty-one original hymns, and about an equal number of translations, together with a few adaptations from earlier German sources.

His life-work, which belongs more to the study of church history, should be studied in some more comprehensive way. He set his nation to singing the Lutheran teachings, and thus kindled

[1] Further information on Luther's music may be found in *Luther's Hymns* by Allyn & Bacon.

the fire that spread its sweeping flames over the nation with powerful effects. We may well regard the sixteenth century as the turning point of Christian hymnody.

Only two of Luther's hymns have a place in our English hymnals of to-day. His "Ein' feste Burg" is his best known hymn. The date of the composition is not definitely known. It was probably in 1529, or when he was in prison or soon after his release. It was widely known to Protestant Germany, and so inspired the people with courage that Heine called it "The Marseillaise of the Reformation"—"A mighty fortress is our God." It is based on the Forty-sixth Psalm, "God is our refuge and strength, a very present help in trouble," which was well versified by Elizabeth Wordsworth and set to a tune provided by Luther. Two other very prominent translations are those by Thomas Carlyle, used in the Canadian and English hymnals, and by Rev. Frederick H. Hedge, made at Cambridge, Massachusetts, in 1852, which is found in American hymnals and is easily accessible. In contrast with Hedge's we give Carlyle's below, as rewritten by J. S. Stallybass, 1857:

A sure stronghold our God is He,
A trusty shield and weapon;
Our help He'll be, and set us free
From every ill can happen.
That old malicious foe
Intends us deadly woe;
Armed with might from hell,
And deepest craft as well,
On earth is not his fellow.

Through our own force we nothing can,
Straight were we lost forever;
But for us fights the proper Man,
By God sent to deliver.
Ask ye who this may be
Christ Jesus named is He.
Of Sabaoth the Lord;
Sole God to be adored;
'Tis He must win the battle.

And were the world with devils filled,
All eager to devour us,
Our souls to fear should little yield,
They cannot overpower us.

Their dreaded prince no more
Can harm us as of yore;
Look grim as e'er he may
Doomed is his ancient sway;
A word can overthrow him.

God's word for all their craft and force
One moment will not linger;
But spite of hell shall have its course;
'Tis written by His finger.
And though they take our life,
Goods, honor, children, wife;
Yet is their profit small;
These things shall vanish all;
The city of God remaineth.

Another popular hymn is his "Gelobet seist Du, Jesus Christ," freely translated:

All praise to Thee, Eternal Lord,
Clothed in the garb of flesh and blood,
Choosing a manger for Thy Throne,
While worlds on worlds are Thine alone.

It is really a translation of a translation of an old Latin hymn which has been written in the nature of a carol for Christmastide.

The Methodist Hymnal contains a hymn of Luther's under the subject of missions:

Flung to the heedless winds,
Or on the waters cast,
The martyrs' ashes, watched,
Shall gathered be at last.

The new Presbyterian hymnal has two others by Luther, both translated in carol style by Miss Catherine Winkworth.

Other writers of Germany have left poetry which has been well translated by Miss Catherine Winkworth and two others, Jane Borthwick and her sister, Sarah Findlater. In fact, the majority of German hymns now used in our hymnal have been given us through the splendid work of translation by this gifted woman. Miss Winkworth was born in London in 1829. Although not the first to publish translations, her work places her among the foremost in this field of service. She has had more to do with the increased use of German hymns in our English language than any other writer.

For what follows we are almost as much indebted to Miss Winkworth as to the author of the original songs which we shall further notice. Her chief works are her volumes, "Christian Singers of Germany," and "Lyra Germanica," which contain the most important of her translated hymns from which we have drawn. Her splendid ability and fine Christian character, together with her poetic gift, enabled her to render a great service during a comparatively short life.

Philip Nicolai (1556-1608)—He was born soon after Luther's death and hence is a product of the latter years of the Reformation. We recognize him because of his music as well as his hymns. Like Luther and other German hymn writers he could well write the music for his text. He is exceptional in that his tunes have been retained with his hymns through these many years, instead of being displaced by more recent compositions.

Nicolai was a Lutheran pastor in Westphalia and given to controversy with both Roman Catholics and Calvinists. When he was living in Westphalia a severe pestilence broke out and he had the sad experience of seeing many funerals pass by his residence. This experience naturally turned him toward the contemplation of the eternal life. His leading hymn as given us by Miss Winkworth is, "Wake, awake, for night is flying." Another is

O Morning Star, how fair and bright
Thou beamest forth in truth and light.

The melodies of both these hymns were Nicolai's own composition, and our hymnals usually offer with them the noble harmonizations by J. S. Bach. They are splendid examples of the German chorale.

Period of the Thirty Years War—During this period (1618-1648) with its prolonged sufferings, came the most prolific German hymn writers, among whom we name:

Martin Rinkart (1586-1649)—About 1640 he wrote his "Nun danket alle Gott," as translated by Miss Winkworth, "Now thank we all our God." This has been called the "Te Deum" of Germany. Rinkart was the son of a poor coppersmith and he made his own way at the University of Leipzig. He was ordained and became precentor at the church in Eisleben. At the age of thirty-one he was offered the position of archdeacon in his native town in Saxony. He was there when war broke out, and died at the close of the Thirty Years War. The plague of 1637 visited the city of Eilenburg with great severity. This was followed by a famine. The two misfortunes brought very trying labours to Rinkart, and his losses and great sacrifices pathetically affected him and his children. Yet out of calamities he breathed the unbounded spirit of trust and readiness to give thanks, and wrote:

Now thank we all our God
With heart, and hands, and voices,
Who wondrous things hath done,
In whom His world rejoices.

The Transitional Period—The next period is the transitional one from the confessional and didactic to that of pietistic period, when individual expression arose to its height. The personal and intense quality of expression came to the front. Among most representative writers of this time is:

Paul Gerhardt (1607-1676)—He occupies a high place after Luther as a hymn writer. Born near Wittenberg, he was educated at the university there. He, too, lived his youth and young manhood during the trying period of the long war, being cast about from one place to another. We find him at the age of forty-five a man of talents, still merely a private tutor and candidate for Orders. When ordained to the ministry he began his work in Berlin. He had already written hymns but was as yet unable to publish them. He lived for a time in the home of an advocate named Berthold, with whose daughter he was in love, but without sufficient income to marry. Later being called to a country place he was at length married to Anna Berthold. Still later he had to endure long illness, the death of his wife and four children. Finally losing his position, he retired to a humble parish at Lubben where he laboured among a rude and unappreciative people. His religion and disposition made him cheerful amidst suffering and disappointments, and instead of becoming embittered with his lot, he took refuge and recreation in writing songs. A number of his hymns have been translated into English. One of his best hymns as translated by Miss Winkworth is:

Since Jesus is my Friend,
And I to Him belong,
It matters not what foes intend,
However fierce and strong.

Another much used hymn is translated by the distinguished John Wesley:

Jesus, Thy boundless love to me
No thought can reach, no tongue declare.

Probably his most important hymn to-day is the Christmas hymn, translated by Miss Winkworth, "All my heart this night rejoices." Another splendid hymn which has been translated by John Wesley is:

Give to the winds thy fears,
Hope and be undismayed.

The famous hymn as translated by James W. Alexander, "O sacred head now wounded," or "O sacred head surrounded," as translated by Henry W. Baker, which has been ascribed to Paul Gerhardt in the past, is now found to be Gerhardt's translation of an earlier hymn by the School of Clairvaux.

The Pietistic and Moravian Period—The next period is that of the Pietistic writers. It produced many hymn writers. It was a kind of second Reformation or revival in Germany. The pietism of Philip Spener and August Franke was a reaction against dry scholasticism and formalism of the Lutheran Church of that day, and it emphasized the need of practical and experimental piety. Among the best of German writers of this movement was

Gerhard Tersteegen (1697-1769)—He was of the German Reformed Church and belongs to the early part of the eighteenth century. He was a ribbon weaver at Mulheim. His life was one of simple habits, by nature ascetic, evangelical, and personally very pious, spending much time in meditation and prayer. His home became known as the "Pilgrim's Cottage," a retreat for many who came for spiritual advice, while others sent to him to come to read and pray with the sick. His hymns numbering over a hundred were conspicuous for simplicity and manifesting the love of God.

Tersteegen's best known hymn in English, as freely translated by John Wesley, is "Thou hidden love of God." Another good one is

God Himself is with us,
Let us now adore Him.

Among the Moravians came the birth of a great missionary movement. They were the descendants of the Bohemian Brethren, followers of John Huss in the fifteenth century. In the latter part of this century the Bohemians had many hymns; some were translations from the Latin, others were original in the vernacular. These Bohemians were later called the Moravians, and were earnest and vigorously missionary in spirit. A certain nobleman of wealth joined these Moravians.

Count Nicolaus L. Von Zinzendorf (1700-1760)—He was born at Dresden in 1700 of a noble, wealthy and religious family, and was educated at the University of Wittenberg where he studied law. His maternal grandmother was the Baroness Von Gersdorff whose house was his home in boyhood. She herself was a writer of hymns and a woman of strict piety. From early years he received strong religious impressions. As a boy in school he founded among his fellows "The Order of the Mustard Seed," which bound its members to promote the conversion of the heathen. After his university course he travelled for some time When in Düsseldorf he saw in the picture gallery a well-known painting of the Saviour crowned with thorns, under which was written, "All this I have done for thee, what doeth thou for Me?" these words struck his heart and led him to adopt as his life's motto, "I have but one passion, and that is He, only He." His private life had its trials, and he devoted the whole of his fortune to the cause of his Master and died poor. Like Gerhardt, he lost his wife and all his sons, but he never lost courage and lived until 1760. He became the Bishop of the Moravian Brethren, and he helped to develop among them that remarkable missionary spirit which has continued among their spiritual descendants until the present time.

During a time of banishment from Saxony on the charge of introducing dangerous novelties, he spent several years in America, mostly in Pennsylvania, where the good work started by him still remains in the institutions in Bethlehem and surrounding community, and also in Winston Salem, North Carolina.

The love of music and devout worship among the Moravians in Bethlehem led the great student of Bach, the late Dr. Fred Wolle, a personal friend of the author, to found the now famous Bethlehem Bach Choir, which gives its noble music festival every spring at Lehigh University.

Although Zinzendorf wrote two thousand hymns, only two are found to-day in the Episcopal and Methodist hymnals, but the new Presbyterian hymnal somehow has omitted them. The Canadian Presbyterian Church hymnal also has two of his hymns.

His best one, which has two translations, of which Miss Jane Borthwick's version, an unusual metred verse, is best loved by all German people and first taught to their children, is as follows:

Jesus, still lead on
Till our rest beyond,
And although the way be cheerless,
We will follow calm and fearless,
Guide us by Thy hand,
To our Fatherland.

Rationalistic Period—This period was contemporaneous with the classic poets of German literature, who, however, produced no hymns. Those who tried to write were naturally affected by the rationalism of the age, and their hymns have failed to survive since rationalism does not naturally produce fervent hymns of lasting worth. But one exception stands out the more prominently, who is

Christian Gellert (1716-1769)—He was a man of distinction and had among his pupils at Leipzig such great men as Goethe and Lessing. His hymns are said to have met the standard lyrics of his time, and won general admiration and soon passed into the hymn books in use in Germany. They were sung by both the Roman Catholic and Lutheran churches.

Gellert's hymn, most favoured in recent years in the translation by Miss Frances Cox, is:

Jesus lives, thy terrors now
Can no longer, death, appall us;
Jesus lives, by this we know
Thou, O grave, canst not enthrall us.
Alleluia.

This has been used for a recessional at funerals of prominent persons, and is one of the good Easter hymns found in that classification in the American Episcopal hymnal and in the Canadian Presbyterian hymnal. It is also classed as an Ascension hymn.

The Classic Period—The last period of German hymnody, we notice here, begins in the early part of the nineteenth century. This late century is a period of classic hymns, coming later than the classical period of German literature and poetry, when lived some of its most distinguished writers. This later period is rich in hymns, which combine the old faith with the new spirit of classical form and expression, or in other words, sound doctrine with refined feeling.

Among hymnists of this time were Frederick Rückert, called one of the greatest masters of German lyric poetry, and Albert Knapp, minister at Stüttgart, one of the most gifted religious poets of his day, and editor of Liederschatz.

Among the most popular German hymnists of the nineteenth century, according to Julian, was

Carl Johann Spitta (1801-1859)—He was a Lutheran pastor and superintendent in the Kingdom of Hanover, educated at the University of Göttingen, and during his early ministry served in various parishes. Spitta's poetic instinct was manifest in early childhood. After his conversion he wrote a friend, "In the manner in which I formerly sang, I sing no more. To the Lord I consecrate my life and my love and likewise my song. He gave to me song and melody. I give it back to Him."

His "Psaltery and Harp" passed through numerous editions, a new edition every year for many years. His hymns are marked by deep evangelical piety and simplicity, and have an excellent translator in Richard Massie.

One of Spitta's best was translated by Massie, of which the following is the first verse:

I know no life divided,
O Lord of life, from Thee;
In Thee is life provided
For all mankind and me;
I know no death, O Jesus,
Because I live in Thee;
Thy death it is that frees us
From death eternally.

Another good hymn of his is, "O happy home, where Thou art loved the dearest."

Among other important German hymnists, whose names we can merely mention are: Baron Friedrich Canitz, author of "Come, my soul, Thou must be waking"; Albert Knapp, a much later writer, author of "Father of heaven, Who hast created all"; Heinrich von Laufenberg, author of "Lord Jesus Christ, our Lord most dear"; Matthaus von Löwenstein, author of "Lord of our life and God of our salvation"; Laurentius Laurenti, author of "Rejoice, rejoice, believers"; Samuel Rodigast, author of "Whate'er my God ordains is right"; Christian Knorr Rosenroth, author of "Jesus, Sun of Righteousness, Brightest Beam of love divine"; Heinrich Schenck, author of "Whose are these like stars appearing"; Benjamin Schmolck, author of "My Jesus, as Thou wilt, O may Thy will be mine"; Johann Schwedler, author of "Ask ye what great thing I know, That delights and stirs me so"; Georg Weissel, author of "Lift up your heads, ye mighty gates." [2]

In conclusion, the nineteenth century is one in which there came a growing interest and popularity of German hymnody. Note also the interest in anonymous hymns of German source, as "When morning gilds the sky," translated by Edward Caswall in 1853; and the favourite, "Fairest Lord Jesus," a seventeenth century hymn, the translation of which in the nineteenth century is anonymous, as well as the original. This period is marked by renewed interest and rediscovery of old German carols, too long hidden, together with their musical settings also.

SUMMARY

In this chapter there is the consideration of the following material: Historical background; Martin Luther; Philip Nicolai; Martin Rinkart; Paul Gerhardt; Gerhard Tersteegan; Count Von Zinzendorf; Christian Gellert; Carl Johann Spitta; Other German writings mentioned.

For Further Reading

Die Melodien der Deutschen Evangelischen Kirchenlieder, Johannes Zahn (6 vols.).

Lyra Germanica, Catherine Winkworth (2 vols.).

Christian Singers of Germany, Catherine Winkworth.

Hymns of Luther, Bacon and Allen.

Paulus Gerhardt as a Hymn Writer, Theodore B. Hewitt.

The Spiritual Sense in Sacred Legend, Brailsford.

A Dictionary of Hymnology, John Julian.

[2] The new Methodist and Presbyterian hymnals contain a beautiful old hymn by Katherine Von Schlegel, translated by Jane Borthwick:

Be still, my soul, the Lord is on thy side;
Bear patiently the cross of grief or pain;
Leave to thy God to order and provide.

PART TWO

VII

ENGLISH PSALMODY AND EARLY ENGLISH HYMNODY

IN THE age of the Reformation in England and for over one hundred years thereafter, psalm singing was the universal rule both in the established an non-Conformist churches.

In the British Empire, as in Germany, there was no Martin Luther, who set the German people to singing in their own language. The people of Germany all began to sing and hence the Reformation soon spread rapidly and effectively throughout the German nation.

The earliest outlet of the common people's singing of songs of praise in the vernacular of their day was in the form of the carol preceding the Reformation, which became largely checked in England some years after the Reformation period. It was to come to silence for a time, or until different days should later come to release the carol from its bounden cords with which this form of self-expression had been firmly tied.

The English people, different from the German, did not depart from the Latin praises, nor the strongly entrenched custom of psalm singing. There was no place given for original composition in the worship of the people of England, nor place given for English hymns until the middle of the seventeenth century. Even then the custom of psalm singing held sway over early attempts of hymnic praise both in England and the American colonies into the eighteenth century or until after the days of Watts and Wesley.

We use the term "psalmody" as applied to the body of songs which were metrical versions of the Hebrew songs adapted to early modern singing. It sometimes included paraphrases of other portions of Holy Writ. Numerous publications of psalms were put into poetic verse. Julian's Dictionary tells us there were three hundred and twenty-six separate publications of the Psalter in English alone, not to mention the attempts made in other languages.

The psalms in metre came into existence first, not in England nor even in Germany, but in France, through the work of Clément Marot, the court poet under King Francis I who reigned from 1515 to 1547. This was the early period of the Reformation and the ascendency of the Spanish Emperor, Charles V. Luther was mightily stirring Germany with his attacks on the papacy, while Cardinal Woolsey was exerting his influence in England.

Marot was a writer of ballads, love songs and court poetry, often regarded as light-hearted, yet at times his serious verses attracted attention. He even espoused the Huguenot faith, and though it would seem his religion did not lead him to a high degree of piety, he did suffer at times because of his Protestant leanings. King Francis was willing to promote him, as he did, because he would serve his cause against the Emperor Charles V. The King appreciated his poetic gifts and willingly rewarded him for his aid. Different in his character and his ways from John Calvin at Geneva, he would not be expected to attract the latter. But Calvin also was willing to use one who would aid his cause. Calvin, bent on extending the effective use of Psalmody, saw in Marot one best fitted to versify the psalms, putting them into "current French metre" for the people to sing. The latter had already versified psalms in the metres of popular songs for court attendants and others to sing. He began to make metrical psalms in 1533. Calvin made his first psalm book in 1539, at Strasburg, which included a dozen of Marot's court songs, together with a few of Calvin's own making. But a subsequent edition of Marot (in 1542) got him into trouble with the Roman authorities who held that this work infringed upon their monopoly of interpreting Holy Scriptures. Marot fled to Geneva where he found Calvin, whose encouragement led Marot to continue his work of Psalmody. In 1543 was published the famous "Genevan Psalter," whose lasting value is discovered by reference to any modern hymn book. The next year he died, and his psalter was enlarged and revised by Theodore Beza, at the request of Calvin, and what was objectionable in its gaiety and references of the French Court was removed. The influence and success of this work were beyond expectation. It was much used among French-speaking people and even extensively used by the Roman Catholics. All the Huguenots were familiar with it. It is said Francis I used it upon his death-bed. It was translated into various languages. It passed through at least a thousand editions, and its influence extended throughout the Protestant world. In England several translations of it appeared, and the versions which succeeded it followed its form and manner of expression.

ENGLISH PSALMODY

The psalms of Marot were carried across the English Channel to England and their influence was soon felt there. In 1538 Myles Coverdale, Bishop of Exeter, had published a metrical version of fifteen psalms and other material named, "Goastly Psalms and Spirituall Songs, drawn out of the Holy Scripture." This we call the beginning of English Psalmody, but the version never secured much attention. Coverdale had spent much time in Geneva, first in the pursuit of learning and later as a refugee during the reign of Queen Mary. But this song book did not follow closely the models of Marot.

The impetus to psalms in England virtually began with Thomas Sternhold who was "groom" to his Majesty the King's robes. His organ playing and singing were pleasing to King Edward VI, to whom he dedicated his new versification of nineteen of the psalms. He followed the model and metres of Marot. A second edition containing more of the psalms was published in the year he died, 1549. This was the year when the first book of Common Prayer was published in English during the reign of the young King Edward VI. His work was continued by another poet, John Hopkins, of whose biography we know little except that he received his education at Oxford and later settled as a minister in Suffolk. The additional psalms which Hopkins and others added to those of Sternhold constituted what is called "The Old Version" of the psalms. Thus arose the English Psalmody which gained much attention and became widely popular in England. The 1562 edition was printed with notes of melodies which were called "Church Tunes," published in completed form in 1562. It was the first to give all the psalms in English verse to the English public, and was appended to the Book of Common Prayer.

The reason for Sternhold's pious labours is well expressed in the preface to the book where it is stated that Sternhold desired the verse should be sung by the English, not only in the worship of the church but "moreover in private houses for their godly solace and comfort; laying apart all ungodly songs and ballads which tend only to the nourishment of vice and corrupting of youth."

For over a hundred years from the first edition there was a succession of many editions. Before the year 1600, says Alice M. Earle, there were seventy-four editions—a large number for the times. From 1600 to 1700 two hundred and thirty-five editions came out. Many subsequent editions were published in the eighteenth century and even twenty-one in the nineteenth century.

As in other versions, many of the psalms were very awkward, and poor poetry, often having metrical renderings which were bad, and difficult to sing smoothly. In some instances the translations from the Hebrew were so free and easy that they were regarded as positive misrepresentations of the sacred writers. Rev. Samuel Wesley, the father of John Wesley, referred to some of it as "scandalous doggerel."

Metrical psalms were set to music by some of the leading musicians of that day, as Thomas Tallis, the contemporary of the famous Palestrina, William Byrd, Parsons, and John Milton, the father of the great poet. Some of their melodies are still found in hymn books. Some of the psalms were also sung to popular street tunes. So not all the early psalm tunes were of the "gravest" type.

The more direct influence of Marot began to be felt when Queen Mary, daughter of Henry VIII and Catherine of Aragon, ascended the throne. Her attempt to restore the Roman Catholic faith is connected with the persecution of Anglican Christians, including the burning of bishops, other clergymen and people. Many refugees fled to the Continent. A congregation of English and Scotch Protestants was organized at Frankfort-on-the-Main, and the famous John Knox was chosen pastor, but the Anglicans and dissenting brethren did not get along well together. Knox and his adherents retired to Geneva in 1555, where a distinct church was formed and the psalms of Sternhold and Hopkins were adopted with many alterations and additions. This Anglo-Genevan Psalter contains songs and tunes in use ever since, to which can be traced "Old Hundredth," so called because it appears for the first time set to "All people that on earth do dwell," ascribed to William Kethe.

In England the public singing of psalms was suspended during Queen Mary's reign, although they were used privately more than ever. When Queen Elizabeth came to the throne the simple versions of Sternhold and Hopkins became the congregational book of praise of the English Church. It is said nothing could exceed the enthusiasm of the people, allowed to sing these psalms again, when in 1559 permission was given that they should be used in public worship.

About this time lesser attempts at versification were made by Elizabeth herself, and by Fairfax, Lord Bacon, and other poets, but these did not obtain wide usage. Sir Philip Sidney, assisted by his sister Lady Pembroke, made a metrical version of the psalms which was never used in public worship although its poetic character was not inferior to other versions.

Another important version was made in 1622 by Henry Ainsworth. It was carried by the Pilgrim Fathers to New England, and thus became the first book of English praise to be used in America. Longfellow refers to it in his "Courtship of Miles Standish," where John Alden "heard as he drew near the door the musical voice of Priscilla." This versification after a few years became unsatisfactory to the early colonists in America and was superseded by a newer translation by representatives of the Congregational churches in New England. Ainsworth's version was the book which the Puritan refugees in Holland published a few years before the Pilgrims departed for the New World in 1620.

BAY PSALM BOOK

The "Bay Psalm Book" was the result of efforts of able men in New England whose work is the first book of praise produced in the New World. It passed through several editions, substantially unchanged, covering a period of one hundred years. Not only did it in its favourable reception supersede the Ainsworth version in New England, but it also gained recognition and favour in Scotland, where it was printed and bound up with the Bible and then imported again into the American Colonies. There are only ten extant copies of the first edition still found, and the author has viewed with interest one of the two known extant copies of the second edition, found in the John Carter Brown Library of Brown University, Providence. The other copy is in the British Museum.

A portion of the work of the "Bay Psalm Book" was supposed to be assigned to each of thirty scholars but the most of it was done by three men, viz.: Richard Mather, Thomas Welde and John Eliot who later became known as "the apostle to the American Indians."

While the work was in progress a printing press was imported from England and placed in the home of President Dunster of the recently founded Harvard College. Stephen Daye was brought over from England to be the printer. Here the "Bay Psalm Book" was printed in 1640. This first edition consisted of 1700 copies, a large number for the small population of those days, which showed faith in the new undertaking. The books sold rapidly and a good profit was realized. For this work a General Court was held in Boston, and Stephen Daye was given a "grant of three hundred acres of land where it may be convenient without prejudice to any town." The men who made this version were scholars but not poets, and a bad sample of their versification with ungrammatical expression is here given:

And sayd He would not them waste; had not
Moses stood (whom he chose)
For him i'th breach; to twine his wrath
Lest that he should waste those.

President Dunster was later expected to improve the versification, but did not go far in this accomplishment. He was willing to accept the excuse the translators themselves offered, "if the verses are not always so elegant as some desire or expect, let them consider that God's Altar needs not our polishings. We have respected rather a plain translation than to smooth our verse with the sweetness of any paraphrase." [1]

A noticeable improvement of President Dunster's, although far from perfect, was his lines:

Likewise the heavens he down-bow'd,
And he descended; also there
Was at his feet a gloomy cloud
And he on cherubs rode apace.

Yet on the wings of wind he flew
The darkness made his secret place
His covert round about him drew.

Other editors soon followed these "polishings" until sixteen editions had been printed. It is said that at least seventy editions were brought out, some of which were printed in England and Scotland.

There were other subsequent versifications attempted in America, but for general use both the American Church as well as the Church in Scotland used more extensively for a time the third chief version produced in Scotland, the Scottish Psalter compiled by Francis Rous, which has been used in Scottish kirks since its publication in 1650 and extensively used in the psalm-singing Presbyterian churches in America. Francis Rous was a

[1] *The Sabbath in Puritan New England,* Charles Scribners Sons, New York.

Presbyterian, a lawyer by profession. He was a member of Parliament during the reigns of James I and Charles I. During the Long Parliament he decided against the king and bishop. He was also a member of the Westminster Assembly. During the period when Parliament was not permitted to assemble he used his time in versifying the psalms. When the Westminster Assembly was called and undertook the selection of a psalter, Rous was the successful competitor. After alteration and revision it was finally published in 1650 and came into use in England as well as in America. Thus it became the song book of psalm-singing churches of the English language for two hundred years.

When published it was superior in some respects to its predecessors, but its literal translations were often lacking in grace of diction which interfered with real poetic merit. Besides, it was mostly in common metre and therefore lacked the wide range of tunes which other metres afforded.

The fourth important version of psalms which in England was destined partially to succeed the Old Version of Sternhold and Hopkins was what was called the New Version, prepared by two Irishmen, Nahum Tate and Nicholas Brady, whose work was published in 1696 and was permitted to be used in churches and chapels at the time of the Restoration. Tate was the son of a clergyman in Dublin where he was educated at Trinity College. He was encouraged in literary work by the poet John Dryden, and later became Poet Laureate. Brady was educated at both Oxford and Trinity College and later was prebendary at Cork. This new version had no special merit over that of Sternhold and Hopkins, except it had in places a better literary style than those preceding it, but was less literal than the version of Rous. It only gained adoption through royal and commercial influence and received the endorsement of King William III. Soon, however, it supplanted the Old Version throughout the Church of England. From England it came to America where it was adopted by the American Episcopal Church in 1789 and bound up with the Prayer Book. The three versions of the First Psalm which the student may compare are given below:

Sternhold and Hopkins

The man is blest that hath not lent
To wicked men his ear,
Nor led his life as sinners do,
Nor sat in scorner's chair.

But in the law of God the Lord
Doth set his whole delight,
And in the same doth exercise
Himself both day and night.

He shall be like a tree that is
Planted the rivers nigh,
Which in due season bringeth forth
Its fruit abundantly.

Whose leaf shall never fade nor fail,
But flourishing shall stand,
E'en so all things shall prosper well
That this man takes in hand.

As for ungodly men, with them
It shall be nothing so,
But as the chaff which by the wind
Is driven to and fro.

Therefore the wicked men shall not
In judgment stand upright,
Nor in assembly of the just
Shall sinners come in sight.

For why? the way of godly men
Unto the Lord is known,
Whereas, the way of wicked men
Shall be quite overthrown.

Rous

That man hath perfect blessedness
Who walketh not astray
In counsel of ungodly men
Nor stands in sinners' way;
Nor sitteth in the scorner's chair;
But placeth his delight
Upon God's law, and meditates
On his law, day and night.

He shall be like a tree that grows
Near planted by a river,
Which in his season yields his fruit
And his leaf fadeth never;

And all he doth shall prosper well.
The wicked are not so,
But they are like unto the chaff
Which wind drives to and fro.

In judgment therefore shall not stand
Such as ungodly are,
Nor in th' assembly of the just
Shall wicked men appear,
Because the way of godly men
Unto the Lord is known;
Whereas the way of wicked men
Shall quite be overthrown.

Tate and Brady

How blest is he who ne'er consents
By ill advice to walk,
Nor stands in sinners' ways nor sits
Where men profanely talk;
But makes the perfect law of God
His business and delight;
Devoutly reads therein by day
And meditates by night.

Like some fair tree, which fed by streams
With timely fruit does bend,
He still shall flourish, and success
All his designs attend.
Ungodly men and their attempts
No lasting root shall find;
Untimely blasted and dispersed
Like chaff before the wind.

Their guilt shall strike the wicked dumb
Before their Judge's face;
No formal hypocrite shall then
Amongst the saints have place,
For God approves the just man's ways,
To happiness they tend,
But sinners and the paths they tread
Shall both in ruin end.

EARLY ENGLISH HYMNODY

We have noted that the Reformation movement in Germany produced a great outburst of hymnody under Luther's forceful leadership. This was more or less true in other European countries, as in Holland and the Scandinavian lands, Denmark, Sweden and Norway. In France also the Huguenots were singing original hymns in addition to their French Psalmody. So in Italy religious leaders were using some hymns in the common language of the people, particularly on special occasions, although not during the services of the Mass. It seems the more strange that in England during the sixteenth century the people did not sing songs of original composition. Even the beautiful Latin hymns were banished from the services in the time of Edward VI against the wish of Archbishop Cranmer. Hardly any hymns were used in public worship for more than two centuries, except the metrical psalms and a few hymns appended to the Old Version. This was likely due more to the influence of Calvin and the Genevan School who held to the principle that only the word of God should have recognition in public worship, while no composition of mere man should be permitted to take its place.

George Wither—One of the first writers of hymns, not psalms, who wrote for the Church, lived in the seventeenth century, but his hymns never found their way into general use. Had they done so, the history of English hymnody might have been a far different story. His life was full of adventure. He was put in prison by James I because he wrote satire. He served in the army under Charles I to fight the Covenanters, and later became a major among the Roundheads.

During the Restoration he was again imprisoned for his outspoken verses concerning the people's rights. Although James I disapproved of his satire, he did approve of his collection of "Hymns and Songs of the Church," which was really the earliest attempt at an English hymn book. Wither obtained a patent from the king in 1643 that these hymns be bound up with the metrical psalms. But this work only brought on him persecution and loss. The book contained paraphrases of Scriptures and hymns for festivals and holy days. Some of them were set to music by the famous musician, Orlando Gibbons. With the exception of one or two, these hymns did not survive, but his sunset hymn still appears in "Hymns Ancient and Modern":

Behold the sun, that seemed but now
Enthroned overhead.

John Milton—Soon following Wither, there lived such distinguished writers as George Herbert, John Donne, Jeremy Taylor, Richard Baxter, Henry Vaughan and the great poet Milton. All these wrote sacred verses good for reading and study but not suitable for church singing. John Milton's life is so well known we may omit his biography. "Paradise Lost" and "Paradise Regained" are perhaps his best known poems. He also wrote the splendid "Ode to the Nativity." His best hymn poem used to-day, based on Psalm 136, "Let us with gladsome mind," was written when a boy of fifteen years and a student at St. Paul's School.

John Mason—Mason was rector of Water Stratford, Bucks, and lived until 1694. He was the author of "Spiritual Songs" which became a household treasure in many families. Richard Baxter called him "the Glory of the Church of England." It is said that Watts was very fond of him. He held millenarian views, and declared he had seen the Lord. His vision was the occasion of his passionate discourse "The Midnight Cry," which excited the village where he preached. He was the author of the hymn, "My Lord, my Love was crucified." Another of his hymns used to-day is:

Now from the altar of my heart
Let incense flames arise;

also his introit hynm,

Lord, for the mercies of the night
Our humble thanks we pay,
And unto Thee we dedicate
The first fruits of the day.

George Herbert—Although among the English poets of the first half of the seventeenth century very little poetry was written for congregational praise, it is claimed that not even the gayest of the Cavaliers failed to write some sacred verse of prayer or aspiration during the Puritan age. Herbert is regarded as the greatest among these poets. He wrote many sacred lyrics, yet these were not to appear in the hymn book. These religious poems were written to be read or studied and not to be sung.

His life was written by Isaak Walton; for Herbert was skilled as an angler as well as a poet. To appreciate fully both the fine character and gentle poetry of Herbert one must read Walton.

Brilliant as he was, his life was not so eventful or distinguished as he deserved. He was born in Wales in 1593 of a noble Welsh family, was educated at Westminster School. From there he went to Trinity College, Cambridge, where he so distinguished himself that he was appointed "Public Orator." After graduation he waited some years for preferment at court and after further struggle against disease, he resolved to enter the Church. Not until he was thirty-seven years old was he ordained and placed over the little church of Bemerton. Here in the little village close to Salisbury he lived among plain people in "this happy corner of the Lord's field, hoping all things and blessing all people, asking his own way to Zion and showing others the way." After a brief ministry he was cut off by the much dreaded disease, consumption. His life showed spiritual strength that shone through physical weakness. His chief literary work was "The Temple," containing over one hundred and fifty short poems suggested by the Church Year, her holidays and ceremonials, and the experiences of the Christian life.

The opening poem is "The Church Porch," full of counsel for the conduct of life. Among other great poems is "The Pilgrimage," having but six stanzas, with its lines so full of thought that it contains the whole substance of Bunyan's "Pilgrim's Progress." Although written before Bunyan was born, it becomes an interesting question, considering the influence of Herbert's poetry, whether or not Bunyan got the idea of his immortal work from "The Pilgrimage."

Among his lines adopted for the hymnal to-day we have his hymn of adoration,

Let all the world in every corner sing,
My God, my King.

The "Canadian Presbyterian Book of Praise" contains another poem adopted as a hymn,

Throw away Thy rod,
Throw away Thy wrath,
O my God,
Take the gentle path.

Bishop Thomas Ken (1637-1711)—Ken was born at Berkhampstead, Hertfordshire. His life while young covered the period of the Commonwealth and later the troubled period of the

Restoration. Ken and his younger contemporary, Addison, are the only major hymn writers of the seventeenth century, as their successor, Isaac Watts, lived most of his life in the eighteenth century. Ken first attended Winchester School where he was brought up under the care of his older sister and her famous husband, Isaak Walton, his parents having died while he was very young. Later he attended Oxford, and after graduation he became chaplain to the Bishop of Winchester and prebendary of the Cathedral. When King Charles II visited Winchester, accompanied by his courtiers, good and bad, the King wanted to use the residence of the chaplain for one of his mistresses. But with characteristic stability Ken emphatically refused, saying, "Not for the King's Kingdom," just as he had once before stood for a principle, incurring the displeasure of the Prince of Orange at The Hague. Charles evidently did not hold a grudge against the chaplain for standing for purity of morals, and when later the Bishopric of Bath and Wells became vacant, the king, instead of preventing Ken's promotion, out of admiration for his courage asked, "Where is the little man who would not give our Nell Gwynn a lodging? Give it to him." At the age of forty-eight he was consecrated bishop. His own words expressed his humble feelings:

Among the herdsmen I, a common swain,
Lived, pleased with my low cottage on the plain,
Till up, like Amos on a sudden caught,
I to the pastoral chair was trembling brought.

Ken was continued in his office under James II, but when William and Mary came on the throne his years of humiliation and suffering began. He was deprived of honours under the new dynasty, having offended William III because he refused the oath of allegiance, as he felt he had already sworn his allegiance to James. Under the good Queen Anne he was offered restoration to his see, but preferred to remain in private life. He was made comfortable in old age with a modest pension.

Ken wrote a number of hymns. He was desirous that church people might praise God in words of his own composition, and not be always limited to Psalmody and Bible canticles only. It was with difficulty that the churches could be led to adopt or use, to any extent, original compositions of modern English writers; but at length, though not until after Ken's day, was his desire widely fulfilled. Ken has left enduring monuments of praise in his celebrated Morning and Evening Hymns. His famous Morning Hymn is very familiar:

Awake, my soul, and with the sun
Thy daily course of duty run.
Shake off dull sloth, and early rise,
To pay thy morning sacrifice.

Direct, control, suggest, this day,
All I design, or do, or say;
That all my powers, with all their might,
In Thy sole glory may unite.

His even more celebrated Evening Hymn, so widely sung to this day, begins:

All praise to Thee, my God, this night

(some hymnals give the first line "Glory to Thee, my God, this night"),

For all the blessings of the light;
Keep me, O keep me, King of kings,
Beneath Thine own Almighty wings.

This hymn is so well-known and universally sung that we need not quote the remaining verses. Ken's wonderful Doxology which, it is said, has been sung more than any other four lines in the English language, is the last stanza of both of these hymns.

Praise God from whom all blessings flow,
Praise Him all creatures here below,
Praise Him above, angelic host,
Praise Father, Son, and Holy Ghost.

Doctor Bodine said, "I had rather written these words than anything else ever written by man."

Joseph Addison—who lived from 1672-1719, is the last of the great seventeenth century writers. His fame rests more on his general literary work. His prose writings were greater than his poetry, although the latter was far from unimportant in the literary world. His essays, contributed to "The Spectator" and "The Tatler," were famous for their wisdom and advocacy of the art of good living. Living in the age following the Restoration, when the tendency of literature was toward the coarse and the corrupt, which tried to make vice attractive and virtue laughable, he set himself against the tendency of the age, stripped off its mask and exposed its ugliness and sin. He so well succeeded in his efforts that since his day English literature has not generally followed false gods, until some twentieth century writers have tried to ignore Addison's example and influence, despite Macaulay's further warning, "That since his (Addison's) time the open violation of decency has always been considered amongst us a sure mark of a fool."

To appreciate this noble man in literature and politics, we must glance at his background and biography. He was born in 1672, son of a scholarly English clergyman, dean of Litchfield, and his mother was the sister of the Bishop of Bristol. He married the Countess of Warwick, and so his life was lived among leaders of both Church and State. He filled one government post after another as Under Secretary, Secretary of Ireland and Secretary of State. His life was divided between political duties which he filled with fidelity, and his work in literature.

He won more literary fame by his tragedy, "Cato," now nearly forgotten. His poems were very popular in his day, but are now little read. Among his many hymns a few still survive. His hymn, proclaiming God in nature, beginning,

The spacious firmament on high,
With all the blue ethereal sky,

appeared first in "The Spectator" in 1712. Another one almost as popular is

When all Thy mercies, O my God,
My rising soul surveys.

Also another one known as "The Traveller's Hymn," which begins:

How are Thy servants blest, O Lord,
How sure is their defense.

This was published in "The Spectator" after a stormy sea voyage on the Mediterranean, when the captain and crew were frightened by terror. It shows that a good hymn can be sung in the same spirit as one would say his prayers, and be equally helped.

He also wrote a hymn based on the Twenty-third Psalm, sometimes used today:

The Lord my pasture shall prepare,
And feed me with a shepherd's care,
His presence shall my words supply,
And guard me with a watchful eye.

SUMMARY

In this chapter we have studied about metrical Psalmody, where first begun; Clément Marot; John Calvin; Genevan Psalter; English Psalmody; Myles Coverdale; Sternhold and Hopkins; Authors' Psalm tunes; Congregation of Protestants at Frankfort; John Knox; Suspension of psalm singing under Queen Mary; Lesser attempts at versification; Version of Ainsworth; "Bay Psalm Book"; Rous's Scottish Psalter; Tate and Brady's version; Comparison of the three versions; Early English Hymnody; Countries where original hymns were sung; George Wither and the first hymn book; John Milton; John Mason; George Herbert; Bishop Thomas Ken; Joseph Addison.

For Further Reading

The English Hymn, Louis F. Benson.
The Sabbath in Puritan New England, T. M. Earle.
The Story of the American Hymn, Edward S. Ninde.
A Dictionary of Hymnology, John Julian.
The History and Use of Hymns and Hymn-Tunes, David R. Breed.
English Literature, W. J. Long.
Hymns and Hymn Makers, Duncan Campbell.
History of the English Hymn, Benjamin Brawley.

VIII

WATTS AND WESLEY

W*ATTS,* 1674-1748; ***Wesley,*** 1708-1788—These two names, so often coupled together, stand out as unsurpassed in the development of English hymnody, and have done more for the Christian Church of modern times than any other authors. Nevertheless they have had to prepare the way and convert the Church to the use of modern lyric poetry, reflecting the highest aspirations of man in his worship of God in the full expression of New Testament teaching. This the English speaking churches needed, but it was difficult of achievement because of the old tradition of congregational praise, and the long-standing adherence to the limitation of Psalmody as the only suitable vehicle of divine praise.

Watts blazed the trail, while hymnody's fuller development depended upon Wesley who widened and improved the road through the vast wilderness of religious song. Watts's chief work was to modernize and improve the old substance of church praise, while Wesley's work was to create much new and original composition in the field of evangelical doctrine, and the human soul's expression of inner emotions in its highest and most varied aspirations when contemplating its relations to God. Watts has been well called the "father of English hymnody," not that he was the first to write modern hymns, but because he gave such distinct impetus to its development and established its hold on church worship.

Ken and Addison, as well as a few lesser lights whom we have previously noticed, had contributed some hymns, but it would have been impossible to compile a suitable church hymnal preceding the contribution of Watts. He so far surpassed, both in quantity and quality, those who had preceded him that he properly deserves the title given him. Watts was born in Southampton where his father was a deacon of the Congregational Church. It was in the troublesome times following the Restoration when the laws against non-conformity to the established religion were enforced with natural bitterness so soon after the iconoclastic period of the Commonwealth. For non-conformity his father was committed to jail, and frequently as a babe the son was carried in his mother's arms to visit his imprisoned father. But when William and Mary ascended the throne, better times came for the family. As a child he was undersized and delicate. The stories of his childhood may be exaggerated, one of which tells of his asking others "to buy a book" when he could hardly pronounce the word. It is said he was learning Greek and Hebrew when eight years old, and was evidently writing poetry at seven or eight years of age. He doubtless was very precocious and entertained his parents with some of his childhood poetry.

Thomas Wright tells us this story of Isaac's childhood that during family prayers he laughed outloud. The solemn household awaited an explanation of his apparent irreverence. Soon the information was given that he saw a mouse run up the bell rope by the fireside on which he made this rhyme:

A mouse for want of better stairs
Ran up a rope to say his prayers.

The boy was given good opportunities for education which he faithfully improved. Because of frail physique he had to strive for his intellectual and religious life. Reared amidst Puritan rigour and strictness, without the deeper Puritan piety he had to struggle to develop his natural inclination to charity and freedom, and stood firmly for his own opinions. University life was offered to him at a time when only Conformists had easy access to university education. But he would not give up his principles and so went to the Academy of one, Thomas Rowe, at Stoke Newington. At twenty he had completed the usual study and retired to his father's home, spending two years there in study for his ministry, and also became tutor to the children of Sir John Hartopp. He became a non-Conformist parson, and on his twenty-fourth birthday preached his first sermon. He became assistant to and later successor of Doctor Chancy, pastor of an Independent church in London. Both while assistant, and later when himself the pastor, he was for periods of time unable to do pastoral work. Between 1712 to 1716 he was disabled by a fever from which he never fully recovered. But his church was always patient and sympathetic. During a period of weakness he was invited to the home of Sir Thomas Abney, near London. Intending to stay a week his visit extended over thirty-six years, or the rest of his earthly life. He was, however, a beloved and welcome guest, and Lady Abney cared for him as she would have done for her own son. He preached occasionally and continued in literary work. Soon he was obliged to resign his parish; but he continued his writing on serious subjects, and so succeeded in accomplishing a great life's work.

Dr. Samuel Johnson has said of Watts, "Few men have left behind such purity of character or such monuments of laborious piety."

His versatility is shown in such literary products, in addition to his poetry, as his "Treatise on Logic," his "Elements of Geography and Astronomy," his "Philosophical Essays," and "Improvement of the Mind." His "Logic" was used till long after his day as a text-book at Oxford and other universities, including American, although he was not a conformist and not a university man.

Timely text-books as these were, he is nevertheless best known to posterity by his poetry, especially his versification of Psalmody and original hymns. When a very young man he ventured to criticize the versification of psalms used in his father's church, when either his father or another church officer retorted: "Give us something which will be better, young man!" He accepted the challenge and wrote a hymn which was sung the next Sunday evening, and was well received. The hymn is not commonly used to-day; yet there are many poorer hymns written since. Its first verse is:

Behold the glories of the Lamb
Amidst His Father's throne;
Prepare new honours for His name
And songs before unknown.

So he continued to furnish one for each succeeding Sunday evening until over two hundred were produced. But his largest work was his versification of the psalms. This required several years of his time until the entire work was done.

In 1707 Watts published his "Hymns and Spiritual Songs." This included his original hymns and versifications of the Psalter, which was less literal and a more free translation than all those attempts made preceding him. Yet this versification was done with fidelity to the teaching and spirit of the old psalms, but in the language of the New Testament colour and expression. This was a great departure from the long standing rule that the English psalm must be literally and meticulously followed. This bold attempt did not arouse so much opposition as would be expected, as the time was ripe for such revolutionary change.

But one opponent of the change did bluntly ask, "Does Watts indeed presume to correct and instruct the Holy Ghost in writing psalms?"

Twelve years later he published his "Psalms of David Imitated." This work was written wholly in the language of the New Testament and by this time he had largely won the victory for the broader freedom and variety in worship, and released the English-speaking communions from their long, hide-bound, literal translations of the Old Testament psalms. He now had largely settled for all time the propriety of free and modern expression of Christian truths and also the right to use original compositions of men in the praise of God, which the opposition always called "songs of human composition," and firmly held that only the "inspired Word of God" was proper for church worship. His arguments were irrevocable.

First: Watts denied that we are required of God to use only the "inspired Scriptures" in song; but on the contrary, that while the Bible is God's message to us, the hymn (of human composure) is our response to God, our word of praise to Him.

Secondly: He denied in particular that the Book of Psalms was a canonical hymn book for the New Testament Church, or adapted to its use. It was a Jewish book rather than a Christian book. In Christian praise, the gospel teaching must be supreme over that of the Old Testament psalms, some of which are even contrary to the spirit of the gospel.

Thirdly: Watts denied the claim of Metrical Psalmody to be the "inspired Word of God." If it be required that in praise we should use only the pure word of God, we should sing only the words of Scripture in English prose, not the metrical version of the psalms, which cannot be said to fulfil that requirement.

Watts might have added another argument for his position, that if it is proper to pray to God with the thoughts and language of "human composition," whether written or extempore, it is also proper to praise God in a similar manner.

It should be observed that Watts's poems, many of them, were based on the thoughts of the psalms, but so freely expressed in poetic simplicity and Christian terminology that these have often been regarded as original hymns. In fact they are Christian hymns as much as free "Imitation" of psalms.

Take for example his poem based on the Seventy-second Psalm:

Jesus shall reign where'er the sun
Does his successive journeys run,

or the one founded on the Nineteenth Psalm:

The heavens declare Thy glory, Lord;

and his greatest of all hymns based on the Ninetieth Psalm:

O God, our help in ages past,
Our hope for years to come,
Our shelter from the stormy blast,
And our eternal home.

This was feelingly sung at the English-speaking church in Berlin by the mixed assembly of people from various countries on the Sunday morning following the outbreak of the World War in Europe, the summer of 1914.

Among other hymns included in the hymnal to-day, the new Presbyterian hymnal contains twenty of Watts's which is a large number for a modern, reduced-sized hymnal of 513 hymns to include. These can be readily referred to in any modern book. Among the most famous are:

Before Jehovah's awful throne

This is the day the Lord hath made

Come, Holy Spirit, heavenly dove

Joy to the world, the Lord is come

From all that dwell below the skies

Am I a soldier of the Cross?

Among Watts's original hymns is the greatest of all his poems, describing the meaning of the Crucifixion:

When I survey the wondrous Cross
On which the Prince of Glory died.

The severe critic of hymns, Matthew Arnold, and Doctor Julian as well, claimed this was the greatest hymn in the English language. Matthew Arnold on his last day on earth, attending the service of the Presbyterian Church in Liverpool, that Sunday morning listened to the hymn sung by the congregation. After the service he was heard repeating to himself the lines, and at luncheon following spoke of it as our greatest hymn, just shortly before he suddenly passed away.

CHARLES WESLEY

We have observed how Watts fought to win a place for original hymns in the worship of the Church, alongside the Old Testament psalms. But Wesley went farther in the path and even composed poems of greater freedom and departure from established praise in England.

Watts had laid a true foundation upon which Wesley was to build even greater. The latter expended little labour on versification of Psalmody, but laboured abundantly on hymns of "human composition," till during his life-time he wrote the almost incredible number of over 6,000 hymns. He wrote all hours of the day and on all occasions; when riding along the road on horseback and often at night in bed. Most of this large number have been forgotten, this being due to elements or characteristics which were not entirely suitable for continued usefulness. Probably as many as two hundred will be regarded as poems of high merit, of which more are included in the modern hymnal than those of almost any other writer.

Charles Wesley's writings are so closely associated with his distinguished brother John, that it is not always possible to separate their poetic work. Yet almost all the poetic writing of John consists of translations from other sources. His able scholarship and poetic ability enabled him to write many splendid versifications from the French, Spanish, and especially the German. Some of his best poetry was translations of the German writer, Paul Gerhardt, as his

Jesus, Thy boundless love to me,
No thought can reach, no tongue declare,

also

Give to the winds thy fears.

Charles Wesley's hymns were in contrast to those of Watts's whose hymns were objective and formal, setting forth the glorious majesty of God, while on the other hand Wesley's were subjective, more personal and intimate. In general the two poets were alike in spirit and purpose, yet different in style and treatment. The one supplemented the other; their work was complementary.

Their education and associations were opposite. Watts was Calvinistic in belief and his work was among non-Conformists, while Wesley was Arminian, and his education was Anglican. He and his brother John were ritualists and high Anglicans in taste. Charles belonged to the great family of the Wesleys who were the most distinguished family in England in their day. This family's influence and vigorous teaching were to England in the eighteenth century what the famous Beecher family's was to America in the nineteenth century.

To explain fully the life and labours of Charles and his famous brother John, we should look first at their ancestry. Their great grandfather and grandfather, John, were Oxford men and Church of England clergymen. At the time of the Restoration they followed their own beliefs and were virtually driven from the Church's ministry.

Their father, Samuel Wesley, was also a clergyman of the Anglican Church. It is said that as a boy he was to debate the side of the dissenters against the Established Church, but upon study of the subject decided he was on the wrong side, and later entered the Established Church. He himself was a poet and man of much influence and wrote several volumes of poetry. His mother was Susannah Annesley, daughter of the famous Doctor Annesley, non-Conformist minister of London. As a very bright and precocious girl she investigated the subject of the Established Church and non-Conformity and decided to leave the faith of her father to enter the larger Church of her country. So naturally Samuel Wesley and she had much in common, and both were sincere and devout. Naturally they were attracted to each other. Mrs. Wesley was in every way the equal of the able Wesley men. Nineteen children were born to this union; Charles was the eighteenth child and five years younger than John. The oldest child, Samuel, too often overlooked, was an able clergyman also in the Church of England; and to the school of which he was the head, the younger brother, Charles, was sent for his early education. Later he entered Oxford.

Charles Wesley married at the age of forty and most happily, in contrast to John Wesley's still later marriage to a most unsuitable wife. Charles's sons, Samuel and Charles, both became men of eminence in the field of music, and a grandson, Samuel Sebastian Wesley, became one of the foremost English composers of church music.

While at Oxford young Charles was a serious-minded and diligent student. He attended every Sunday the service of Holy Communion and took a few intimate fellow students with him. He set himself to following the method of the proscribed curriculum of the university. This brought him and his companions the name of "Methodist," six months before his brother John joined them at Oxford. Soon after John joined them as leader, these associates were called in derision "The Holy Club." Its rule was to study the Greek Testament and prayer, and to work for the uplift of the slum children, who in that day were much neglected. When their father heard his boys were leaders in what was called "The Holy Club," he was pleased to hear about it. A few years later the Wesley brothers went on a missionary journey to Georgia. Before going Charles was ordained to the priesthood in the Church of England by the Bishop of London. Because of the hardships of the journey and his labours performed amid difficult surroundings, he returned to England in one year, his brother remaining a little longer in the South.

But an incident occurred during his American trip which had lasting influences on the Wesleys. The two brothers came in contact with a devout Moravian, named Peter Böhler. Charles began to instruct the Moravian in English, while Böhler demonstrated to the Wesleys the effective use of the German hymnody in the original composition and vernacular of the common people, with its stirring music, as yet new to the Englishmen, but making a deep impression upon them.

This American trip also resulted in deep, searching spiritual experience which thereafter quickened the zeal of the Wesleys. The zeal and character of Charles's preaching in London soon incurred the disapproval of the Bishop of London, for those were days of rigid and uncompromising standards and domination by the bishops over their clergy. He was, therefore, deprived of his curacy in St. Mary's, and never given another.

What a great change has come to the Church during the two hundred years since! Had Wesley lived to-day the present Bishop of London would have utilized Wesley's zeal and talents. The work of Wilson Carlile, who began a half century ago to preach in the slums of London, was more irregular and radical in method than that of the Wesleys, and Carlile has enjoyed the freedom of doing his difficult evangelical work in his own way.

Doctor Carlile became the founder of the "Church Army," which consists to-day of young lay evangelists within the Church of England and the American Episcopal Church, who do itinerate and evangelistic work both inside and outside of the Church with complete freedom. In England today this group has the patronage and staunch support not only of the Bishop of London, but also of the Archbishop of Canterbury, the Prime Ministers of England and high ecclesiastical officials. This illustrates the difference between the present time and the time in which the Wesleys lived.

Meanwhile, the Wesleys' Oxford companion, George Whitefield, the great orator and eloquent preacher, had started his religious crusade in England, and the Wesleys soon joined him. In many instances the use of the parish churches was denied them. Anyhow in most places these were too small.

So for a long time these great crusaders drew thousands to hear their outdoor preaching, but would not hold services at the hour to conflict with services in the parish churches. But their personality and gifts drew such large audiences that the theatres were much reduced in attendance. The methods and strong influence among the masses aroused the displeasure of the non-Conformists and the Anglicans alike. The enemies of these ardent preachers were very active. Wesley tells us that their lives were in jeopardy much of the time. "Such threatenings, curses and blasphemies I have never heard." On a certain occasion their lives were spared, as Wesley felt, only by a miracle of God. After some years of itinerating, Charles Wesley gave up his joint evangelistic work with John, after both had separated their labours from those with Whitefield, as Charles's health now necessitated a less strenuous life. This gave him even more time for his poetic work. He has furnished us hymns of lasting value, found among those for different seasons of the year. In Advent we sing his version of Cennick's:

Lo, he comes with clouds descending,

also his

Come, Thou long-expected Jesus.

At Christmastide:

Hark the herald angels sing.

At Easter:

Christ the Lord is risen to-day,
Sons of men and angels say.

At Ascensiontide:

Our Lord is risen from the dead,
Our Jesus has gone up on high,
The powers of hell are captive led
Dragged to the portals of the sky.

He gave us such famous hymns as

Love divine, all loves excelling

O for a heart to praise my God

A charge to keep I have

Soldiers of Christ, arise

Ye servants of God, your Master proclaim.

Other hymns of his still in use are found by reference to the index of any hymnal to-day. His two greatest hymns are his Christmas hymn already referred to:

Hark! the herald angels sing
Glory to the new-born King;
Peace on earth, and mercy mild,
God and sinners reconciled!

Joyful, all ye nations, rise,
Join the triumph of the skies;
With the angelic host proclaim,
Christ is born in Bethlehem!

and his "Jesus, Lover of my soul." The former hymn ranks among the "great four," as previously seen in the list of the Anglican hymnology. Yet others claim his "Jesus, Lover of my soul" as his greatest:

Jesus, lover of my soul,
Let me to Thy bosom fly,
While the nearer waters roll,
While the tempest still is high.

Hide me, O my Saviour, hide,
Till the storm of life be past;
Safe into the haven guide,
Oh, receive my soul at last!

It needs no stories of its origin to give it added greatness. The late Doctor Bodine said: "It is the finest heart-hymn in the English tongue." Henry Ward Beecher said: "I would rather have written that hymn of Wesley's than to have the fame of all the kings that ever sat on earth; it is more glorious, it has more power in it. I would rather be the author of that hymn than to hold the wealth of the richest man in New York. He will die after a little while, pass out of men's thoughts, what will there be to speak of him? But that hymn will go on singing until the last trump brings forth the angel band; and then I think it will mount upon some lips to the very presence of God."

Wesley not only has given the world a treasury of praise, but also used that praise for the additional purpose of teaching Christian doctrine and instructing the minds of his disciples, giving in verse, "a body of experimental and practical divinity."

Charles Wesley lived to a serene old age, ever loyal to the Church in which he was baptized, confirmed and ordained. He died a clergyman of the Church of England, as did his brother John, and was buried in the grave-yard of his parish church.

For Further Reading on Watts and Wesley

Some Hymns and Hymn Writers, William B. Bodine.
Studies of Familiar Hymns, Second Series, Louis F. Benson.
English Hymns, Samuel W. Duffield.
The Hymn as Literature, Jeremiah B. Reeves.
The Hymn Lover, W. Garrett Horder.
Some Favorite Hymns, H. E. Langhorne.
Favorite Hymns, W. E. Hutton.
Life of Isaac Watts, E. P. Hood.
The Life of Charles Wesley, John Telford.
Charles Wesley, D. M. Jones.
Charles Wesley, Evangelist and Poet, 1932, F. Luke Wiseman.
Lyric Religion, H. Augustine Smith.
History of the English Hymn, Benjamin Brawley.

IX

OTHER EIGHTEENTH CENTURY WRITERS

PHILIP DODDRIDGE (1702-1751)—Beginning with the contemporaries of Wesley, who are among the other eighteenth century hymn makers, we name first of all Doddridge. He was born in London only a few years before Wesley, but did not live nearly so long into the century. His grandfather before him suffered under the Commonwealth. His father was a devout layman of the Independent Church. Philip was the youngest child of a very large family and gave much promise when a child. The Duchess of Bedford, recognizing his talent, offered to educate him at either Cambridge or Oxford. But like Watts he declined the opportunity in order to stay among the Dissenters. He was educated for the ministry in a non-Conformist seminary at Kibworth, where he first became pastor. He received calls from Presbyterian congregations, but accepted the call to the Independent Church in Northampton. In addition to his regular church work he taught in the theological academy, preparing many candidates for the ministry. At length his health failed, and he sailed for Portugal, arriving at Lisbon where he died and where he lies buried.

Doddridge was a volumnious writer and left valuable contributions in both prose and poetry. He had many friends, among whom were Bishop Warburton and Colonel Gardiner whose life he wrote. His most useful prose writing was "The Rise and Progress of Religion in the Soul," long held in evangelical circles as the best aid to the devout life. He wrote a commentary on the New Testament, called the "Family Exposition," a favourite of many people. He wrote many hymns, some of which endured the test of time. His hymns were the expression of his high Christian character and learning. His noble character may be briefly expressed by calling him "a man of God who always walked closely with his God." Many of his hymns were based on Bible passages and were scriptural paraphrases. His hymns still surviving in modern hymnals may be said to be almost equally good, with none standing out as a great favourite above all the others. Probably the most used in past years is his Advent hymn:

Hark! the glad sound! the Saviour comes,
The Saviour promised long:
Let every heart prepare a throne,
And every voice a song.

Other equally good hymns found in the hymnal to-day are:

Awake, my soul, stretch every nerve,
And press with vigour on.

How gentle God's commands,
How kind His precepts are.

O God of Bethel, by whose hand
Thy people still are fed.

My God, and is Thy table spread
And does Thy cup with love o'erflow.

Triumphant Zion, lift thy head
From dust and darkness, and the dead!

The Methodist Episcopal hymnal retains a hymn which has been extensively used by the Methodists:

O happy day that fixed my choice
On Thee, my Saviour, and my God!

The new Presbyterian hymnal has restored one not commonly found in hymn books:

Great God, we sing that mighty hand,
By which supported still we stand;
The opening year Thy mercy shows;
That mercy crowns it till it close.

Anne Steele (1716-1778)—Miss Steele was also contemporaneous with Wesley, born only a few years later in Broughton, her father being both a merchant and Baptist minister. Having an established business he could serve his congregation without much remuneration. Miss Steele was the earliest among women in the field of English hymnody. Her life was full of trouble and she endured much poor health. Early in life she had a tragic experience. Just before her prospective wedding day her lover, to whom she was deeply attached, was drowned. She does not appear to have begun her hymn writing till past forty years. In 1757 her father writes of her sending a poem to London for inspection, which in accordance with the prayer of her father was readily accepted for publication. She continued to write more good lyrics which were highly acceptable for publication and of much usefulness in the Church. So she could truly have said in the words of a recent book, "Life begins at forty." Thirty years after her death, when Trinity Church in Boston became tired of singing Tate and Brady's version of psalms, with only a few hymns appended, the vestry ventured to obtain a parish hymnal. The result was that their hymnal was made up with one-third of its hymns written by Miss Steele. But of her once popular hymns, the two which seem destined to survive the longest are:

Father, whate'er of earthly bliss
Thy sovereign will denies,
Accepted at Thy throne of grace,
Let this petition rise.

Give me a calm, and thankful heart,
From every murmur free;
The blessings of Thy grace impart,
And make me live to Thee.

This seems to contain reference to her early bereavement and of her Christian attitude and reconciliation toward it. Also

Father of mercies! in Thy Word
What endless glory shines!
Forever be Thy name adored
For these celestial lines.

William Williams (1717-1791) and ***John Cennick*** (1718-1755)—These two names may be somewhat associated together, although one was Welsh and the other English. They were almost the same age, of similar spirit, adopted the same faith, and were both instrumental in later organizing the Calvinist Methodist Communion which Cennick later abandoned to enter the Moravian Church. Both had been identified for a time with the Wesleyan Movement, and each has given us one outstanding hymn.

Williams was the pre-eminent hymn writer of Wales and wrote hundreds of hymns. He chose the medical profession for his career. But one Sunday morning, passing through a village and hearing the church bells, he went into church. To him the service seemed cold and dull, but as he came out of church he noticed the people standing around waiting for something, and soon a tall, dark-looking man stood up on a stone and began to preach. It was the famous Whitefield whose preaching stirred the Welsh people to enthusiasm. Young Williams, also deeply impressed, altered his life's course then and there and became both an able preacher and a gifted Christian poet. He was ordained deacon in the Church of England but never advanced to the priesthood. He spent most of his years with the Methodists in Wales as a travelling evangelist. Most of his hymns were written in his native language. His greatest hymn was also written in Welsh, which we know by its English version, and which the author himself helped Peter Williams to write:

Guide me, O Thou great Jehovah,
Pilgrim through this barren land,
I am weak, but Thou art mighty:
Hold me with Thy powerful hand.

John Cennick, who was not serious-minded in his youth, was fully converted in London after months of spiritual perplexity. For a time he was associated with John Wesley and then with Whitefield before he joined the Moravians. A well known original hymn of his begins:

Children of the heavenly King,
As ye journey, sweetly sing!
Sing your Saviour's worthy praise,
Glorious in His works and ways!

His greatest hymn, as one of the "Great Four" according to the rank in the Anglican Hymnology, which was altered and improved by Charles Wesley, follows

Lo, He comes with clouds descending,
Once for our salvation slain;
Thousand angel-hosts attending
Swell the triumph of His train:
Alleluia!
Christ, the Lord, returns to reign.

It is worth while to compare this with Williams's aforementioned hymn and see how they were associated in their hymns as well as in experiences of their lives. The two hymns are written in the same metre. There is similar high sentiment and the imagery is of similar merit. One gives the experience of the Israelites in the wilderness. The other brings to attention the scenes of the last great day, the Lord's Second Advent with its attending circumstances.

Thomas Oliver (1725-1797)—Oliver began as a shoemaker but did not "stick to his last." Early an orphan, he lived a wild and reckless youth until at Bristol he happened to hear Whitefield preach from the text, "Is not this a brand plucked from the burning?" The sermon changed his whole life. After paying all his debts incurred during his reckless life, he soon joined John Wesley as one of the latter's evangelists. He wrote several hymns, but his famous one is, "The God of Abraham praise." It is a free rendering of the Hebrew doxology, called "Yigdal," which in reality is the Hebrew creed; and its composition, or at least revision, is attributed to Daniel ben Judah of the fourteenth century. It is chanted in synagogue services. Oliver by his rendition gave it Christian character. He called upon a Jew named Leoni to suggest a melody for its revised Christian text. The tune was named for Leoni and is found in hymnals to-day, although John Stainer's tune is often sung to this hymn instead of the old Hebrew melody "Leoni." It is a lyric of majestic style and James Montgomery called this hymn "the noble ode of an unlettered man."

Edward Perronet (1726-1792)—His name indicates he was of French extraction. His grandfather went from Switzerland to England, and his father entered the Anglican Church. He became vicar of Shoreham in Kent two years after his son Edward was born. The father followed the methods of the Wesleys and so continued till the end of his long life. The son continued in the footsteps of the father and entered heartily into the revival of the eighteenth century. But he was well aware of the defects of the Established Church in that age, and wrote a satire called "The Mitre," dealing with ecclesiastical faults, which was so critical that John Wesley even sought to suppress it.

Perronet, being too self-willed to work with Wesley, left the Methodist movement. He would not abide by the law of John Wesley, namely, that his evangelists should not administer the sacraments, but direct their followers to make their own communion in the regular parish churches. This disagreement between Perronet and Wesley did not break their friendship, nor their mutual admiration, but Wesley would not admit Perronet's hymns to his collection. Perronet left the Anglican Communion and joined the "Countess of Huntingdon's Connection," and at length became pastor of a small Congregational church in Canterbury, living in a part of the Archbishop's old palace. When he died he was buried in the cloister of the historic cathedral.

The name of Edward Perronet might have been forgotten, had it not been for the casual discovery of his poetic writings, and one immortal hymn therein which is one of the most used hymns to-day:

All hail the power of Jesus' name!
Let angels prostrate fall;
Bring forth the royal diadem,
And crown Him Lord of all.

THE OLNEY HYMN WRITERS

John Newton (1725-1807) and ***William Cowper*** (1731-1800)—These two men were closely associated and are called the "Olney Hymn Writers," as it was at Olney they produced most of their hymns. Their early experiences were very unlike, but their characters were similar, and their later spiritual experiences had much in common, as their tastes and temperaments were nearly identical. Both were motherless at an early age; Newton at seven and Cowper when six years old. They both spent a reckless and sinful youth, but with different effects. The former developed strength and self-reliance, while the latter became timid and melancholy. Newton, for a time, became an unbeliever and even a blasphemer, while Cowper became irresolute and inclined toward suicide. One was turned toward his Saviour by the violence of his sins, the other by the depth of his sufferings. Later both obtained the grace of God, and put into song their religious experiences.

John Newton was born in London and his good mother improved the few years she was spared in teaching her little boy the truths of Scripture. When he was eleven years old he went to sea with his sea-captain father and followed this life for eighteen years —years full of adventure, narrow escapes and sinful recklessness. He at times seemed to reflect seriously upon his sinful life, but would relax into indifference and scepticism. When eighteen years old he was vulgar and blasphemous. After a time he left the ship on which he was seaman and became technically a deserter. He was brought back and savagely whipped. Later he became a sailor on a vessel bound for Africa, where he remained for two years in misery and almost starved. He was treated with contempt and harshness, with his only relief the study of an old book of mathematics. At the end of this period he received a message from his father and sailed for home. On this homeward voyage, danger harassed the ship in a storm, and he with others worked to save the ship from sinking, till he was exhausted and gave up in despair.

He began to reflect upon his wicked life and concluded his sins were too great to be forgiven, so he waited to receive his seeming doom. But at length the ship righted itself and there was now a ray of hope. He began to cry out in prayer to his God and soon was able to say, "I began to know that there is a God who hears and answers prayer." His prayer was followed by praise and meditation and study of the Holy Scriptures, which enabled him to grow in knowledge at least. Again he went back to sea and engaged in the slave trade as captain of a slave ship; one of his African cargoes was later landed at Charleston, South Carolina. He at first regarded this trade as a respectable occupation in accordance with much of the thinking of that period. Yet later his nature shrank from its inhumanity, and his eyes were opened and he soon wrote words of condemnation of the iniquitous trade.

After six years as slave trader he spent the nine years following in Liverpool in office work, study, and occasional religious service. At thirty-nine he was ordained a clergyman in the Church of England, and there remained a long life of forty-three more years of devout service for his Master. He had occasional contact with Whitefield and the Wesleys and felt their evangelical spirit. He was settled in the curacy at Olney where for sixteen years some of his best work was done, and much of his poetical work in conjunction with Cowper, the literary genius, until he removed to London as rector of St. Mary's, Woolworth. Here he continued to preach almost till the end of his eighty-two years, declaring, "Shall the old African blasphemer stop while he can speak?"

Newton was buried in London, but later his body was removed to Olney and buried in the churchyard there. He wrote an obituary to be placed on a tablet in his London church after his death, as follows:

JOHN NEWTON, CLERK

ONCE AN INFIDEL AND LIBERTINE,
A SERVANT OF SLAVES IN AFRICA,
WAS BY THE RICH MERCY OF OUR
LORD AND SAVIOUR JESUS CHRIST,
PRESERVED, RESTORED AND PARDONED,
AND APPOINTED TO PREACH THE FAITH
HE HAD LONG LABOURED TO DESTROY.

William Cowper (whose name the English pronounce "Cooper") was only a few years younger than Newton. He was born in his father's rectory at Berkhamstead. His family had persons of distinction belonging to the Whig nobility. His mother was a Donne of the family of the poet, and having royal blood. Cowper was born, as was Newton, at a time when iniquity abounded; when ignorance, drunkenness, and gambling prevailed alike in palace and cottage. It was the age of criminal law which hanged men for petty thievery, and life-long imprisonment for debts was often inflicted.

Cowper and Joseph Addison were the two hymn writers who were also distinguished in classic literature, especially Cowper who was one of the outstanding literary writers of the eighteenth century. His life is a pathetic story. He was a delicate and sensitive youth. At six he was sent away to a boy's school where the rougher character of other boys made his life miserable. Among them was an atrocious bully into whose face Cowper could not look, but could recognize this enemy's approach by his shoe buckles. His school life affected both his mind and health. Later he studied law, but at the approach of a public examination for an office he was so scared that he attempted suicide and for many months was confined to an asylum at St. Albans. When his father died he received a small patrimony which removed him from the fear of not securing sufficient daily bread.

After his mental recovery he made his home with family friends, the Unwins in Olney, who cared for him as one of the family, and the devotion of the good woman, Mrs. Unwin, furnished him his first earthly happiness, and she was the "Mary" of his poems. Through the influence of the Unwins he became intimately associated with Newton, who was then curate of the parish church, St. Paul's and St. Peter's, and lived near the church, some distance from the Unwins' residence around by the street, but only a short distance across the back garden and field. The field between the two homes was soon purchased so the two men could have their private way of access to each other's devoted fellowship, and could daily mingle together in the garden and write their sacred poems. But they did not live together "under the same roof" as is often reported. A parishioner of the author has described the location and given the facts as a result of her sojourn in Olney.

Within Cowper's large three-story home (the Unwins' residence) is now the Cowper Museum, one of the very best literary museums in Europe. His poem called "The Task" is his longest and was published in 1785, which showed his striking originality. His most famous literary poem is "John Gilpin," the story of which was suggested by Lady Austen. His largest single literary work was his translation of Homer, superior to other more famous translations, but which never received the recognition it rightly deserved. His later years were distinguished for his poetry and he died renowned and honoured in his sixty-ninth year.

The "Olney Hymn Book," which these two companions produced together, contained 348 hymns to which Cowper contributed 68 and Newton 280. Doubtless poor health or frequent melancholia prevented Cowper from writing more. From this volume of hymns the Church has drawn a larger proportionate number than from almost any other volume.

By examination of certain hymns written by these two men one is struck with their similarity in thought, and dissimilarity in the way of expressing the same topic. Their religious experiences, as already noted, were different. Newton's two most favoured hymns are; first,

How sweet the Name of Jesus sounds
In a believer's ear!
It soothes our sorrows, heals our wounds,
And drives away our fear.

It makes the wounded spirit whole,
And calms the troubled breast;
'Tis manna to the hungry soul,
And to the weary rest.

Dear Name, the rock on which I build,
My shield and hiding place,
My never-failing treasury, filled
With boundless stores of grace.

Jesus! my Shepherd, Guardian, Friend,
My Prophet, Priest, and King,
My Lord, my Life, my Way, my End,
Accept the praise I bring.

Weak is the effort of my heart,
And cold my warmest thought:
But when I see Thee as Thou art,
I'll praise Thee as I ought.

Till then I would Thy love proclaim
With every fleeting breath:
And may the music of Thy Name
Refresh my soul in death.

And his strong hymn with its splendid tune by the famous composer, Haydn, gives it a highly favoured place in church worship:

Glorious things of thee are spoken,
Zion, city of our God.

Other favourite hymns are:

Come, my soul, thy suit prepare;
Jesus loves to answer prayer.

Amazing grace! how sweet the sound
That saves a wretch like me!

Among Cowper's most favoured hymns we have what is probably the first in rank, an outgrowth of his experiences and perplexities as follows:

God moves in a mysterious way
His wonders to perform;
He plants His footsteps in the sea,
And rides upon the storm.

Deep in unfathomable mines,
With never-failing skill,
He treasures up His bright designs,
And works His sovereign will.

Ye fearful saints, fresh courage take;
The clouds ye so much dread
Are big with mercy, and shall break
In blessings on your head.

Judge not the Lord by feeble sense,
But trust Him for His grace;
Behind a frowning providence
He hides a smiling face.

His purposes will ripen fast,
Unfolding every hour:
The bud may have a bitter taste,
But sweet will be the flower.

Blind unbelief is sure to err,
And scan His work in vain;
God is His own interpreter,
And He will make it plain.

Another one of his much used hymns of aspiration is

O for a closer walk with God,
A calm and heavenly frame,
A light to shine upon the road
That leads me to the Lamb!

Another of Cowper's, a popular hymn with many in past years, now less used and omitted from some new hymnals because of its extravagant imagery, begins,

There is a fountain filled with blood,
Drawn from Emmanuel's veins;
And sinners, plunged beneath that flood,
Lose all their guilty stains.

Other very acceptable hymns are

Hark, my soul! it is the Lord;
'Tis thy Saviour, hear His word

Jesu! where'er Thy people meet,
There they behold Thy mercy-seat;
Where'er they seek Thee, Thou art found,
And every place is hallowed ground.

Augustus M. Toplady (1740-1778)—Last but not least among the very prominent writers of the eighteenth century is Toplady. His "Rock of Ages" is as well known and as much beloved as any hymn in the English tongue. He was born at Farnham, son of Major Richard Toplady, who died in the service while his son was in infancy. His mother was a woman of ability and character, who with her son moved to Ireland. His conversion at sixteen years of age happened when visiting his mother and together they attended a revival meeting held in a barn in the little village in Ireland. He said of his conversion, "Strange that I who had so often sat under the means of grace in England should be brought right with God in an obscure part of Ireland, midst a handful of people met together in a barn, and by the ministry of one who could hardly spell his own name. Surely it was the Lord's doing and is marvellous."

Toplady was later in Trinity College, Dublin. He was ordained to the priesthood in the Established Church in 1762 and remained in this work for some years. Later he served as vicar of the Chapel of the French Calvinists in London. He had a weak constitution and gave up the active ministry in a short time to live an easier life, but not "a quiet life" by any means, as he was always a controversialist during his life of short duration. He was never active in the Methodist Movement, yet in spirit was very evangelical. He was such a pronounced Calvinist that he vigorously differed with the Wesleys on doctrinal points. His attacks upon John Wesley were vehement. In those days controversialists spoke in a harsh manner. To-day the angry epithets which Toplady and Wesley used in speaking of each other would sound amazing. They are both remembered as evangelists and writers of deep devotional songs.

Some of Toplady's good lyrics were unsuitable for common praise because of their too rigid Calvinistic doctrines, but he has written able hymns which have been highly acceptable for general Christian usage. One of his fine hymns which is rapidly going out of use, but is still included in the American Episcopal hymnal, begins

Inspirer and Hearer of prayer;
Thou Shepherd and Guardian of Thine,
My all to Thy covenant care,
I, sleeping or waking, resign.

Another is found in the Methodist Episcopal hymnal

If on a quiet sea
Toward heaven we calmly sail,
With grateful hearts, O God, to Thee
We'll own the favouring gale.

His great hymn, ranked as one of the foremost of all English hymns and well known to every congregation, is his "Rock of Ages." Doctor Robinson declared it to be "the first hymn of the first rank." William E. Gladstone thought so much of it as to take pains to make a fine Latin translation of it. It has occupied a deep place in millions of human hearts, hardly excelled by any other of the most famous hymns. The author entitled it, "A living and dying prayer for the holiest believer in the world." It was sung by passengers after their ship had sunk in the Bay of Biscay. It was also sung by the Armenians when they were being cruelly murdered by the Turks in Constantinople in the first part of this century. The poem originally had four verses, but since then parts of two verses have been combined and the rest omitted. The chief image of the hymn may have been taken from a marginal rendering of Isaiah, "In the Lord Jehovah is the rock of ages"; or the author may have had in mind I Cor. x:4,

They drank of that spiritual rock
that followed them;
And that rock was Christ,

and possibly the words of the Psalmist, 31:2,

Be thou to me a strong rock
A house of defense to save me.

SUMMARY

In this chapter the writers considered are: Philip Doddridge; Anne Steele; William Williams; John Cennick; Thomas Oliver; Edward Perronet; John Newton; William Cowper; Augustus M. Toplady.

For Further Reading

Lyric Religion, H. Augustine Smith.
Some Hymns and Hymn Writers, William B. Bodine.
Hymns and their Stories, S. P. C. K. (London).
Studies of Familiar Hymns, First and Second Series, Louis F. Benson.
A Dictionary of Hymnology, John Julian.
English Hymns, Samuel W. Duffield.
Familiar Hymns, W. E. Hutton.

X

NINETEENTH CENTURY HYMN WRITERS

WITH the dawning of the nineteenth century came a large growth and expansion of lyric literature—more writers and more poems from the pens of those writers, which were suitable for worship in the Church of God. It was during the time of the Romantic Period in English literature. Whatever may be said against the lack of any connection between the hymnody of the seventeenth and eighteenth centuries and the "classic" literature of these periods, it can hardly be denied that the influence of the Romantic Period which began some years preceding the nineteenth century had a wholesome effect upon the hymn-poets who followed.

The Romantic Period was a revolt against the long Classic or Augustan Age of literature. This movement which Victor Hugo called "liberation in literature" turned more to nature and common humanity for its subject matter, with its sympathetic understanding of man and the world in which man lives, together with its deeper expression of the feelings and imaginations of mankind. The larger variety in writing, or "literature in art," did not lower its beauty nor finished style in language, but among the religious poets, especially, there was even more regard for style and skill in the use of poetry. The hymns were more restrained in feeling and less personal, and as Dr. F. J. Gilman says, "They (hymns) brought our hymnody into line with the Romantic revival which was then imparting a new charm and appeal to English poetry." [1]

Moreover, the outstanding movements of this great century did most to enrich our hymn writings. Just preceding 1800 A.D. was the founding of the Sunday School movement with recognition of the rights of childhood, and at the very dawn of the century came the modern missionary and evangelistic movements which produced urgent songs.

Then followed the nationalistic spirit, especially in America, when the "Star Spangled Banner" and "My Country, 'tis of Thee" gave impetus to this type of song. This was added to, about the

[1] *Evolution of the English Hymn,* Macmillan Company.

middle of the century, and later more noble lyrics of this kind were produced. Then in the eighteen thirties came the Oxford Movement which sought to bring men back to devout worship and deeper reverence in reaction against the careless and indifferent religious spirit of the time. This movement was a glorification or reinterpretation of the Church as an institution, in a revival of its ancient languages, its Holy Days, its sacraments in a first recognition of the social aspects of the Gospel.

Later came the Gospel Song, somewhat in protest against the Oxford Movement, and emphasizing the individual soul as distinct from the institutional consciousness of the former. Also during the latter half of the century were added a few additional hymns dealing with social aspects of the gospel; and the Civil War had its influence upon the yearning of the human heart. Such great movements were stimulating causes resulting in virile and effective songs.

While without moving causes the tendency is towards decadence in influential hymns, as in the latter part of the century, the weaker, more sentimental type of lyric was produced, and fewer writers of outstanding merit could be found.

Among the large list of able writers of sacred poetry, whose contribution to the hymnals of the Church furnish us a veritable treasury of song during the first half of the nineteenth century, we name,

James Montgomery (1771-1854)—While Montgomery lived and began his labours in the eighteenth century, most of his active hymnic life belongs to the nineteenth century. He was born in Ayrshire, the community famous as the birthplace of Robert Burns. He was the son of a Moravian minister. While he was a boy his parents went as missionaries to the West Indies where they died, leaving the son at a Moravian school in Yorkshire. Secular poetry and fiction were barred at this school, but the boy found ways of borrowing and reading secular poetry, including Burns.

He even as a boy began to write poetry himself. Not being a student satisfactory to the Brethren, he was apprenticed to a grocer near Wakefield from whom he ran away. All the time he was writing verses which he unsuccessfully tried to get London publishers to print. One publisher refused his manuscript but engaged him to work in the newspaper shop. At length he went to Sheffield as assistant to the publisher of the "Sheffield Register." The editor was threatened with prosecution for his political writing and fled to America. Montgomery secured the paper as his own and changed the name to "Sheffield Iris." His ideas of reforms did not meet with the favour of the authorities. He was punished with a fine and six months' imprisonment. His prosecution together with the publication of his poems widened his fame. The poetry of Montgomery attracted the attention of such literary writers as Wordsworth, Southey, Byron, and Moore. He lectured on poetry in various cities and at the Royal Institute, London. He was in demand as lecturer, particularly at religious meetings and missionary organizations.

He did not take his own writings very seriously. Once asked, "Which of your poems will live?" he replied, "None, sir, except a few of my hymns," and his prophecy proved true. He was not only one of the great hymn writers, but also one of the best literary critics of his day. He ably criticized the hymn writings of his predecessors, usually kindly criticism, and his insight and impartiality made his criticisms valuable. Like Wesley, he owed his impulse toward hymnody to the Moravians.

He greatly helped one Thomas Cotterill who had been discredited for trying to press the use, in the Anglican Church, of the hymns of Watts, Cowper and Newton by helping Cotterill to revise and remodel the latter's hymnal. When Archbishop Harcourt saw the revised hymnal he gave permission for it to be dedicated to himself and allowed its use in St. Paul's Church. This resulted in breaking down the opposition which persisted in the Anglican Church ever since the days of Calvin, as all over England Harcourt's attitude was accepted as authorizing the general use of hymns in the services of the Church. Thus we to-day are gratefully indebted to both Montgomery and Archbishop Harcourt for the increased and unhampered usage of modern hymns in the general worship of the English Church.

In Montgomery's old age, when he had won general admiration for his poetic work and for the influence of his noble character, not only among his fellow townsmen, but even with the government itself, the government, as if to atone for its harshness in his earlier life, gave him an annual pension of two hundred pounds. He also had been in the running for the Poet Laureateship, which he did not attain. When he died the people of Sheffield revered his memory and erected a bronze statue in his honour.

Montgomery has contributed some of the best hymns in the hymnal. He wrote many lyrics covering a wide variety of subjects and is one of the largest contributors to the present day hymnal. Perhaps his best hymn is the one based on Psalm 72:

Hail to the Lord's Anointed,
Great David's greater Son!
Hail in the time appointed,
His reign on earth begun!
He comes to break oppression,
To set the captive free,
To take away transgression,
And rule in equity.

Among other great favourites are—

For ever with the Lord!
Amen! so let it be!

His famous Holy Week hymn is

Go to dark Gethsemane,
Ye that feel the tempter's power.

His hymn of comfort also appropriate for Holy Week,

In the hour of trial,
Jesus, plead for me.

His Holy Communion hymn,

According to Thy gracious word
In meek humility.

His Christmas hymn is

Angels, from the realm of glory,
Wing your flight o'er all the earth.

His hymn for Saints' days

Who are these in bright array,
This innumerable throng.

Other good hymns of his are

O Spirit of the living God

Songs of praise the angels sang

God is my strong salvation

Call Jehovah thy salvation

Be known to us in breaking bread

Lord, forever at Thy side

Lord, pour Thy Spirit from on high.

Thomas Kelly (1769-1854)—Kelly was exactly contemporaneous with Montgomery, passing away in the same year as the former. His hymn writing began early and continued till near the end of his long life. His first writings were in the eighteenth century, but like Montgomery's, his best labours belong in the nineteenth, and his hymns found in the hymnals of to-day were nineteenth century productions. He wrote a large number of hymns totalling more than seven hundred. As his name indicates, he was of Irish descent, son of an Irish judge. The son was expected to follow in the footsteps of the father, so he studied for the bar. But the young man, after having read the works of Romaine (the same works which much affected Newman), went through a change in his spiritual life. He was ordained to the priesthood in the Anglican Church, but was said to be too evangelical to suit the Archbishop of Dublin, and was inhibited from preaching in his diocese. As a consequence Kelly was led to associate with the Congregationalists, for whom he built several churches, having the financial means to assist very substantially in this kind of work.

Kelly's contribution to hymnody was even more lasting than his contribution to church building. His able hymn, "We sing the praise of Him who died," appealed strongly to Lord Selborne. He said of it, "I doubt whether Montgomery ever wrote anything quite equal to this hymn."

But among his other hymns, the two probably sung more often to-day are his two famous Ascension hymns,

Look, ye saints; the sight is glorious;
See the "Man of Sorrows" now;
From the fight returned victorious,
Every knee to Him shall bow;
Crown Him! Crown Him!
Crowns become the Victor's brow.

Also his equally good one,

The head, that once was crowned with thorns,
Is crowned with glory now;
A royal diadem adorns
The mighty Victor's brow.

Two other of his hymns should not be overlooked, as his good Holy Week hymn,

We sing the praise of Him who died,
Of Him who died upon the Cross,

and his earlier written Easter hymn which has been somewhat altered, as follows:

Come, see the place where Jesus lay,
And hear angelic watchers say.

Harriet Auber (1773-1862)—Miss Auber was born in London and was a member of the Church of England, and her life was one of reticence. Her death occurred at Hertfordshire in 1862. Her one book of poems was a metrical version of the Psalter which she called "The Spirit of the Psalms," the same title as afterwards adopted for a metrical version of Psalms by Lyte.

This work of Miss Auber's was first published anonymously. From this book her hymns are mostly derived. For example a good missionary hymn of hers, based on Psalm 72, is as follows;

Hasten, Lord, the glorious time,
When beneath Messiah's sway,
Every nation, every clime,
Shall the gospel call obey.

Her greatest outstanding hymn is one found in almost all hymn books of English speaking countries, and which has been translated into many other languages, her famous Pentecost hymn:

Our blest Redeemer, ere He breathed
His tender, last farewell,
A Guide, a Comforter bequeathed,
With us to dwell.

The author, Cuthbert Haddon, in one of his biographical writings, tells us that at least part of the verses of this poem were written upon a pane of glass in the house in which she lived at Hoddesdon, but the pane of glass has nowhere since been found.

Richard Mant (1776-1848)—Mant was a bishop in the Irish Episcopal Church and did much writing both prose and verse. Poetic by nature, he even versified parts of his sermons, and wrote a volume, entitled, "The Gospel Miracles," a series of poetic sketches. He performed the special service of bringing the rich hymn stores of the Roman Breviary to English readers.

More of his work was versification based on psalms and on the Latin sources of hymnody. The early Latin hymn of Fortunatus, "See the destined day arise," is a paraphrase by Mant. Another Holy Week hym[illegible] taken from a later Latin source was translated by Mant and further improved by Caswall is,

At the Cross her station keeping.

His "God, my King, Thy might confessing" is based on Psalm 145. His original verse includes the hymns

For all Thy saints, O Lord,
(altered to)
For Thy dear saints, O Lord
We strove in Thee to live.

But his leading original hymn is—

Round the Lord in glory seated,
Cherubim and seraphim.
Filled His temple and repeated
Each to each th' alternate hymn.

It should be remembered that Mant lent influence to Heber's hymn book of 1827. After the book of Heber's, nearly 600 authors were listed in Sedgwick's catalogue of hymn writers of 1863, and hymnists rapidly multiplied in the Church of England following the Oxford movement.

Reginald Heber (1783-1826)—In Heber we come to one of the most outstanding writers of the last century. He was recognized as a man of great ability, and his poetry commands attention for its literary merits; and the classic writers of his day were ready to recognize the literary quality and genius of his poetry. Heber marks a new era in hymn worship within the Established Church, which the influence of the non-Conformist Montgomery and the help of the Archbishop of Canterbury merely started, as seen in a preceding chapter.

As we have already seen the hymns of the eighteenth century were for the most part given us by the non-Conformist Churches. But from the time of Heber onward by far the largest number of good hymns were produced by the members of the Anglican Church, by her clergy or members of their families.

When Heber desired to compile a hymn book for Anglican usage he first asked to secure a copy of the "Olney Hymn Book, taking this as a basis and adding to it his own initiative. So his labours and influence made the English Church for the first time a truly hymn-singing Church, only a little over a century ago, although his hymn book was not published till after his early death.

The youth of Reginald Heber is of unusual interest. He was the son of Rev. Reginald Heber, Sr. The father being a man of means and scholarship, the son was given every opportunity for learning and culture, and the young man well improved his opportunities. In 1800 he entered one of the colleges of Oxford. During his first year he took the prize for the best Latin poem. Two years he later took the Newdigate prize for the best English poem, entitled "Palestine," one of the few undergraduate poems which has lived and is considered unsurpassed both before and since his day. But he also excelled in high moral character and religious devotion, as well as in the sphere of intellect. With vice prevalent around him, he kept himself pure and reverent, and as a leader among young men helped many of them over the road of temptation.

After his distinguished graduation he went on tour of the Continent. Later he was ordained to the priesthood in the Anglican Church, and was settled at Hodnet, where he remained for sixteen years and where he wrote most of his hymns and was much beloved by his people.

He knelt "often at sick beds at the risk of his life; where there was trouble, the peacemaker; where there was want, the free-giver."

In 1815 he was appointed Bampton Lecturer, later prebendary at St. Asaph, and in 1822 removed to London as preacher at Lincoln's Church. Twice he was urged to take the bishopric of Calcutta. Being of very devout and missionary spirit, after twice declining for good reasons, he finally consented to go to India with Ceylon and Australia added to all India for a diocese. There he laboured hard for the spread of Christ's Kingdom. His episcopate was brief, lasting but three years, but they were of fruitful labours. In his vast diocese with his enthusiastic labours and the hot climate, his strength was heavily taxed. After a busy period of pastoral visitation and confirmation of a large class, he retired, took a bath and, the shock of cold water being too much, he soon expired.

Heber's great fame resulted from his writing of a variety of hymns of high rank. His hymns show a large variety of topics. Not only did he give us one of our greatest missionary hymns, but also a great martial hymn, a great Epiphany hymn, a famous Eucharistic hymn, and the finest hymn of adoration. The story of his writing his missionary hymn, "From Greenland's icy mountains," is as follows. When Heber went to visit his father-in-law, the Dean of St. Asaph, the two being together in the latter's study, on Saturday before Whitsunday (1819) each preparing a missionary sermon for the Sunday services, Doctor Shipley, the Dean, said, "Heber, write something appropriate to sing to-morrow." So Heber, sitting down on the other side of the room, wrote quickly three verses, which he read. The Dean responded, "There, that will do very well." "No, no, the sense is incomplete," replied Heber. So he added a fourth verse despite the objection of his father-in-law. The next morning it was sung in Wrexham Church for the first time. It was, for that day, written in unusual metre, and required a new tune to fit it. The story of young Lowell Mason's being asked to write the tune is equally interesting.

Another example of unusual metre for that time, and a fine example of Heber's noble literary style, is his

Bread of the world, in mercy broken,
Wine of the soul, in mercy shed,
By whom the words of life were spoken,
And in whose death our sins are dead.

It may possibly be objected to as too indefinite in its reference, and bordering on transubstantiation in teaching, but the objection is not clearly established. Be that as it may, his martial hymn, "The Son of God goes forth to war," written for the martyr St. Stephen's holy day is surely not an exhortation to national and physical warfare against fellowmen, but rather an exhortation to spiritual warfare, against "the world, the flesh, and the devil."

Written at a time when there was international warfare in Europe and when men were taking their lives into their own hands, the figurative language was used to reflect the martial spirit, and apostolic zeal in the spiritual realm, as illustrated in the life of St. Stephen. Thus in contemplating what apostles, martyrs, and self-sacrificing Christians had done before, his prayer for the modern generation was, "O God, to us may grace be given To follow in their train," as the refrain of the hymn so well expresses.

But Heber's greatest, of all his great hymns, is his Trinity hymn of adoration, based on the rhythm of the Apocalypse (Rev. iv, 8), and having more Catholic usage than almost all other hymns with but few exceptions:

Holy, holy, holy! Lord God Almighty!
Early in the morning our song shall rise to Thee;
Holy, holy, holy! merciful and mighty!
God in three persons, blessed Trinity.

The last line of this first verse may not be purely poetic, yet the simplicity and dignity of the hymn as a whole are pure adoration with nothing of the subjective element in it. It is said Tennyson considered it one of the finest ever written.

This poem which is invariably sung to Dykes's famous tune, "Nicæa," furnishes us an example of a sacred lyric almost unsurpassed. Other good hymns of Heber's in use to-day are the Epiphany hymn,

Brightest and best of the sons of the morning

and

Hosanna to the living Lord

By cool Siloam's shady rill

Lord of mercy and of might.

The evening hymn, "God that madest earth and heaven," was written in part by Heber and later completed by Richard Whateley.

Robert Grant (1785-1838)—Grant is another pre-eminent hymn writer, following soon after Heber and deserving very high rank. He was born in the surroundings of high political life. His father was a member of Parliament from the district of Inverness, Scotland, and at forty-one years of age introduced a bill of rights for the Jew. He was graduated from Cambridge, 1806, and practiced law for nineteen years.

In 1834 Sir Robert became Governor of Bombay which office he held for the few years more that he lived. Strong testimony was given of the high character of his labours as governor. But he also preserved the simplicity and ardour of his Christian faith. Upon his death a public meeting of the citizens of Bombay paid tribute to his memory. He became known also through his volume of "Sacred Poems."

Grant wrote various fine hymn poems. His hymn of first rank is,

O, worship the King all glorious above!
O, gratefully sing His power and His love!
Our shield and defender, the Ancient of days,
Pavilioned in splendour, and girded with praise.

This hymn is splendid for its adoration, as "King," "power," "might," "grace," "bountiful care," and "ineffable love." Its spiritual element is praiseworthy, and God's faithfulness to those who put their trust in Him is highly emphasized. The imagery of the hymn is splendid, and its literary features are commensurate with its spiritual ones. It should be noted that these lines have double rhyme, in the middle as well as at end of the lines, which only adds to the poetic beauty. Taken all in all, there are not many such hymns which could be called superior lyrics.

Another hymn of Grant's, scarcely inferior to the foregoing, is his famous litany hymn which is a paraphrase of the ancient litany and is an example of an uncommon form of prayer in lyrics known as "pleading." It begins,

Saviour, when in dust to Thee
Low we bend the adoring knee;
When, repentant, to the skies
Scarce we lift our weeping eyes.

A third hymn of his, better known in the past than at present, as not all the new hymnals contain it, but worthy of note, is,

When gathering clouds around I view,
And days are dark, and friends are few,
On Him I lean who not in vain
Experienced every human pain;
He sees my wants, allays my fears,
And counts and treasures up my tears.

All three of these hymns are well worth careful reading and comparison for their majesty and graceful expression, on the points they treat, and their inspiring sentiments.

Charlotte Elliott (1789-1871)—Miss Elliott is one of the best of female hymn writers. She was a lover of nature and of souls, and after her conversion was a devout lover of her Lord. These qualities enabled her to write hymns which were greatly helpful to other souls. After her death a great many letters were found in her repositories, which expressed appreciation and gratitude for her greatest hymn, "Just As I Am." One of these letters tells of how the poet Wordsworth's daughter had been comforted on her death-bed by this hymn.

Charlotte Elliott was born in Brighton and lived to the age of eighty-two, although she was an invalid much of her life. She was the granddaughter of the Rev. Henry Venn, himself a prose writer. She lived a quiet life, yet had many friends, some of whom were prominent characters. None influenced her so much as the famous Genevan evangelist, Cæsar Malan, with whom she corresponded during the many years they both were alive. She kept the anniversary of their first meeting as a festal day, commemorating "the birthday of her soul."

The story of her writing "Just As I Am" should be told (even though in part some doubt has been cast upon it in recent years).

From Doctor Robinson's "Annotations of Hymns" we are told that when Doctor Malan was visiting the house of the young lady's father, one evening as they sat conversing, the clergyman asked Miss Elliott "if she thought herself to be an experimental Christian." Her health was poor at the time and she was annoyed by pain, and the question made her petulant at the time. She resented the question, and told him that she did not want to discuss religion. Doctor Malan replied in his sweet manner that he would not pursue a subject displeasing to her, but would pray that she might "give her heart to Christ, and become a useful worker for Him." A few days later the young lady apologized for her bluntness to the minister and said, "I do not know how to find Christ and I want you to help me." He answered, "Come to Him just as you are," never expecting that that simple advice would be repeated in song the world over.

Further spiritual instruction resulted in opening her mind to spiritual light, followed by faith and action. Having literary gifts, she was asked to assume charge of the "Yearly Remembrance," and she inserted original poems, including this hymn without revealing authorship, which supposedly expressed her personal religious experience after Doctor Malan's words of advice. After its publication a philanthropic woman, realizing its spiritual value, had it printed on a leaflet and circulated throughout the cities and towns of the country. When Miss Elliott, in feeble health, was at the watering place of Torquay her eminent physician and a good Christian, visiting her handed a leaflet to his patient, telling her he felt sure she would like it. The surprise and pleasure were mutual when she recognized her own hymn, and he discovered she was the author.

No other hymn is more completely evangelical, and its figures of speech and its spiritual teachings put it foremost among hymns of that type. Its boundless love on the divine side and the full surrender on the human side are perfectly set forth in poetic force and faultless rhyme, and can so adequately express the condition and needs of the doubtful or troubled heart.

Another great hymn by Miss Elliott is almost equally valuable to the devout Christian under trials or sadness, and very appropriate for funeral occasions as well,

My God, my Father, while I stray
Far from my home in life's rough way,
Oh, teach me from my heart to say,
Thy will be done.

Another similar type of hymn expressing the burdened heart's desire is

Jesus, my Saviour, look on me,
For I am weary and oppressed;
I come to cast myself on Thee;
Thou art my rest.

One other of her well-known hymns is

"Christian, seek not yet repose,"
Hear thy guardian angel say;
"Thou art in the midst of foes:
Watch and pray."

James Edmeston (1791-1867)—Another writer, worthy of attention, is James Edmeston. He was a London architect who wrote many volumes of verse. His volume, entitled, "The Cottage Minstrel," was written in response to an advertisement by a Christian philanthropist, Thomas Thompson. The father of Mrs. Jemima Luke who wrote one of our well-known hymns, offered a reward for fifty simple hymns which would be suited for cottage meetings. In fact he prepared a new hymn every week for Sunday worship in his own home, and these were the collection, entitled, "Cottagers' Hymns." One of these evening hymns is the well known "Saviour, breathe an evening blessing."

The cause of his writing it was his reading of a book, "Travels in Abyssinia," in which was given a description of the setting up of the traveller's tent in the evening at the close of the march for the day, and the mention of the natives singing an evening hymn, entitled, "Jesus, Forgive Us." This gave him the thought of an evening hymn which would pray for forgiveness and also for divine protection, and Edmeston expanded these thoughts by writing them in the words of this famous hymn. But Edmeston also wrote another fine hymn praying for protection and peaceful guidance over life's journey, which to-day is found in new hymnals, and is not to be confused with other hymns, beginning with similar language:

Lead us, heavenly Father, lead us
O'er the world's tempestuous sea;
Guard us, guide us, keep us, feed us,
For we have no help but Thee,
Yet possessing
Every blessing
If our God our Father be.

Henry Hart Milman (1791-1868)—When Milman was a student at Oxford he won various honours, among them the Newdigate for English verse, which greatly appealed to Dean Stanley. While a student he wrote his first drama, which proved a success in both England and America, yet it stood against him during his first parish work because of a feeling against a clergyman who was also a playwright.

Later three religious dramas added fame to his career as poet and dramatist, "The Fall of Jerusalem," "The Martyr of Antioch" and "Belshazzar." But he became more famous in later life as a historian by his "History of the Jews" and his "Latin Christianity" which made a new era in ecclesiastical history. He was a brilliant author, a poet, playwright, historian, theologian, scholar; professor at Oxford and lastly Dean of St. Paul's. As Dean he was much sought after because of his brilliant scholarship, his social charm and his earnest Christianity. As a boy he had witnessed the burial of Nelson from St. Paul's, and as Dean he officiated at the burial of the Duke of Wellington.

It was through Heber that Milman became a hymn writer. When Heber planned to compile a new hymn book in the Anglican Church he appealed to Scott, Southey and Milman. While Heber waited, Milman sent a dozen poems to Heber, but Southey failed to send any as promised. Heber was so pleased with Milman's hymns, he wrote the latter, referring especially to his "Ride on, ride on in majesty," saying "a few more such hymns and I shall neither need or wait for the aid of Scott and Southey."

His style was similar to Heber's, with "lyric grace and literary finesse," such as would naturally be expected from one who held the chair of Poetry in Oxford.

His most famous hymn, used on Palm Sunday, already referred to, was based on the story of Jesus' triumphal entry, riding on the ass, into Jerusalem when the people waved their palm branches, and called Him "Son of David," and "Lord," and cried "Hosanna in the highest!" The hymn expresses the thought of sacrifice and the strife to the ultimate triumph picturing Christ as coming to reign victorious.

A second outstanding hymn of Milman's in the list of hymns for "Burial of the Dead," and very appropriate and consoling for those in sadness to sing, begins,

When our heads are bowed with woe,
When our bitter tears o'erflow,
When we mourn the lost, the dear,
Jesus, Son of Mary, hear.

John Bowring (1792-1872)—Bowring was born in Exeter, the son of Charles Bowring, a woollen manufacturer, who carried on a successful trade with the Spanish and Chinese. The father expected his son to carry on the business; and to increase his efficiency he took up the study of foreign languages, and at sixteen years of age could write and speak in Spanish, Italian, Portuguese, French and German. Before starting on a commercial career he became a pupil of Jeremy Bentham in political economy. Upon the death of the latter he went into the Mediterranean trade and obtained large contracts for supplying the British Army. His young man companion was George Borrow who also made great linguistic attainments, and the two young men studied much together. In 1870 these two men wrote conjointly an article on "Danish and Norwegian Literature." Later Bowring made translations of lyrics from Bohemian, Bulgarian and other Slavic languages. Because of his attainments he had been honoured with high degree by the University of Groningen in Holland. Later he was elected as a Radical from Kilmarnock to the House of Commons. Afterwards he was Governor of Hongkong, and in 1854 he was knighted. When he died his wife had inscribed on his tombstone the first line of his hymn, "In the Cross of Christ I glory."

Although his business and political achievements were conspicuous, yet his lasting fame is on account of his hymns. The one already referred to has been widely sung and is still much used to-day as a favourite hymn with many people, and is appropriate for Holy Week.

Another widely known hymn to-day is

Watchman, tell us of the night,
What its signs of promise are.

Still another hymn is found in new hymnals and worthy of use,

God is love; His mercy brightens
All the path in which we rove;
Bliss He wakes, and woe He lightens;
God is wisdom, God is love.

Henry Francis Lyte (1793-1847)—While Montgomery and Heber were among the greatest writers of the nineteenth century, Lyte was surely the equal of any writer of the century. Two of his hymns are included in the first ten of Benson's list of "Best Hymns," an honour accorded to none other except Wesley. Two of his are accorded first rank in the "Anglican Hymnology." He was full of the evangelistic and missionary spirit, representing the best devotion of his time.

Lyte was born near Kelso, Scotland, of English parents, but educated at Trinity College, Dublin, where he took the English prize for poetry three times.

He was ordained to the priesthood of the English Church, and after being moved from one small parish to another he was settled at the village of Brixham on the Devonshire coast, England. During his early ministry he had an experience at the deathbed of a brother clergyman, which deepened his spiritual outlook on life, and he henceforth studied his Bible and preached in a more ardent manner than he had done before.

In Brixham he spent the remainder of his twenty-five years of labour, interrupted with poor health, which occasionally required his absense from home, seeking health on the Continent. But with all his strength he laboured devotedly among his humble people who were rather crude fishermen, uneducated, and unappreciative of Lyte's talents and scholarship. He had many trials among them. Here he wrote most all his hymns, and they were the outgrowth of his own religious experiences, yet with the personal element carefully obscured. At the end of his last summer of suffering he returned to his parish, and against the protest of friends, he insisted upon holding a final Holy Communion and preaching a farewell sermon to his beloved congregation, when just afterwards he admitted "he was scarcely able to crawl."

During his later days he wrote a poem, entitled, "Declining Days." As he looked back over life he felt its sorrows and disappointments, and with never having such mutual companionship, as other writers of note and never having the conspicuous honours and recognition such as Montgomery, Heber, and others had, still in humble spirit and resignation to fate he gave expression to his only remaining ambition in his "Declining Days," when he wrote,

Some simple strain, some spirit moving lay,
Some sparklet of the soul, that still might live
When I have passed to clay.

The poem closes with the prayer,

O Thou, whose touch can lend
Life to the dead, Thy quickening grace supply,
And grant me, swanlike, my last breath to spend
In song that may not die.

Not often are the prayers and language of a disappointed heart so completely and literally fulfilled as this, but not till shortly after death. His swan song was written the evening of the Sunday of his farewell service mentioned above. During the afternoon the villagers had seen their pastor, walking among the flowers of his garden which he loved so well, and out of the grief of farewells which helped to make that final morning service so difficult; out of the experiences of the whole day he carefully wrote the immortal hymn which stands among the very first in the English language,

Abide with me, fast falls the eventide;
The darkness deepens; Lord, with me abide;
When other helpers fail, and comforts flee,
Help of the helpless, O abide with me.

Every one of the five verses should be carefully and meditatively read, and their great worth can be appreciated. The fourth verse begins:

Swift to its close ebbs out life's little day,
Earth's joys grow dim, its glories pass away.

This too was fulfilled in Lyte's experience. The next day after writing the hymn he started for Italy, but died soon after he reached Nice, France, and he lies buried there in the English cemetery.

Of course, it is dealing with the heart and soul at the eventide of life, and not merely of the eventide of the day. Its depth of emotion, its poetic beauty, and imagery, and its richness in Christian experience make it a hymn of rare value.

Lyte's second hymn of highest rank, according to the "Anglican Hymnology," is "Praise, my soul, the King of heaven," and to-day a half century later it is often selected by compilers of new hymnals. But according to Benson's "Best Hymns," the hymn of second highest rank is

Jesus, I my cross have taken,
All to leave and follow Thee.

This surrender of self to God and aspiration to be a complete follower of the Master are also the outgrowth of Lyte's inward experience, as a result of his deepened spiritual insight when he found his own spiritual deficiency with nothing to offer when serving at the deathbed of his fellow clergyman, referred to above.

This hymn has been compared very favourably with Charlotte Elliott's great evangelistic hymn, "Just as I am," and both of these hymns have a wonderful history in influence over the sinful and penitent souls of men and women. This hymn of Lyte's has never fully come into its own for the lack of an adequate tune.

Because of Lyte's Christian experiences and his able poetic skill, refined imagery and deep spiritual insight, he was able to write other great hymns which still live and are much appreciated by users of hymns. Any good hymnal to-day should include several of Lyte's hymns.

Another of Lyte's best hymns should be noted, not only because it is a fine missionary lyric, but especially because it is one of the few hymns which pray for the redemption of the Hebrew people and which are not so much used to-day as they might be.

O that the Lord's Salvation
Were out of Zion come,
To head His ancient nation
And lead His outcasts home.
How long the Holy City
Shall heathen feet profane?
Return, O Lord, in pity
Rebuild her walls again!

Other hymns of his are taken from his metrical version of the Psalter, entitled, "The Spirit of the Psalms," the same in title as Harriet Auber's work. It is a free paraphrase of the psalms, and some of these poems are much used, as his

Pleasant are Thy courts above,

based on Psalm 84, and

God of Mercy, God of Grace,

based on the 67th Psalm.

John Keble (1792-1866), Oxford Hymn Writer—We come now to a new movement which had wide effect on both church history and the development of hymnody. It was a revolt against looseness and irreverence in church worship, and the indifference and spiritual negligence of the times. Furthermore, it was a movement to bring the Anglican Church back to its inheritance of the historic Catholic faith and practice. Regarding its inspiration to a larger production of church hymns, Doctor Benson says, "To say that the High Church Movement has inspired a large proportion of the best hymns of the nineteenth century is simply to acknowledge the truth." It is usually called the Oxford Movement or the Tractarian Movement which began in 1833.

Keble was the first of the chief actors in the movement, which was started, according to general consent, by the famous "Assize Sermon," preached by Keble at Oxford. John Keble was the son of a clergyman in Gloucestershire. The father tutored his own sons, John and Thomas, till they went to college. They entered Oxford and John began his brilliant career. At only eighteen he took double first class honours, which had never been done before, except by Sir Robert Peel. The next year he was Fellow at Oriel, and also took the university prizes in both Latin and English composition. Later he was ordained to the priesthood in the Anglican Church, and still later became tutor at Oriel College. He was subsequently elected Professor of Poetry, his lectures being delivered in Latin, as was the custom. Previously his mother had died, and he stayed at Fairford to care for his aged father and sisters. He was offered several appointments in the Church which he declined because he would not leave his family, which showed his devotion to family duty. After his father's death he accepted the vicarage at Hursley for the rest of his days, as it seems no further offer of advancement was given him, and he sought none.

This shy, modest and unambitious man was deeply concerned with personal humility, but despite this fact his life and work made its mark on English history, and on all the churches.

In 1827 was published his "Christian Year," which made a memorable step in English hymnody. It was a wonderful collection of poems by which the church calendar was supplied with appropriate poems for each Sunday, holy days, and saints' days of the year, intended as a poetical companion to the book of Common Prayer. His purpose was to delay publication till after his death, but friends who saw them urged that they be given to the world at once and he finally consented for his father's sake, who desired it to be published before he died. It was remarkable that it passed through ninety-six editions in the author's life time.

From this book most of Keble's hymns have been taken, and chiefly on the reputation and merits of this book of poetry was Keble elected to the professorship of Poetry at Oxford.

In his "Christian Year" Keble followed the example of his predecessors, such as Ken, and introduced his poems with a morning and evening hymn. From these two poems we get his most famous hymns. The morning poem originally contained sixteen verses and we should realize, in singing or reading it, that the verses selected to form a hymn, both in the case of the morning hymn and evening, are wrested from their context and somewhat abrupt in continuity. For example between the third and fourth verses in the hymnal a number of original verses are omitted. It begins;

New every morning is the love,
Our waking and uprising prove;
Through sleep and darkness safely brought,
Restored to life, and power, and thought.

Still even more popular is his evening hymn:

Sun of my soul, Thou Saviour dear,
It is not night if Thou be near;
O may no earthborn cloud arise
To hide Thee from Thy servant's eyes.

Keble was more of a religious poet than a writer of sacred hymns, but he has written other poems suited to be adopted as hymns, as his famous hymn for the marriage office;

The voice that breathed o'er Eden.

Others of his hymns are,

Lord, in Thy name Thy servants plead

Blest are the pure in heart

God the Lord a King remaineth.

John Henry Newman (1801-1889)—Cardinal Newman, born a few years later than Keble, was another very conspicuous actor in the Oxford Movement, although probably Edward Pusey was the most versatile scholar and teacher among the Oxford leaders, and remained in the Anglican Church, as did Keble; but Newman and one other hymn writer among the group, Frederick William Faber (whom we sketch later), went over to the Roman Catholic Church. It was a source of sore disappointment to Keble that Newman seceded to Rome, although the former had feared and expected the latter would do so.

Newman was born in London, and was graduated with honours from Trinity College, Oxford. He was ordained to the English ministry in 1824, and it was twenty years later before he entered the Roman Church. A few years later he became rector of the new Roman Catholic University at Dublin, and in 1879 became a Cardinal, and lived to 1890 when he died in Birmingham. His going over to Rome is only the more striking when one remembers that in his younger days he was strongly anti-Roman and even held the view that the Pope was anti-Christ, which idea the most ultra-Protestant to-day does not believe. From early childhood Newman was interested in religion, and was converted at fifteen years. He delighted in reading the Bible, and knew his Catechism well. As a young clergyman in the English Church he was always delving into church doctrines in mystical contemplation. After a few years he became Vicar of St. Mary's and an important figure at Oxford, and his sermons almost always closely read, made deep impressions on men of divergent types. William E. Gladstone was an undergraduate there at the time and, like others, was impressed with Newman's preaching. He soon threw himself vigorously into the Oxford Movement and wrote the famous "Tract XC," which advocated extreme church doctrine.

The first year of the Oxford Movement Newman made a journey to Italy, and upon his return voyage on the Mediterranean a dead calm ensued and there were no breezes to move the sails of the vessel. He had been ill and away from friends. As the calm continued there was nothing for the passengers to do but wait and meditate and pray, if so inclined. As a clergyman of England he was perplexed over the state of religion in his country, and lack of spirituality in the Church. And having just visited in Rome and conversed with a cardinal of the Roman Church, he set to wondering whether the Church of England or the Church of Rome was right in its teachings. So in wonder and perplexity he at length began to write. Thus his one very famous hymn was produced,

Lead, kindly Light, amid th' encircling gloom,
Lead Thou me on!
The night is dark, and I am far from home;
Lead Thou me on!
Keep Thou my feet; I do not ask to see
The distant scene; one step enough for me.

But this hymn was written twelve years before Newman went over to the Roman Church and forty years before he was made a Cardinal by Pope Leo XIII.

The hymn was a record of his own personal struggle, his doubt and the uncertainty of his future course. His title for this hymn was "Light in Darkness," and it reflects the condition and perplexity of many human hearts. Its mood is that of fervour and humble aspiration with its poetic words, although it has been criticized as being little removed from prose, of which Newman was a better writer than he was of poetry.

Many years later, when a Romanist, he was asked to explain the meaning of one or two of the obscure lines of his hymn, and he replied, "I may plead that I am not bound to remember my own meaning—whatever it was—at the end of fifty years." But there is no denying that the popularity of the hymn has been due in large measure to its very musical tune. When late in life as Cardinal Newman he was congratulated on being the author of such a favourite hymn, he was generous enough to reply, "But you see it is not the hymn but the tune that has gained the popularity." The tune is Dykes's, and Doctor Dykes was a great master. Many people will agree that there is much truth in what Newman said, and he is to be given much credit for saying it.

Newman wrote one other original hymn which is in use, although he thought so little of it that he put it in the waste basket. A friend rescued it, and it has been used ever since.

Praise to the Holiest in the height,
And in the depth be praise.

Sarah Flower Adams (1805-1848)—This author was a daughter of Benjamin Flower, editor of "The Cambridge Intelligencer." She was married to William B. Adams, a civil engineer; and they settled in London where she came under the pastoral care of a Unitarian minister, the Rev. W. J. Fox. Mrs. Adams, only three or four years before writing her hymns, achieved triumph in drama, which seemed to be her great ambition. But ill health soon developed and she was obliged to give up the stage and turned to poetic writing. She attained recognition by her dramatic poem, "Vivia Perpetua," founded on the story of a Christian martyr in the third century.

Her pastor published a volume of poems in 1841, entitled "Hymns and Anthems," to which Mrs. Adams contributed thirteen poems. Only one of them is to-day in general use. But because of her one great outstanding hymn of much fame, she is given a place of high recognition among hymn writers.

This hymn, "Nearer, my God, to Thee," taking as its scriptural background the story of Jacob's vision at Bethel, brings forth the loftiest aspiration of the soul, but recognizes that what often seems to hinder, may be used to help, the spiritual life. Because of its lofty aspirations and its resignation to disappointment or affliction, it has been used universally on the occasion of funerals and in the crises of life.

The ship's band, in the last moments during the sinking of the Titanic, played the music of this hymn; and the martyred President McKinley quoted its words on his death-bed. It was a favourite of Theodore Roosevelt and many other good people. But it has had many criticisms at the hands of the critics, just as almost all the great hymns have been found fault with, and their supposed defects pointed out. One of these criticisms is that it sticks too closely to the story of Jacob at Bethel, which in truth it does, if that be an adequate criticism. Think more of its deeper meaning. Likely "the cross that raiseth me" was the closed door to her early life's ambition.

So the hymn goes on through the darkness, and the dream that even difficulty and the hard journey of life may be the very steps unto heaven. So whether by a cross or in the midst of trials or by soaring to "cleaving the sky," the prayer along life's journey must be

Nearer, my God, to Thee,
Nearer to Thee!
E'en though it be a Cross
That raiseth me;
Still all my song shall be,
Nearer, my God, to Thee,
Nearer to Thee!

Christopher Wordsworth (1807-1885)—Although Wordsworth was born only two years after Mrs. Adams, his hymns were written much later. He was the Bishop of Lincoln, and a nephew of the distinguished poet William Wordsworth. Christopher was an honour graduate of Trinity College, Cambridge. In fact he won the prize for scholarship, but won in athletics also. Having obtained so many prizes he was spoken of as "The Great Christopher." Still under thirty, he was elected Headmaster of Harrow School and was Canon of Westminster, and for fifteen years Bishop of Lincoln.

His capacity for work was prodigious. He wrote a "Commentary on the Whole Bible" which in itself was a life-time labour for one man, and his was characterized by great learning.

As Canon of Westminster he arranged a series of hymns which he published under title "The Holy Year," many of which were his own authorship. But as he was more concerned with teaching doctrine than writing poetry only a few of his hymns attained common use. He wrote a hymn of almsgiving and thanksgiving which has had few equals on stewardship.

O Lord of heaven and earth and sea,
To Thee all praise and glory be,
How shall we show our love to Thee
Who givest all?

Probably his most used hymn is his fine one, emphasizing the blessing of keeping the Lord's Day,

O day of rest and gladness
O day of joy and light.

Also his hymn for holy days, especially "All Saint's Day,"

Hark the sound of holy voices
Chanting at the crystal sea.

Another good hymn of his, appropriate for Ascension, is

See the Conqueror mounts in triumph,
See the King in royal state.

Another one of his hymns worthy of frequent use, setting forth the desire of world peace, is

Father of all, from land and sea
The nations sing, "Thine, Lord, are we,
Countless in number, but in Thee
May we be one."

One more of Wordsworth's hymns should be mentioned, which is a paraphrase of St. Paul's great chapter on love (I Cor. 13) with the first verse as introducing the topic, "Gracious Spirit, Holy Ghost," and the second verse is as follows

Love is kind, and suffers long,
Love is meek, and thinks no wrong,
Love than death itself more strong;
Therefore give us love.

Horatius Bonar (1808-1889)—Bonar was born a year later than Wordsworth, but his hymns for the most part were written before the latter's. His birth-place was Edinburgh. He was the son of James Bonar, Solicitor of Excise, an elder in the Church of Scotland and a man of learning.

Ancestors on his father's side were clergymen of the Church of Scotland. Thus it is not surprising that he chose the ministry, and one of his poems expresses his gratitude for the influence of his ancestry as follows:

I thank Thee for a holy ancestry,
I bless Thee for a godly parentage;
For seeds of truth and light and purity,
Sown in this heart from childhood's earliest age.

He was educated at the schools in his home city and was graduated at the University of Edinburgh. One of his classmates there was Archbishop Tait, and among other student intimates was the able Robert McCheyne. Upon being ordained, he settled at Kelso which place is associated also with the name of Henry F. Lyte. A revival soon developed at Dundee under the preaching of his friend Robert McCheyne in which Bonar joined enthusiastically; and to promote this work he published and widely circulated the Kelso tracts, which also added to Bonar's reputation.

In the early days of his ministry, his preaching was stern in tone, but he naturally mellowed in his dogmatic theology and ecclesiastical associations.

When the strong controversy came in the old Kirk and there followed disruption, Bonar went with the Free Church, and his congregation being able to hold their church property, his church became a centre of influence. In 1865 he removed to Edinburgh where he banded a new congregation which he built up by his able pastorate.

He lived to a ripe old age and his last days were serene and beautiful, and when he died he was mourned as much as any man of his generation.

Yet he disliked publicity and counted honours from men as an empty thing. He was of humble spirit and his chief aim in life was to bring men to Christ. With him the Second Advent was an absorbing problem and he became an ardent "premillenarian." He believed Christ was to return in person soon and restore Israel and to inaugurate an earthly kingdom for a thousand years. His sense of separation from the world and his desire for other-worldliness are the background for the hymns which he wrote, most of them during his quiet life at Kelso. Bonar is one of the largest contributors to our hymnals and foremost among Scottish hymn writers. Several of his hymns are special favourites with many people. Probably the greatest favourite among his hymns is

I heard the voice of Jesus say,
"Come unto Me and rest."

This hymn is one of spiritual depth and of well-balanced parts. The words of Jesus are put before the soul and the human response to Christ's gracious invitation. The author entitled it, "A Voice from Galilee," an appropriate name; and thrice the words are repeated, "I heard the voice of Jesus say." Dykes's splendid tune, "Vox Dilecti," also helps to make the hymn a great favourite to sing.

His early hymns written for the Sunday School, "I lay my sins on Jesus" and "I was a wandering sheep," are not in general use to-day. His first hymn written for adults was

Go labour on! spend and be spent!
Thy joy to do the Father's will.

His beautiful communion hymn is very impressive,

Here, O my Lord, I see Thee face to face;
Here would I touch and handle things unseen.

Here is another hymn of Bonar's, sometimes criticized and frequently not sung because it looks to the next world and gives little emphasis to the importance of this world; yet it does have its proper appeal and should be appreciated by any Christian who sees life in a prospective whole:

A few more years shall roll,
A few more seasons come.

A beautiful and expressive hymn, which Bonar entitled "Resignation," showing the interpretation of the difference between the mere passive idea of resignation and the inspiring activity of of an obedient and submissive life, begins thus:

Thy way, not mine, O Lord,
However dark it be;
Lead me by Thine own hand:
Choose out the path for me.

The new Presbyterian hymnal has restored for use the following:

Glory be to God the Father,
Glory be to God the Son,
Glory be to God the Spirit,
Great Jehovah Three in One.

and

Come, Lord, and tarry not;
Bring the long-looked-for day;
O why these years of waiting here,
These ages of delay?

Also

Blessing and honour and glory and power,
Wisdom and riches and strength evermore
Give ye to Him who our battle hath won,
Whose are the Kingdom, the crown, and the throne.

One more

Upward where the stars are burning,
Silent, silent in their turning
Round the never-changing pole.

One of the strange things in history is that this great hymn writer did not use his hymns in his own church, while the outside world (except Scotland) acclaimed his sacred poems. Not until near the end of his active ministry did he venture to introduce his own poems in his own insistent psalm-singing congregation, and even then there was a protest on part of some of his laity, and at least two officers immediately strode out of church. Such was the lack of appreciation of this man's original hymns.

Alfred Tennyson (1809-1892)—We have noted previously how few of our distinguished literary poets have contributed to hymnody. But Lord Tennyson did write one conspicuous hymn during his last days.

His life and poetic works are well known to the reader of literature, and his biography and his famous poems belong to the books on the history of English literature, and need not be narrated here. Suffice to say, he was Poet Laureate of England and lived to an old age.

Two of his religious poems, written when approaching middle age, have in recent years been regarded as possessing qualities which permit their adoption into the list of modern hymns, and are more apt to be found only in the newer hymnals. One of these is

Strong Son of God, Immortal Love,

taken from the opening verses of his famous religious poem "In Memoriam." The other is his

Ring out, wild bells, to the wild sky,
The flying cloud, the frosty light.

This hymn is now appropriately used for the end of an old year or beginning of a new year. But his chief hymn lines are his

Sunset and evening star

which was in reality his "swan song" (and he desired that it be such), written in his eighty-first year, and read to his son who said to him, "That is the crown of your life's work." To this the father replied, "It came in a moment." He explained that "the Pilot was the Divine and Unseen who is always guiding us." The son tells us further that a few days before his father's death the latter told him, "Mind you, put 'Crossing the Bar' at the end of all editions of my poems." It is indeed significant that Lord Tennyson should have selected these solemn and devout lines as his "swan song."

Henry Alford (1810-1871)—Alford, Dean of Canterbury Cathedral, was born in London, son of a clergyman of the Church of England. He was graduated from Trinity College, Cambridge, was successful in different positions and became Dean of Canterbury in 1857 where he remained until his death. He is known chiefly today as Dean, and as a writer of good hymns. But to students of the last generation he was known equally for his monumental work of a critical commentary on the Greek Testament upon which he laboured for twenty years. He had great capacity for scholarly work and he was ever writing. At six he wrote "Travels of St. Paul," at eleven "A Collection of Hymns for Sunday Occasions." He was interested and sympathetic with almost any good movement, a member of the Evangelical Alliance, and always in friendly association with the non-Conformists of England. He was a man of deep devotion and full of gratitude to God for His many blessings.

Alford was much interested in hymnology. After his boyish effort, he compiled several hymn books and for these he translated and wrote various hymns. Only a few of them have been cherished by the Church, but three stand out prominently.

The first one of these, written when he was young, is a good hymn of thanksgiving, and appropriate for Thanksgiving Day;

Come, ye thankful people, come,
Raise the song of harvest home.

During his last years he wrote the other two, and both are appropriate as processional or recessional hymns. One begins,

Forward! be our watchword,
Steps and voices joined;
Seek the things before us,
Not a look behind.

The other one is,

Ten thousand times ten thousand
In sparkling raiment bright,
The armies of the ransomed saints
Throng up the steeps of light:
'Tis finished; all is finished,
Their fight with death and sin:
Fling open wide the golden gates,
And let the victors in.

The hymn proclaims the Everlasting Life and it gives courage to the Church Militant, which is to become the Church Triumphant. This hymn was appropriately sung at the funeral of Dean Alford in Canterbury Cathedral.

John Samuel Bewley Monsell (1811-1875)—Monsell was another writer of this period who contributed several splendid hymns, much used. He was born in Ireland, the son of an archdeacon. His education for the priesthood was at Trinity College, Dublin. Most of his ministry in the Church of England was at Egham, England.

For some time he was chaplain to Bishop Mant. His last

years were spent as Rector of Guildford, Surrey, where occurred the tragedy which ended his active life. During repairs on the church he, being much interested in the progress of the work, was climbing in the church watching the workmen. Suddenly a mass of stone came down from the roof upon him. He was carried unconscious to the rectory but soon died. The first lines of his last poem, written to raise funds for rebuilding, had these ominous words,

Dear body, thou and I must part,
Thy busy head, thy throbbing heart
Must cease to work, and cease to play
For me at no far distant day.

Monsell held the view that our hymns should be "more fervent and joyous." He thought we were too restrained in our praises, "We sing not as we should sing to Him and of Him who is chief among ten thousand, the Altogether Lovely."

His hymns therefore reflect his ideas of praise. His joyous processional hymn is

On our way rejoicing,
As we homeward move,
Hearken to our praises,
O Thou God of love.

Probably the chief favourite of his hymns is

Fight the good fight with all thy might,
Christ is thy strength, and Christ thy right;
Lay hold on life, and it shall be
Thy joy and crown eternally.

This hymn seems to be inspired by the text, "Fight the good fight of faith, lay hold on eternal life, whereunto thou art also called."

Its figures of speech change quickly, and Christ is presented as "the fighter's strength, the runner's path and prize, the guide of the care-worn traveller, and the trusting soul's life and love."

With all the changing scenes of life the contrast is suggested of an unchanging Christ, who is the same yesterday, to-day and forever.

Other hymns of Monsell's are his Holy Communion hymn,

I hunger and I thirst;
Jesus, my Manna be,

and his hymn of offering and service,

Holy offerings, rich and rare,
Offerings of praise and prayer,
Purer life and purpose high,
Claspèd hands, uplifted eye,
Lowly acts of adoration,
To the God of our salvation;
On His altar laid, we leave them;
Christ, present them! God receive them!

Also his hymns,

Worship the Lord in the beauty of holiness

O'er the distant mountains breaking

Sweet is Thy mercy, Lord

Light of the world, we hail Thee.

SUMMARY

In this chapter we have considered: Introduction to nineteenth century hymn writers; James Montgomery; Thomas Kelly; Harriet Auber; Richard Mant; Reginald Heber; Robert Grant; Charlotte Elliott; James Edmeston; Henry Hart Milman; John Bowring; Henry Francis Lyte; John Keble; John Henry Newman; Sarah Flower Adams; Christopher Wordsworth; Horatius Bonar; Alfred Tennyson; Henry Alford; John S. B. Monsell.

XI

LATER NINETEENTH CENTURY WRITERS

F*REDERICK WILLIAM FABER* (1814-1863)—After the first decade of the nineteenth century there were born a succession of writers whose hymns were written for the most part after the middle of the century, and these writers' works consisted partly of translations and partly of original hymns which were not so vital in type as those preceding. The Romantic Period of English literature had closed and the Victorian Age succeeded it. The women writers now came to the front and with them the more sentimental and often more devotional type of hymn. By the middle of the century the Oxford group took the lead over the evangelical leaders in the Church of England, and the hymnody of all churches became modified. There were not the stirring movements after the middle of the century as before, except the Civil War in America, and the rise of the hymns proclaiming social justice.

Among the Oxford party, whose writers now appear again following the early leaders of that movement, is the outstanding writer, Frederick William Faber. There have been various opinions of his poems. but nevertheless he has been most frequently quoted, and some of his lines have become "proverbial." He was a friend of Newman and later followed him to the Church of Rome.

Faber, the son of an Anglican clergyman, was born in Yorkshire. He was graduated from Balliol College, Oxford, ordained the next year after graduation and became rector of Elton in 1843. He joined the Roman Church in 1846. He published a volume of travels, called "Sights and Thoughts in Foreign Churches and among Foreign People," before his secession, but this showed evidence that his mind had been turned Romeward. When Faber told Wordsworth that he intended to enter the Roman Church, the latter replied, "I do not say you are wrong, but England loses a poet," and the poems he left support Wordsworth's opinion.

His hymns number one hundred fifty. Various editions of his hymns have been published, some of which, because of being addressed to the Virgin Mary and the saints, have not been used for Protestant worship. But many of them need no change for they were written before his secession.

Faber's hymns show much poetic genius. He is inclined to exaggeration. He mixes phraseology that seems incongruous. He uses words in unusual meanings, and sometimes of such familiarity that they offend conservative taste. But whatever is said about the language he often employs, his spirit is almost above reproach. He was willing that his hymns be used by anyone and did not object to omissions which others preferred to make, but he did object to alterations which changed his meaning and doctrines.

It is claimed he derived language from other poets and used words so as to attain spiritual teaching greater than the average hymn writer. Two of his hymns which have become great favourites with many people show his poetic ability and peculiar style, as

Hark! hark, my soul! Angelic songs are swelling
O'er earth's green fields and ocean's wave-beat shore;
How sweet the truth those blessèd strains are telling
Of that new life when sin shall be no more!

then the refrain:

Angels of Jesus, angels of light,
Singing to welcome the pilgrims of the night.

How effective is this song with either Smart's tune, "Pilgrims," or Dykes's tune, "Vox Angelica," among the best tunes in our hymnals. Also

O Paradise, O Paradise, who doth not crave for rest?
Who would not seek the happy land, where they that loved are blest;

with refrain,

Where loyal hearts and true stand ever in the light,
All rapture, thro' and thro', in God's most holy sight?

The effect of this hymn is increased by its good tune by Barnby.

Another of Faber's leading hymns is

There's a wideness in God's mercy
Like the wideness of the sea;
There's a kindness in His justice
Which is more than liberty.

Here we have the unusual use of language in the "kindness in His justice," and "There is joy for all the members In the sorrows of the Head"; also his closing lines, "And our lives would be all sunshine In the sweetness of the Lord." In this hymn his imagination is very vivid and also unusual in its expression.

Among the other hymns of Faber's which possess striking language are

My God, how wonderful Thou art

Jesus, gentlest Saviour, God of might and power

Faith of our fathers, living still
In spite of dungeon, fire and sword

O come and mourn with me awhile;
And tarry here the cross beside;
O come, together let us mourn;
Jesus, our Lord, is crucified.

The last one is justly a favourite hymn for Holy Week and peculiarly appropriate for Good Friday services.

Edward Caswall (1814-1878); ***John Mason Neale*** (1818-1866)—This period is conspicuous for its able translators of hymns. We have already mentioned under German Hymnody the work of translators—Catherine Winkworth, Jane Borthwick and her sister, Mrs. Sarah Borthwick-Findlater—who have done so much for our hymnals by their able translations.

Contemporaneous with these women we have two great hymnists who have given us some of our best English hymns, translated from early sources of the Greek and Latin. These men were mentioned in an earlier chapter but need further consideration here. Caswall and Neale continued the group of able hymn writers of the Oxford Movement, although Caswall seceded to the Roman Communion, while Neale remained in the Anglican Church.

Caswall was born in Hampshire, the son of a clergyman. He was educated at Oxford, and graduated with honours. After the sudden death of his wife, he joined Newman in founding the Oratory at Edgbaston, and to the end of his days devoted himself to the duties of that order, showing unusual sympathy for the sick.

Neale was born in London four years later than Caswall and he too was the son of a clergyman. He attended Trinity College, Cambridge, where he was the leading scholar in his class. He was given various honours, chiefly classical and gave primary attention to mediæval church history. He became one of the most learned hymnologists of the Church. Yet the Church of England offered him no preferment and he was practically ignored by the patrons of the Church of England; even his degree of "Doctor of Divinity" came from America. He was offered the Wardenship of Sackville College, which in reality was an obscure almshouse, paying the meagre salary of twenty-seven pounds per year. Here he formed institutions after the Roman model, the most important being a sisterhood. His work brought him into disfavour instead of appreciation from the ecclesiastical authorities, but he lived down opposition by his gentle and devout character and the splendid charity he showed to all Christians. He was an advanced ritualist and a pronounced mystic which made him seem like a mediæval saint. He contributed much to the literature of the Church. It is really not too much to say that he and Caswall together have done more to give us a knowledge of ancient and mediæval hymnody than all other authors combined.

Their knowledge of both English and Latin so excelled that few men in history, if any, have equalled them in translating from one poetic language into the poetry of another language. Their hymns in English have been referred to previously, but they have also written original hymns. Not many of Caswall's original ones are in use now: one of them is worthy of note:

O Jesus Christ, if sin there be,
In all our former years,
That wrings the soul with agony
And chokes the heart with tears,
It is the deep ingratitude
Which we to Thee have shown,
Who did for us in tears and blood
Upon the Cross atone.

This has been criticized for its referring to a special kind of sin as ingratitude. But that quality is generally the most common defect in character, and the real source of many special sins. Moreover, the hymn filled a place in English hymnody, as its theme is sadly neglected in sacred song and we need more hymns dealing with the general sin of ingratitude, this type of hymn having been overlooked by almost all of the hymnists (as well as by many preachers). He wrote another original hymn, "Days and Moments quickly flying." Caswall's most famous hymns are (translated)

Jesus, the very thought of Thee

When morning gilds the skies

Earth has many a noble city

O Saving Victim.

Neale's most famous translated hymns are:

O come, O come, Emmanuel

All glory laud and honour

The day of resurrection

O sons and daughters, let us sing

Come, ye faithful, raise the strain

Christian, dost thou see them

Christ is made the sure Foundation.

His hymns, "Those eternal bowers" and "Art thou weary," are not so much versions of Greek, as they are adaptations from early sources. In addition he is the translator of the three famous hymns taken from the De Contemptu Mundi, ascribed to Bernard of Cluny, as mentioned previously:

Jerusalem the golden

Brief life is here our portion

and

The world is very evil.

An original hymn of Neale is:

Holy Father, Thou hast taught me.

Thomas Toke Lynch (1818-1871)—Exactly contemporaneous with Neale was Thomas Toke Lynch, a Congregational minister. He was said to be a man of personal charm and originality, despite his poor health, which often interrupted his work. But he always returned to his work as soon as the pain subsided. He ministered to several small congregations and never received calls to large churches. His strength usually permitted him to preach but one sermon a Sunday, but often he wrote a second sermon to read to his Sunday evening congregation. While not a popular preacher in the usual sense of the word, it is said he gathered around him, by the individuality, freshness and spirituality of his pulpit work, a congregation of thoughtful and devoted people. He published a column of verse, called, "The Rivulet," containing his own works, hymns which were attacked as wanting in vital religion. Spurgeon also denounced his hymns, but the author met these attacks with sweet spirit.

Lynch was a musician as well as poet and he composed tunes for his own hymns and was heard humming one of them on his death-bed. His hymns have not been so extensively used as many others, possibly because unconventional, but they are still found included in hymnals recently edited. The new Pilgrim Hymnal contained but one which is probably his most favoured hymn,

Gracious Spirit, dwell with me,
I myself would gracious be.

Other hymnals contain such hymns as:

The Lord is rich and merciful;
The Lord is very kind,

and

A thousand years have come and gone,
And near a thousand more

also

Where is thy God, my soul?
Is He within thy heart?
Or ruler of a distant realm
In which thou hast no part?

Another hymn of his which shows his unconventional writing and teaches us a deeper appreciation for hearing the Holy Scriptures read is:

Christ in His word draws near;[1]
Hush, moaning voice of fear,
He bids thee cease;
With songs sincere and sweet
Let us arise and meet
Him who comes forth to greet
Our souls with peace.

And then the last verse ends:

O let us hush and hear
His holy word!

[1] From *Lyric Religion.*

Sir Henry Williams Baker (1821-1877)—Sir Henry W. Baker was born in London and was graduated from Trinity College, Cambridge. Baker was ordained priest in the Church of England in 1844 and was knighted in 1859. He became vicar of Monkland in Herefordshire a few years after ordination and remained there until his death in 1877. He was not only a hymn writer of distinction, but even more a genius in editing a hymnal. He was the chief editor and leader, in giving to the Church the famous collection, "Hymns Ancient and Modern." Thirty-three of his best known hymns are included in that book. He was the leader of a company of clergy who met in 1857 to compile a hymnal which they hoped might be used by a few dozen parishes. At that time in England there was no general book of praise, but many books, none of which were used by more than a few individual churches. All was chaos, so far as any one book having general recognition. After this famous hymnal, to which many poets of the day were asked to contribute, was published, its worth and usage grew by leaps and bounds, until it became the leading book of the nineteenth century in point of general usage, and until today is referred to as a standard of judgment.

The late Dr. William Bodine, the American hymnologist, informs us that the chairman of the committee of compilers told him that at the time it was compiled they would have been satisfied and thankful if it should be adopted in twenty churches besides their own parishes.

Baker was one of the greatest hymnology scholars of his time; and what added much to the favour of the book was the musical settings arranged for it by another genius, Dr. William H. Monk, one of the foremost church musicians of the nineteenth century. Small wonder that the committee with two such geniuses for editors as Baker and Monk, with their able assistants, produced one of the most famous hymnals of modern times.

Not only did it contain the best of the modern English writers, but also included selections from Latin and Greek sources from the fourth century downward, which had long been practically ignored. Although Baker's greatest talent was as a critic of hymns, and he did not hesitate to alter and "improve" versions of other writers, yet he was a hymn writer of no small merit.

Among his good hymns, which are well known, are:

O God of love, O King of Peace,

Praise, O praise our God and King

I am not worthy, holy Lord

Of the Father's love begotten

There is a blessed home

Lord, Thy word abideth.

His "Praise, O praise our God and King" is based on John Milton's version of the 136th Psalm. His most famous lines, beginning, "The King of love my Shepherd is," may be regarded as a hymn, although it is an expanded paraphrase of Psalm 23. Each verse of the hymn corresponds to each of the six verses in the King James version of the psalm, adding the New Testament teaching to the figures of the Old Testament, as in the last couplet of the fourth verse:

Thy rod and staff my comfort still,
Thy cross before to guide me.

Edward Hayes Plumptre (1821-1891)—Plumptre received his higher education at King's College, London, and University College, Oxford, and distinguished himself as a scholar. He was a man of talents, preacher of ability and won favour. He advanced upward till he became Dean of Wells, which position he filled admirably. He was not only theologian, but also biographer, exegete, translator and poet. His life of Bishop Ken is a standard work. His sermons and studies on "Life after Death" were the foremost utterances up to his day on the subject and his book on this topic was dedicated to Frederick Denison Maurice.

His famous sermon on "Eternal Hope" was epoch-making, on the text: "He went and preached unto the spirits in prison." It did more than any other sermon to bring to life the then dormant article of the Apostles' Creed, "He descended into hell."

His poetic gifts, imagination and accurate scholarship pervaded his writings of whatever kind. Of the ten hymns which he wrote, four are preserved in some of our hymnals:

O Light whose beams illumine all

Thine Arm, O Lord, in days of old

Thy Hand, O God, has guided

and

Rejoice, ye pure in heart!
Rejoice, give thanks and sing!

Your festal banner wave on high,
The cross of Christ your king!
Rejoice, rejoice,
Rejoice, give thanks, and sing!

The last named is his best known and was written in 1865 as a processional for a choir festival at Peterborough Cathedral. This hymn has been appropriated by all evangelical churches and is often used as a processional and is well suited for such purpose; or it is also a good children's hymn, as well as adapted for general congregational singing. It is said that Dean Plumptre based this hymn on the words of Psalm 20:5 which reads, "We will rejoice in thy salvation, and in the name of our God we will set up our banners."

Cecil Frances Alexander (1823-1895)—This woman was the wife of the Archbishop of Armagh, Dr. William Alexander. To her he dedicated his Bampton Lectures, the Witness of the Psalms to Christ. She is another who represents the Oxford group of writers, and was influenced by the Oxford movement, and wrote for its expansion before marriage, when known by her maiden name, Miss Fanny Humphreys. When young she became intimate with the sister of the Dean of Chichester, through whose influence she had been taught the truth and seeming necessity of the English Reformation, and her balance was preserved by the Dean's influence. She was married in 1850 to her distinguished husband, through whom she naturally came into contact with some of the best Christian leaders of her day. She was especially fond of Bishop Wilberforce, and while she naturally enjoyed most those of her own type of churchmanship, yet she admired Dean Stanley, Matthew Arnold and Mr. Lecky and was indignant when she heard criticisms of any one of them. In later years she came more in contact with the non-Conformists, especially the Presbyterians, and learned to like and associate with them.

Mrs. Alexander is famous for the large amount of poetry written by her especially for children, which purpose partly accounts for its simplicity of language. But it was not childish poetry, for it contained profound doctrine and her poetry has been greatly appreciated by both young and old.

Her first volume was "Hymns for Little Children," published in 1847, and subsequently appearing in seventy or more editions. These poems had hymns on Baptism, Apostles' Creed, the Ten Commandments and the Lord's Prayer.

She is one of the leading contributors to our hymnals. She could write the finest kind of sacred lyrics. The most famous of her large poems was the well-known "Burial of Moses," which ends thus:

O lonely grave in Moab's land!
O dark Beth-Peor's hill!
Speak to these curious hearts of ours
And teach them to be still.
God has His mysteries of grace
Ways that we cannot tell;
He hides them deep, like the secret sleep
Of him He loved so well.

Still these majestic lines are little superior to her hymn which has become a great favourite, so much used in Holy Week,

There is a green hill far away,
Without a city wall,
Where the dear Lord was crucified,
Who died to save us all.

Next to this great hymn is another almost equal to it in general usage. It is as descriptive as the former and has been adopted as the hymn of the Brotherhood of St. Andrew, a fine organization for men and boys:

Jesus calls us; o'er the tumult
Of our life's wild, restless sea,
Day by day His sweet voice soundeth,
Saying, "Christian, follow Me."

Among others of her splendid hymns are:

Once in royal David's city

He is risen, He is risen

Forsaken once and thrice denied

All things bright and beautiful

Saw you never in the twilight

Thou Power and Peace, in whom we find.

Different from what you might expect, she was more deaf to applause and the praise of friends, including friends of great distinction, than almost any other character in history that one can recall. She did not wish to hear praise for her noble poetry. But on one occasion when some one wrote to tell her of the change in heart and life which had come to a worldly man through hearing one of her hymns sung, she sprang to her feet, joyfully exclaiming: "Thank God! I do like to hear that." Those who knew her intimately felt that her life was even more beautiful than her hymns.

Miss Adelaide Anne Procter (1825-1864)—Miss Procter was the eldest daughter of Bryon W. Procter, who was known as Barry Cornwall, himself a poet, biographer and dramatist. She became interested in poetry at an early age; before she learned to write, her mother wrote down some favourite verses her child composed. She was an able student. Her parents were friends of Charles Dickens. When the latter was editor of "Household Words," he received one day a poem for his magazine which he deemed of more than ordinary merit, and whose author signed herself as "Mary Berwick." He published it in the magazine. Dickens became much interested in his unknown contributor and formed in his own mind an imaginary picture of her as being a governess, and that she was an English girl who travelled in Italy. Dr. William B. Bodine in his book on hymnology gives a full account of the story of her identity as later revealed.

Dickens, going to dine before Christmas 1854 with his friends, the Procters and their daughter, took with him the Christmas issue of the magazine to show them a new poem included in it, and remarked, "There is a pretty poem in this number by a Miss Berwick." The poem was entitled, "The Seven Poor Travellers." The following day he received a letter from Mrs. Procter informing him that what he had said, about the poem he mentioned, was done in the presence of the author, who was none other than her daughter Adelaide, and that there was no such author in existence as "Mary Berwick." This surprise only deepened his interest in his contributor and Dickens always regarded his publication of Miss Procter's poems as among the most pleasing of his experiences.

Miss Procter was an English Roman Catholic, who devoted herself to a variety of charitable objects—visiting the sick, sheltering the homeless, teaching the underprivileged and rescuing the wandering. Eager to help and to sympathize with those in need of assistance, she was very unselfish and self-sacrificing. The last fifteen months of her life she was bed-ridden, yet her cheerfulness and patience never failed and her resignation at death was brave and firmly confident. How well she had been able to write concerning death,

Why shouldst thou fear the beautiful angel Death,
Who waits thee at the portals of the skies,
Ready to kiss away thy struggling breath,
Ready with gentle hand to close thine eyes?

She was also an author of popular songs, as "The Lost Chord" and "Cleansing Fires." The new Congregational and Presbyterian hymnals and the American Episcopal and Methodist hymnals, all contain the same three, and the "New Baptist Praise Book" contains four of Miss Procter's hymns. Probably her best known is

My God, I thank Thee, who hast made
The earth so bright,
So full of splendour and of joy.

It is useful for the visitation of the sick and Bishop Bickersteth regarded it as our best hymn to touch the heart of thankfulness in time of affliction.

The other two as well known are

The shadows of the evening hours
Fall from the darkening sky.

and

I do not ask, O Lord, that life may be
A pleasant road.

And the Baptist hymnal adds:

One by one the sands are flowing,
One by one the moments fall;
Some are coming, some are going,
Do not strive to grasp them all.

William Walsham How (1823-1897)—How is another writer included among the Oxford group who lived during the same years as Mrs. Alexander, but two years longer. He was Bishop of Wakefield, although better known as Bishop of Bedford (East London). He is said to have been offered the bishopric of Durham, a more conspicuous position. How was born in Shrewsbury, and was graduated from Oxford. He did not win distinction as a scholar as did Bishop Heber or John Keble, but thought at first he had failed in his final examinations. He first became the rector of Whittington, where he spent twenty-eight years; then became Suffragan Bishop of East London. As a prose writer, he wrote commentaries and works on pastoral theology, yet poetry constituted his major writings. In East London he became known as the "Poor Man's Bishop," or the "People's Bishop." At first he was a curious sight, with his episcopal dress of flat hat, apron and gaiters, which led the people on the streets to enquire what he was. And they came to hear it said, "That is a bishop." But his good and impressive life soon caused them to say, "That is *our* bishop."

The English Church had had various types of famous bishops. There had been such men as Archbishop Usher and Lightfoot; men like Bishop Butler and such eloquent men as Jeremy Taylor and Wilberforce. But a new type was found in Bishop How. Without great eloquence or distinguished scholarship, that many predecessors had, he was more like his early prototype, St. Barnabas, "a good man full of faith and of the Holy Ghost." His ministry was greatly blessed of God.

Probably his greatest legacy to the Church was his hymns, for he was another of the leading contributors to our hymnals. For the sixteenth anniversary of the Coronation of her Majesty Queen Victoria, he was asked to write the hymn to be sung throughout Great Britain. He produced a noble hymn for this occasion (for which Sir Arthur Sullivan composed the tune), beginning, "O King of Kings, whose reign of old." But even greater was his hymn so favoured to-day, sung at Trinity Church, Boston, at the funeral of Phillips Brooks, and which has been sung at many funerals since, "For all the saints, who from their labours rest." The vision of all saints gave him inspired power in such phrases as "O blest Communion fellowship divine," "The golden evening brightens in the west," "But lo! there breaks a yet more glorious day," and finally,

From earth's wide bounds, from ocean's farthest coast,
Through gates of pearl streams in the countless host,
Singing to Father, Son and Holy Ghost,
Alleluia.

Another great favourite hymn to-day is

O Jesus, Thou art standing
Outside the fast closed door.

Jean Ingelow, in an English fishing village, wrote a sermon poem, "Brothers and a Sermon," which fell into the hands of Bishop How. He said of it "The pathos of the verses impressed me forcibly at the time. I read them over and over, and finally closing the book, I scribbled on an old scrap of paper my first idea of the verses, beginning, 'O Jesus, Thou art standing' "; and he wrote out this hymn, never revised or altered since. His second and third verses follow logically:

O Jesus, Thou art knocking,

O Jesus, Thou art pleading.

Another fine hymn begins:

O Word of God incarnate
O Wisdom from on high.

And what a list of other great hymns!

O One with God the Father

Lord Jesus, when we stand afar

On wings of living light

Jesus, Name of wondrous love

Soldiers of the cross, arise

To Thee, our God, we fly

We give Thee but Thine own

Lord, Thy Children guide and keep.

Godfrey Thring (1823-1903)—Thring was prebendary of Wells. He is better known as the editor of the "Church of England Hymn Book," probably the most widely used of any hymnal in the English Church, except "H. A. & M." Concerning this hymnal Doctor Julian writes: "Its literary standard is the highest among modern hymn books and its poetical merits are great."

Thring was born at Alford, Somersetshire; another son of the rectory. He graduated from Balliol College, Oxford. His work as curate in various places followed graduation. For some years before he was a prebendary of the Cathedral at Wells.

We have some of his own notes on his hymns which give us information about them. He tells us that what started him to writing hymns was the fact that his mother could not find any suitable hymn to sing to an old tune which was a favourite with her, and the son offered to write a hymn for her, if he could. The result of his effort was his hymn to fit the melody his mother wished to sing—an instance of writing a poem to fit a tune—and which began, "We all had sinned and gone astray." This was only the beginning of more and better poems for our hymnals.

His hymn, "The radiant morn hath passed away," was written for afternoon and early evening services, as he felt the need of such hymns, because most of the evening hymns were written with a view to singing at services after the sunset. Among the other popular favourites are his Epiphany hymns:

From the eastern mountains,
Pressing on they come,
Wise men in their wisdom,
To His humble home.

Another dealing with the Future Life:

Saviour, blessed Saviour,
Listen while we sing.

And another equally good processional:

Hear us, Thou that broodest
O'er the wat'ry deep.

Other hymns are contained in our hymn books as:

Heal me, O my Saviour, heal;
Heal me as I suppliant kneel.

Thou to whom the sick and dying
Ever come, nor come in vain.

Edward Henry Bickersteth (1825-1906)—This one of the eminent Bickersteths was born in Islington, the son of Rev. Edward Bickersteth, Secretary of the Church Missionary Society, and rector of Watton—one of four brothers who became eminent in their day. The son, Edward Henry, was graduated from Trinity, Cambridge, and distinguished himself for poetic ability. Later he became Vicar of Christ Church, Hampstead, where he laboured diligently for thirty years, both in his parish and for foreign missions.

He was also interested deeply in social and charitable movements. He became Bishop of Exeter, upon which office he entered vigorously at the age of sixty, in 1885, and continued his arduous labours for fifteen more years. He is said to have "ruled with zeal and diligence, with meekness of wisdom, winning victories by his gentleness and fairness, disarming prejudice and opposition by his single-mindedness." The cause of missions in Great Britain, especially the advancement of foreign missions by the English Church is much indebted to the three Edward Bickersteths, representing three generations; for the bishop's son, Edward Bickersteth, became Missionary Bishop of South Tokio. Edward Henry Bickersteth was like his father, but greater as a poet and hymn writer. His book, "From Year to Year," contained his collected hymns assigned to various portions of the Christian Year. Perhaps his leading hymn is the very familiar one, "Peace, perfect peace, in this dark world of sin." This hymn is taken from his book referred to above, and is based on the Prayer Book "Collect for Peace," in the service of Evening Prayer, and like the collect, gives calm assurance to the perplexed soul.

The circumstances which produced this hymn are as follows: Canon Gibbon had preached before Doctor Bickersteth on the text, "Thou wilt keep him in perfect peace, whose mind is stayed on thee." This sermon set Bickersteth to thinking on the subject. That same Sunday afternoon he went to visit a dying relative, Archdeacon Hill of Liverpool. He found the sick man somewhat troubled in mind, and as it was easy and natural for Bickersteth to express in verse what he desired to say, he took up a piece of paper and there wrote on it the words of the hymn just as they stand to-day, and read his poem to the dying relative.

In reading this hymn, one will notice that the first line of each of the two line verses is in question form, referring to different troublesome experiences of life, and the second line gives answer to each question.

His other good hymns which still live, are

O brothers, lift your voices
Triumphant songs to raise,

and his

O God the Rock of Ages,
Who ever more hast been.

Also it is worth noting that he added the third verse to Edmeston's famous hymn, "Saviour, breathe an evening blessing," which begins:

Father to Thy holy keeping
Humbly we ourselves resign.

John Ellerton (1826-1893)—Only a few men have written more hymns to enrich English hymnody than Ellerton, but as most of his hymns were written for special occasions and saints' days, only a few are preserved for general use and ordinary occasions.

He was born in London and died in Torquay. He studied at Trinity College, Cambridge, and for a time he was influenced by the writings of Frederick D. Maurice, but never became attracted to any special school in the Church. He was sympathetic with the good found in the Evangelicals, the Liberals and the Ritualists. In addition to parochial work, he spent time in literary work, especially in preparation of "Church Hymns" and the "Children's Hymn Book." He was a man of wide culture, of noble character and was greatly beloved. Matthew Arnold called him the greatest living hymnologist, and he was one of the greatest. His studies in hymnology show profound judgment and his biographical notes on other hymn writers show his research, knowledge and sympathy.

Among the large number of his hymns possessing high merit, we have

Saviour, again to Thy dear Name we raise
With one accord our parting hymn of praise.

And others,

The day Thou gavest, Lord, is ended,
The darkness falls at Thy behest.

This is the day of light,
Let there be light to-day.

O Son of God, our Captain of salvation,
Thyself by suffering schooled in human grief.

God of the Living, in whose eyes
Unveiled Thy whole creation lies.

Joy because the circling year
Brings one day of blessings here.

O Father, all creating,
Whose wisdom, love and power.

Behold us, Lord, a little space
From daily tasks set free.

And his very popular Easter hymn:

> *Now the labourer's task is o'er;*
> *Now the battle day is past.*

This hymn was appropriately sung at the burial of the great Earl of Shaftsbury, as it has been at the funerals of many others. It is more used in England than in America.

The striking thing about Ellerton's hymns is that, instead of decreasing in use as years go by, they are seemingly increasing in usage.

Christina Georgina Rossetti (1830-1894)—Miss Rossetti was the youngest of a brilliant family. Her father, Gabriel Rossetti, was an Italian refugee. He became a Protestant professor of the Italian language in King's College, London.

Miss Rossetti's education was received at home among artists and literary folk. Her life was unusual among hymn writers, for her face became known to many who did not know her poetry. This was because she sat as a model for several famous artists who were friends, and also for her able artist-brother, Dante Gabriel. In his "Ecce Ancilla Domini" the face is hers.

In her younger days, she broke off an engagement to a man whom she loved because he became a Roman Catholic. Disappointed in love and because of much sorrow in later years, her deeply religious nature was increased. She found relief, however, for her troubled spirit in befriending the poor children of the parish where she regularly worshipped, near Regent Park.

In the "Encyclopedia Britannica," her biographer says: "Hers was a cloistral spirit, timid, nun-like, bowed down by suffering and humility. Her character was so retiring as to be almost invisible. All that we really need to know of her, save that she was a great saint, is that she was a great poet."

In her later years, Miss Rossetti published devotional books in prose, including a devotional commentary on the Apocalypse toward the end of her life.

Her hymnic poems are short, simple lyrics of which several are included in the new Presbyterian hymnal, and also in the Scottish Church Hymnary.

Doctor Benson in his book "The English Hymn" [2] speaks of her poems as "intense and generally subjective lyrics." Among her poems which depart from the old form of the hymn, but which have been accepted as hymns in recent years are such verses as:

[2] Hodder and Stoughton, 1915.

None other Lamb, none other Name,
None other Hope in heaven or earth or sea.

The shepherds had an angel,
The Wise Men had a star.

We know not a voice of that river,
If vocal or silent it be.

Love came down at Christmas,
Love all lovely, Love divine.

Another poem, used as Christmas carol in "Songs of Praise" (English), begins:

In the bleak mid-winter
Frosty wind made moan,
Earth stood hard as iron,
Water like a stone.

Frances Ridley Havergal (1836-1879)—The three leading female hymnists are Miss Havergal, Miss Charlotte Elliott and Mrs. Cecil F. Alexander, according to the number of valuable hymns contained in our hymnals.

Miss Havergal was the daughter of the Rev. W. H. Havergal of the Church of England, who was both poet and music composer. The daughter was born at Astley in Worcestershire. When a young woman, she gave herself to her Master's service and said: "I committed my soul to the Saviour, and earth and heaven seemed brighter from that moment."

She began poetry at seven years of age; and she was also an able linguist, having knowledge of both ancient languages and several modern. She was like her father an able musician and played from memory some of the best strains from Beethoven, Handel and Mendelssohn, but her greatest achievement was her consecrated Christian life. She was an invalid most of her life, but still she accomplished much more than many talented people of good health. Her writings of prose and verse have had large circulation. Her letters showed her sympathetic nature and her eager spiritual life. Few have lived up to her aspirations, as she succeeded in doing. Her hymns are very devotional; she once said, "Writing is praying with me." Her earliest poems were not so deeply spiritual until her devotional life became more developed. She tells of a certain painting which greatly influenced her. When in Germany she attended a school in Düsseldorf. When weary she sat down and gazed upon the original painting, or perhaps a copy, of the famous "Ecce Homo" in the art gallery, which represented Christ crowned with thorns, and bore the words written above it, "I have done all this for thee, what doest thou for Me?"

The hymn founded on this motto came to her suddenly and she wrote it on a piece of paper with pencil: "I gave my life for Thee." The version in our hymnals is a recast by the compilers of "Church Hymns," with the approval of the authoress. Bishop How calls it "one of our few delightful meditation hymns."

Thy life was given for me,
Thy blood, O Lord, was shed,
That I might ransomed be,
And quickened from the dead.
Thy life was given for me:
What have I given for Thee?

All the following verses are equally expressive. She speaks and lives in all her poetry and the above was followed by other similar hymns expressing complete resignation and self-surrender. One of her best known hymns is:

Lord, speak to me, that I may speak
In living echoes of Thy tone,

followed by logical step in first lines of succeeding verses:

O lead me, Lord, that I may lead

and

O teach me, Lord, that I may teach

and

O use me, Lord, use even me.

Other fine hymns of hers are

O Saviour, precious Saviour

I am trusting Thee, Lord Jesus

I could not do without Thee.

A favourite children's hymn is

Golden harps are sounding,
Angel voices sing.

Her splendid Advent hymn is of a different tone, expressing pure adoration, which really precedes the element of consecration.

Thou art coming, O my Saviour,
Thou art coming, O my King.

William Chatterton Dix (1837-1898)—Among English laymen Dix in his day was the best known of hymn writers, who wrote sacred poetry for over thirty years. Dix was born in Bristol, England, the son of a surgeon. The son was trained for commercial life, and was head of a marine insurance company in Glasgow. When Lord Selborne read a paper on "English Church Hymnody" at the Church Congress he quoted one of Dix's leading hymns and claimed that from such hymns "the most favourable hopes may be entertained of the future prospects of British hymnody." He wrote over forty hymns and at least three or four of these are to be found in modern hymnals. Probably his most used hymn now is his famous

As with gladness men of old
Did the guiding star behold.

He was only twenty-three years old when he wrote this during convalescence following a serious illness; which expresses desire for more light and guidance. It was included in the 1875 revised edition of "Hymns Ancient and Modern," although like most famous hymns it did not become well known for about twenty years after writing. Another of his best hymns written in 1864, the same year as "Onward, Christian soldiers," and given recognition by James King in his "Anglican Hymnody," published in 1885, is as follows:

Come unto Me, ye weary,
And I will give you rest.

Duncan Campbell says it is worthy of rank with Bonar's, "I heard the voice of Jesus say," and Neale's translation, "Art thou weary, art thou languid." Another is,

Allelulia! sing to Jesus,
His the sceptre, His the throne.

His thanksgiving hymn in the "New Baptist Praise Book" begins,

To Thee, O Lord, our hearts we raise
In hymns of adoration.

The Episcopal hymnal gives us a Christmas carol beginning,

Joy fills our inmost hearts to-day,
The royal Child is born.

George Matheson (1842-1906)—Matheson is the author of a hymn which has increased in popular favour, and which he describes as "The fruit of pain":

O Love that wilt not let me go.

He was one of Scotland's outstanding preachers and pastors, greatly esteemed in Edinburgh. Despite the fact that he became blind in youth, he took his education with a brilliant career in the University of Glasgow and under his great handicap entered the ministry of the Church of Scotland. He became pastor at Innellan on the Firth of the Clyde and at forty he was called to St. Bernard's Parish in Edinburgh. After his retirement he devoted himself to additional writing of books, among the best devotional literature in the English language, as "Moments on the Mount," "Voices of the Spirit" and "Rests by the River." He also wrote works on theology and was once chosen to preach at Balmoral before Queen Victoria, who said she was "immensely delighted with the sermon and the prayers."

Fortunately Doctor Matheson has furnished an account of his writing of his great hymn, mentioned above: "My hymn was composed in the manse of Innellan on the evening of 6th June, 1882. I was at that time alone. It was the day of my sister's marriage, and the rest of the family were staying over night in Glasgow. Something had happened to me, which was known only to myself, and which caused me the most severe mental suffering. The hymn was the fruit of that suffering. It was the quickest bit of work I ever did in my life. I had the impression rather of having it dictated to me by some inward voice than of working it out myself. I am quite sure that the whole work was completed in five minutes, and equally sure it never received at my hands any retouching or correction."

Probably it is because the words of the hymn lend credence, that the imaginative story has grown up concerning it that he wrote this following the loss of his sight, with the result that his fiancee on learning of his blindness broke off their engagement. But Dr. W. J. L. Shepperd [3] himself investigated by inquiry of Matheson's own family, who assured him this wide-spread legend was unfounded. As a matter of fact, he did not write this hymn until over twenty years after he had become blind. Doctor Matheson, like Cardinal Newman, was both humble and generous

[3] *Great Hymns and their Stories,* The Religious Tract Society, London.

enough to give large credit to the composer of the tune, set to his hymn by Dr. A. L. Peace, for its wide-spread popularity.

Matheson has another hymn included in the new Presbyterian hymnal which is an unusual expression of words and thoughts:

Make me a captive, Lord,
And then I shall be free;
Force me to render up my sword,
And I shall conqueror be.
I sink in life's alarms
When by myself I stand;
Imprison me within Thine arms,
And strong shall be my hand.

Sabine Baring-Gould (1834-1924)—Baring-Gould was born before either Frances Ridley Havergal or George Matheson, but lived long after these two had passed away and (though Miss Havergal began writing hymns before Baring-Gould)—well into the twentieth century. Thus we think of him as a more recent writer.

This very versatile man, who was squire, clergyman and famous prose writer, used to write a book or more every year of his active life, on a wide variety of subjects—novels, histories, religious books, volumes of folk-lore and mythology and legends. His "Lives of the Saints" made fifteen volumes. When he inherited "the living" at Lew Trenchard and there came a vacancy, he appointed himself as the rector and it can only be admitted that he made a suitable choice for the parish.

When he wrote his most famous hymn "Onward, Christian soldiers," he was the young curate at St. Peter's Mission, at Horbury Bridge in Yorkshire under the Rev. John Sharp, vicar of Horbury.

At Whitsuntide in 1864 when it was the custom for the mission school to join with the parish at Horbury for celebrating Whit-Monday, Baring-Gould wanted his school children to sing when marching to the neighbouring village, and as he could not think of any song which quite suited him, he sat up at night to write something himself. His "Onward, Christian soldiers" was the result. In the procession next day every class carried a banner, the big boys carrying the large banner leading the procession. This was at the close of the Civil War in America, thus its soldier language and spirit added to its appeal. The author had never expected its publication and was the one most surprised by its fame, which it attained much more quickly than most hymns. In 1868 it was placed in the appendix of "Hymns Ancient and Modern"—a very influential sponsor. At the same time, the American Episcopal Church desired a better hymn book and eyes were on "Hymns Ancient and Modern." A new appendix printed in Philadelphia in 1869 included this hymn. Soon it was included in the hymnals of other communions. In 1871 it was printed in the "Musical Times," with Sullivan's stirring tune set to it for the first time, and this marriage has helped to give it such wide fame.

One day during Lent a few years ago when the writer was giving a series of lenten addresses on familiar hymns in St. Paul's Protestant Episcopal Church at Pawtucket, R. I., he told of the author and the usage of this hymn and happy was his surprise when an elderly lady stepped up after the service and said she knew its author and was one of the small children who marched in the procession of school children on that Whit-Monday when it was first sung at Horbury Bridge.

Concerning his unusual marriage, little is revealed by most hymnologists. The author is indebted to the above-mentioned woman [4] for the facts given here and for the privilege of reading correspondence between Baring-Gould and his former parishioner written in later years.

Our informant says of him: "He was one of the finest ministers that ever was." She had worked in the mill at Horbury with two brothers of Grace Taylor, who also worked there and whom she described as a beautiful girl of fine character. The young clergyman's attentions to the girl naturally aroused interest and curiosity. When a flood occurred in the village he promptly went to see that his sweetheart had gotten home safe. After his continued attentions, Grace Taylor's father called upon the clergyman to know what his intentions were, but no gossip learned the facts of that interview. Wealthy men who had eligible daughters wanted to know what the young clergyman's intentions might be and appealed to his uncle, who had educated him (instead of his parents who did not have the means) to see if he would influence the young man, but the uncle refused to interfere as he had married a poor working girl and could only reply, "It is what I did myself." The young man married the girl he loved and then sent her to a boarding school for further needed education. Their married life was one of happiness and devotion to each other;

[4] Mrs. Elizabeth Hawkhead, Pawtucket, R. I.

fifteen children were born to them and two of the sons served faithfully in the World War.

In the latter years of her life Mrs. Baring-Gould became a confirmed cripple and her husband provided a nurse for her, night and day, and tenderly ministered to her needs and comfort. When she died in 1916 Doctor Baring-Gould had inscribed on her tombstone *"Dimidium Animae Meae"* (Half my Soul).

Baring-Gould was author of more than one famous hymn. There was his children's evening hymn,

Now the day is over
Night is drawing nigh.

His famous hymn, translated from the Danish hymn of Bernardt S. Ingemann, is a great favourite to-day:

Through the night of doubt and sorrow
Onward goes the pilgrim band,
Singing songs of expectation,
Marching to the promised land.

Rudyard Kipling (1865-1936)—After Baring-Gould we can pass over a period of years before we record the next hymn poet, whose life has extended far into the twentieth century, but whose now most famous hymn was written in 1897. Rudyard Kipling has long been one of the conspicuous citizens of the British Empire, both as author and educator He was born in Bombay in 1865; was graduated from United Service College, North Devon, in England and became assistant editor in India on the "Civil and Military Gazette." He travelled in China, Japan, Australia, Africa and America. He published many books of stories, ballads, current history articles, letters of travel; compiled songs from various books and wrote children's stories. His books have been written both in the nineteenth and twentieth centuries, as he has been a constant writer during his life. At first he failed to find a willing publisher in England or America. Suddenly in London in 1890 he found himself famous. Since that time his reputation has been extraordinary.

In 1892 he married a girl in New York City and settled in Vermont where he lived until 1896. Upon returning to England the following year, he wrote one of his most famous books, "Captain Courageous." The same year he wrote also his famous poem, "The Recessional," written on the occasion of Queen Victoria's

Jubilee. Two years later he wrote another widely read poem, entitled "The White Man's Burden."

Kipling is regarded as having more original genius than any other writer of the last part of the nineteenth and the first part of the twentieth century. He represents the spirit of the times and of the Anglo-Saxon race. He was a master of language, ranging from the vivid slang of the barracks to the noble diction of a high educator and Hebrew prophet. His "Recessional," written in 1897, gained notice very rapidly and the writer heard it recited in a Thanksgiving Day sermon in Pittsburgh by the late Dr. David Breed the year it was written. Since then it has had wide recognition and inclusion in modern hymn books. It begins: "God of our Fathers, known of old," and the refrain for four of the verses is;

Lord God of hosts, be with us yet,
Lest we forget, lest we forget.

and the last verse's refrain prays, "Thy mercy on Thy people, Lord."

Kipling's next most famous hymn, written during the first part of the twentieth century (1906), is

Father in heaven, who lovest all,
O help Thy children when they call,
That they may build from age to age
An undefilèd heritage.

The nineteenth century, rich in the production of English hymns, includes many more worthy hymns than have been named in the last two chapters, for which we have not space for individual paragraphs or extended notice. We can only make mere mention of some fine hymns and some distinguished men who have enriched the Christian Church and our treasury of Christian praise, as follows:

Adler, Felix—Hail, the glorious golden city.
Bode, John Ernest—O Jesus, I have promised.
Bridges, Matthew—Crown Him with many crowns.
Bright, William—And now, O Father, mindful of the love.
Burns, James Drummond—Hushed was the evening hymn.
Clephane, Elizabeth Cecilia—Beneath the cross of Jesus.
Croly, George—Spirit of God, descend upon my heart.
Elliott, Ebenezer—When wilt Thou save the people.
Elliott, Emily Elizabeth Steele—Thou didst leave Thy throne.
Hughes, Thomas—O God of truth, whose living Word.

Julian, John—Hark! the voice eternal.
Kingsley, Charles—From Thee all skill and science flow.
Littledale, Richard Frederick—God, the Father, God the Son.
Luke, Jemima (Thompson)—I think when I read that sweet story of old.
Maclagan, William Dalrymple—The saints of God! their conflict past.
Marriott, John—Thou, whose almighty word.
Palgrave, Francis Turner—O light of life, O Saviour dear.
Pollock, Thomas Benson—Jesus, with Thy Church abide.
Jesus, we are far away.
Reed, Andrew—Spirit divine, attend our prayers.
Stone, Samuel John—The Church's one foundation.
Symonds, John Addington—These things shall be; a loftier race.
Tuttiett, Laurence—Father, let me dedicate.
Twells, Henry—At even, when the sun was set.
Waring, Anna Laetitia—In heavenly love abiding.
White, Henry Kirke—Oft in danger, oft in woe.
Whiting, William—Eternal Father! strong to save.

SUMMARY

In this chapter we have considered the following: Frederick W. Faber; Edward Caswall and John Mason Neale; Thomas Toke Lynch; Henry W. Baker; Edward Hays Plumptre; Cecil Francis Alexander; Adelaide Anne Procter; William Walsham How; Godfrey Thring; Edward Henry Bickersteth; John Ellerton; Christina Georgina Rossetti; Francis Ridley Havergal; William Chatterton Dix; George Matheson; Sabine Baring-Gould; Rudyard Kipling.

For Further Reading on Nineteenth Century Hymn Writers

Lyric Religion, H. Augustine Smith.
Some Hymns and Hymn Writers, William B. Bodine.
English Hymns, Samuel W. Duffield.
The English Hymn, Louis F. Benson.
The History and Use of Hymns and Hymn-Tunes, David R. Breed.
Hymns and Hymn Makers, Duncan Campbell.
A Dictionary of Hymnology, John Julian.
Some Favorite Hymns, H. E. Langhorne.
The Story of the Hymns and Tunes, Theron Brown and Hezekiah Butterworth.
The Hymn Lover, W. Garrett Horder.
History of the English Hymn, Benjamin Brawley.

XII

AMERICAN HYMNODY THROUGH THE NINETEENTH CENTURY

(Including Brief Mention of Gospel Songs)

WHEN the early colonists came to America, especially the Pilgrims of New England, they brought with them their Ainsworth Version of the psalms. Soon the Puritans from England brought their copies of the Sternhold and Hopkins version. Not long afterward there was produced the American book of psalms, called "The Bay Psalm Book." Later came the hymns of Watts and Watts's "Psalms Imitated." These became widely used among the Colonies.

But American hymnody is mostly embraced within the nineteenth and twentieth centuries. It is true that in earlier days there was some interest in original hymns and newer versions of the Psalter. Among those in America who showed deep interest in lyric worship, or sought to improve praise in the Church, were Dr. Samuel Davies, the able American orator and fourth president of Princeton, who frequently added an original hymn at the close of his vigorous sermons, but only two of his hymns became widely known and used for a time; and Timothy Dwight, the distinguished president of Yale, one of the ablest of the early scholars in this country, a theologian, possessing poetic talents, who did much to improve the use of Psalmody in American churches. He left one outstanding hymn, "I love Thy Kingdom, Lord." Such able men as Joel Barlow, Mather Byles, and the famous Connecticut Indian preacher, Samuel Occum, did their work of versification and hymn-writing during the eighteenth century. These men helped to prepare the way for the nineteenth century American hymnody and called the attention of distinguished men to the value of such labours.

George Washington, in one of his letters, copied a hymn. His successors, John Adams and Thomas Jefferson, were deeply interested in hymns. After retirement, these two statesmen, who lived many years, continued a discussion of hymns in their personal correspondence. It should be remembered that Benjamin Franklin's first issue of a book from his printing press was Watts's "Psalms and Hymns."

Thomas Hastings (1784-1872)—With Hasting came the beginning of a more distinctive American hymnody, for he brought out the hymnal and tune book. He was born at Washington, Connecticut, but his parents moved to Clinton, New York, the seat of Hamilton College, when he was a child. The country there was still primitive and the boy made the best of his limited educational advantages. His greatest work was the improvement of singing in American churches, so greatly needed at the time. He was regarded as the foremost choir trainer of his day, and was constantly in demand for this purpose in many places. He published a number of sacred song books, but is best known as the composer of "Toplady," the usual tune sung to "Rock of Ages," written in 1830. He wrote many original hymns, several of them becoming popular in America. His hymns well belonged to his time and were usually missionary or evangelistic in spirit. His leading missionary hymn, written in the metre of Heber's famous "Brightest and best are the sons of the morning," begins,

Hail to the brightness of Zion's glad morning!
Joy to the lands that in darkness have lain!

An evangelistic hymn, with deep appeal to the sinner, is his

Return, O wanderer, to thy home.

He also revised and added to the words of the famous hymn,

Come, ye disconsolate.

Hastings wrote other good hymns of the evangelistic type and hymns of praise, not now usually found in the hymnals. But his most lasting service was in conjunction with Dr. Lowell Mason, who together changed the poor and barren music of the early days of the nineteenth century to the (advanced) modern type of hymn tunes which has been such a blessing to American praise. Further study of their work belongs to the other side of hymnody not treated here.

William Cullen Bryant (1794-1878)—Bryant, the famous New England poet, was the first of a line of hymnists among Unitarians, although he was identified at different periods with both the Episcopal and Presbyterian churches. His life and writings are well known to readers of poetry. He wrote the famous poem

"Thanatopsis" when nineteen years old. It was first printed in "The North American Review" without the author's name and at once attracted attention with one critic remarking, "That was never written on this side of the water." Bryant was educated for the law but soon turned to journalism, and was the able editor of the "New York Evening Post" for over fifty years. He began writing poetry at ten and continued until his last poem was written at eighty-three years of age. He also wrote fine lyric poetry, and a few of his hymns still live. The one written for the dedication of a church is

Thou whose unmeasured temple stands,
Built over earth and sea,
Accept the walls that human hands
Have raised, O God, to Thee.

Another favourite hymn he wrote is

O North, with all thy vales of green
O South, with all thy palms!

He also wrote a good home missionary hymn

Look from Thy sphere of endless day,
O God of mercy and of might!
In pity look on those who stray,
Benighted in this land of light.

The remaining verses are equally fine and should be read or sung, as found in the new Congregational book, "The Pilgrim Hymnal," or in the old Episcopal hymnal. It ought to be included in other hymnals.

William Augustus Muhlenberg (1796-1877)—Doctor Muhlenberg was born in Philadelphia and was graduated from the University of Pennsylvania. He had a virile ancestry. His great-grandfather was Henry M. Muhlenberg, a graduate of Göttengen and friend of Frederick the Great. He came to America in 1742 and became the founder of the American Lutheran Church, and with missionary zeal travelled through the states extensively. Doctor Muhlenberg's grandfather was president of the Convention which ratified the Constitution of the United States and the first speaker of the House of Representatives.

The subject of our sketch was not so much a great hymn writer, as a man of full life and great deeds, and left an influence upon American hymnody. Little over a hundred years ago, when the Methodists had their Wesleyan collection of hymns, and other communions had their collection from Watts, the Episcopal Church had only their Psalms, and a small collection of fifty-seven hymns. Doctor Muhlenberg felt the need of a wider selection and was the leader in widening and improving the collection of original hymns for use in his Church. He was on the first committee of General Convention in 1822 for preparing a new hymnal. Francis Scott Key, author of "The Star-Spangled Banner," was also a member of that committee.

Doctor Muhlenberg, after a short and useful rectorship at Lancaster, Pennsylvania, went to New York where as rector of the Church of the Holy Communion he was the first to introduce the novelty of free pews, and also started the first boys' choir in New York City. He also started raising funds to start a hospital, and the large St. Luke's Hospital on Cathedral Heights is the result. He also founded the Flushing Institute for Boys. He established a then unique charitable institution for boys on Long Island at St. Johnsland, and his many noble and charitable deeds make one of the outstanding records in American history. The last-named institution was established when he was seventy years old, and his prayer was for ten more years in which to do this work. His Lord granted him just ten more years of earthly life, and then he passed away.

His hymn so popular in the nineteenth century was

I would not live alway, I ask not to stay
Where storm after storm rises dark o'er the way.

It was written like most of his hymns in his youth, and it is the more surprising that when older he came to dislike its sentiment and revised it with a view of advocating living longer in the service of the work, and was most disappointed that the people would not substitute the amended form for the original. His most appreciated hymn to-day is one appropriate for infant baptism,

Saviour, who Thy flock art feeding
With its Shepherd's kindest care.

Another of his, a Christmas hymn, begins,

Shout the glad tidings, exultingly sing,
Jerusalem triumphs, Messiah is King.

George Washington Doane (1799-1859)—Bishop Doane was born in Trenton, New Jersey, was graduated from Union College in 1818 and ordained in 1821. He became professor at Trinity College, Hartford. Soon afterward he was advanced to the rectorship of the famous Trinity Church in Boston, and succeeded in filling this prominent position, which has been held by many distinguished men. At the early age of thirty-three he was chosen to be second bishop of New Jersey. He began his work with devotion and zeal, and splendid results followed his labours. He was a very gifted man and became a leader in religious education, as he thought for the good of the Church. He established two schools of learning in his diocese. But soon the disastrous panic of 1837 swept over the country. He pulled through the panic, but later the expanded debt forced him into bankruptcy. The mercenary creditors harshly criticized the bishop and even impugned his motives and integrity. But the bishop signed over all his property for the benefit of the creditors. Both the diocesan Convention of New Jersey and the House of Bishops unanimously dismissed charges against him. Moreover, one of the most able defences uttered in American history was made by a distinguished Presbyterian divine, as a neutral in the controversy and not too friendly a neighbour of the bishop's because of the latter's "High Church" tendency, when he preached from the text in his Presbyterian pulpit, "Let us fall now into the hand of the Lord, for his mercies are great, and let me not fall into the hand of man."

Next to Doane's hymn his most lasting service in the Church was his forceful missionary preaching and program in 1835, which included the appeal to all baptized members, as such to support the cause of missions on the ground of their baptismal vows. His efforts proved to be the real beginning of the past neglected cause of missions to progressive efforts within the American Episcopal Church.

But his work for hymnody is important to-day. His leading hymn is his forceful missionary lines, written in 1848 and more appreciated now than before, which begin,

Fling out the banner, let it float
Skyward and seaward high and wide,
The Sun that lights its shining folds,
The Cross on which the Saviour died.

Another is the beautiful evening hymn,

Softly now the light of day
Fades upon my sight away.
Free from care, from labour free,
Lord, I would commune with Thee.

John Greenleaf Whittier (1807-1892)—One of America's ablest lyrical and most distinguished poets, Whittier, was a Friend or Quaker who wore the quaint garb of the Society of Friends, and continued to use often their peculiar forms of speech. Whittier was the son of a Massachusetts farmer at Haverhill, Mass., who possessed few books. He received his first literary impulses from the poems of Robert Burns which he read when fourteen. His elder sister encouraged him to begin writing verses, some of which she sent to the newspaper of William Lloyd Garrison. He was so impressed by their quality that he rode fifteen miles to make the personal acquaintance of the young writer, and a friendship developed which influenced young Whittier to adopt journalism as a profession in Boston. He was an upright, patriotic and talented man. His early poems were taken from early colonial records and Indian stories. He became an ardent supporter of the anti-slavery movement, and was the outstanding literary man of New England against slavery.

He used his pen to oppose this movement from which he first suffered harsh criticism and loss of friends, but in the end gained fame and applause. After the Civil War the beauty of New England scenery and rural life inspired his poetry. His most famous poem is "Snowbound," which was followed by others as "The Tent on the Beach," "Among the Hills," "Barbara Frietchie" and others. He produced much writing in prose also. He did not write directly for public worship, as then the Quaker meeting-houses did not have any singing. Whittier once said, "I am not a hymn writer for the good reason that I know nothing of music. A good hymn is the best use to which poetry can be devoted." Among his hymnic poems he wrote, "O Lord and Master of us all," and "We may not climb the heavenly steeps." He wrote the hymn, "All things are Thine, no gift have we," "Immortal Love, forever full," and "The harp at nature's advent strung, Has never ceased to play," which has been overlooked by most compilers of recent hymnals. His most popular hymn to-day is his famous hymn of five-line stanzas,

Dear Lord and Father of mankind,
Forgive our foolish ways;
Reclothe us in our rightful mind,
In purer lives Thy service find,
In deeper reverence, praise.

This is taken from the poem, "The Brewing of Soma," which begins with a description of a sensuous Hindu religious rite under influence of the drink, but when the author reaches the sixth verse he rises to a strain of hymnic poetry and this hymn constitutes the remainder of the stanzas of the poem, with the exception of one verse which is omitted from the hymn.

Ray Palmer (1808-1887)—We come now to two outstanding American writers from the same year, Dr. Ray Palmer and Dr. Samuel F. Smith. These two were near the same time and were contemporaneous with Mrs. Sarah F. Adams, Bishop Wordsworth, Dr. Horatius Bonar, Lord Tennyson and Henry Alford, in Great Britain. Palmer was a distinguished minister of the Congregational Church, well-known in both England and America as author of "My faith looks up to Thee," written in 1830, before he entered the ministry, when but twenty-two years of age. He was born in Little Compton, Rhode Island, the son of Hon. Thomas Palmer. When thirteen years old he became clerk in a store in Boston, and soon connected himself with Park Street Church. His thoughts turned toward the ministry, and he prepared for college at Phillips Andover Academy and entered Yale from which he was graduated in 1830. He first began to teach in a private school for young women in New York, then located downtown on Fulton Street, near Church Street. It was in the quiet of his own room, in the home of the Christian who was head of the school, that he wrote his famous hymn. The occasion of writing this hymn had no external meaning but came out of his inmost soul, when not in good health, expressing his religious feelings. He wrote for himself with no thought of its ever being known or used in public:

My faith looks up to Thee,
Thou Lamb of Calvary,
Saviour Divine.

Doctor Benson says, "It is as well-known and beloved as any American hymn. It seems to many people like a part of their own [illegible] lives." It would never have been known to the Church, had it not been for Dr. Lowell Mason, who together with Dr. Thomas Hastings were preparing to publish a new "Hymn and Tune Book." Doctor Mason, meeting young Palmer on a Boston street, requested that he write a hymn for the contemplated book. The two men stepped into a store and a copy was written of this hymn which Palmer had placed in his note book the year before. Doctor Mason took it home. When looking it over he was deeply impressed with the poem and wrote a tune for it—the well-known tune, "Olivet." A few days later when Mason again met Palmer on the street he exclaimed, "Mr. Palmer, you may live many years and do many good things, but I think you will be best known to posterity as the author of 'My faith looks up to Thee.'" The prophecy proved to be very accurate.

Yet Palmer did do many good things. He was ordained to the ministry and became pastor of the Central Congregational Church at Bath, Maine; later at the First Congregational Church in Albany, New York. In 1866 he became corresponding secretary of the American Congregational Union, removing to New York City, and was greatly esteemed and honoured in his own denomination. He was the author of several books of praise, generally of a devotional character. His hymns and other verses appeared at frequent intervals, the first in 1865, entitled "Hymns and Sacred Pieces," being hymns and short poems on a wide variety of religious subjects. It should be borne in mind that all these works were done while Doctor Palmer was busy and devoted to the manifold labours of a city pastor for forty years. He wrote other hymns of high merit, scarcely inferior to his most famous one. His hymns were usually of evangelistic type. His version of St. Bernard's great hymn, *"Jesu, dulcis memoria"*—"Jesus, Thou joy of loving hearts," became more favoured than did Neale's or Caswall's versions, and is a favourite Holy Communion hymn with many people. Another which is a beautiful original hymn of Palmer's and one which he preferred to all others which he wrote, is included in new publications of hymnals, begins,

Jesus, these eyes have never seen
That radiant form of Thine;
The veil of sense hangs dark between
Thy blessed face and mine.

Samuel Francis Smith (1808-1895)—Doctor Smith was a prominent Baptist minister who was noted for his national hymn, "My country, 'tis of thee." He was a Boston boy, born within the sound of Old North Church chimes. He was graduated from Harvard in 1829, in the same class with Oliver Wendell Holmes, who once referred to his class-mate in the famous quatrain,

And there's a fine youngster of excellent pith,
Fate tried to conceal him by naming him Smith;
But he shouted a song for the brave and the free,
Just read on his medal, "My Country, of thee!"

After graduation he studied for the ministry; and it was while a student at Andover Theological Seminary in February, 1832, that he wrote the national hymn at the request of Lowell Mason to fit some tune in a German song book. Smith picked up a scrap of waste paper and at once wrote the poem, and the hymn stands to-day as it was written on the bit of waste paper. On the Fourth of July, Lowell Mason had it sung at a children's celebration in Park Street Church. Then it soon found its way into the public schools of Boston, then into other places, and finally into hymn books.

Doctor Smith served in different churches, and at length became secretary of the Missionary Union for a number of years, spending two years abroad visiting missionary stations. He also spent time editing and writing, and for a few years was editor of the "Christian Review." In addition to his many duties he wrote poetry rather as a recreation, which included able hymns. Few realize that the author of patriotic verses was also deeply interested in foreign missions, and gave a son to the foreign field. He wrote the famous missionary hymn when he heard that the famous missionary Judson had written "The light was breaking and hundreds were accepting" in Burma:

The morning light is breaking,
The darkness disappears;
The sons of earth are waking
To penitential tears.
Each breeze that sweeps the ocean
Brings tidings from afar
Of nations in commotion
Prepared for Zion's war.

The student should study also the remaining three verses of equal or greater merit. Near the close of Smith's life he wrote another noble hymn in present-day hymnals, which should give increased courage to all churchmen:

Founded on Thee, our only Lord,
On Thee, the everlasting rock,
Thy Church shall stand, as stands Thy Word,
Nor fear the storm, nor dread the shock.

The noble character and wide influence of this distinguished man was often felt very strikingly when later in life, as the busy, excited Board of Trade in Chicago one day learned of his presence in the gallery as a spectator and suddenly stopped their mercenary trading and in his honour began to sing,

My country, 'tis of thee.

Oliver Wendell Holmes (1809-1894)—In 1809, the year following the birth of these American authors, Holmes was born. This year was distinguished by the birth of other famous persons, such as Elizabeth Barrett Browning, Alfred Tennyson, Charles Darwin, William E. Gladstone and Abraham Lincoln. Holmes was also of New England ancestry of which he was proud, and Dr. Edward Ninde says "he was a bit of an aristocrat." [1]

He was the son of the Rev. Abiel Holmes, pastor of the First Congregational Church of Cambridge. His distinguished son, Oliver Wendell Holmes, Jr., was later a judge of the Supreme Court of the United States.

Oliver Wendell Holmes attended Harvard and was graduated in the class of 1829, a class he helped among others to make famous. He entered the profession of medicine, but as, he said, "he was too sympathetic to practice medicine," he became professor of anatomy and physiology. His assistant said of him, "When it became necessary to have a freshly killed rabbit for his lecture, he always ran out of the room, left me to chloroform it, and besought me not to let it squeak." It is reported that in old age he confided to a friend, "Outside I laugh, inside I never laugh: it is impossible; the world is too sad." It was natural for such a sensitive soul to become interested in some appealing avocation and it was literature which appealed most.

He was one of the founders of "The Atlantic Monthly" in which first appeared his "Autocrat of the Breakfast Table," and later "The Poet" and "The Professor," which constituted a series of witty and wise essays on the questions of the day given in conversational form. How often quoted are his well-known lines from his "Chambered Nautilus" which begin,

[1] *The Story of the American Hymn,* The Abingdon Press.

Build thee more stately mansions, O my soul,
As the swift seasons roll!

Doctor Holmes did not attempt many hymns, but wrote several recognized ones. The new hymnals do not use the same ones, but are different in their selection of his hymns. The new Presbyterian hymnal includes only his most famous one, found in almost all hymnals,

Lord of all being, throned afar,
Thy glory flames from sun to star.

This hymn was written for "The Atlantic Monthly," not for the hymnal, yet it well sets before us the omnipresence of our Lord.

The "Pilgrim Hymnal" also contains his second most famous hymn:

O Love divine, that stooped to share
Our sharpest pang, our bitterest tear.

A third hymn in this hymnal is

Angel of peace, thou has wandered too long;
Spread thy white wings to the sunshine of love.

"Hymns for the Living Age" instead of containing the last-named hymn uses for its third selection from Holmes, the following:

Thou gracious Power, whose mercy lends
The light of home, the smile of friends,
Our families in Thine arms enfold,
As Thou didst keep Thy folk of old.

The American Episcopal hymnal, with two from Holmes, uses as the second hymn one for national days, written when his son, Justice O. W. Holmes, responded to the call of his country at the time of the Civil War:

O Lord of hosts, Almighty King,
Behold the sacrifice we bring;
To every arm Thy strength impart,
Thy spirit shed through every heart.

Edmund Hamilton Sears (1810-1876)—He was descended from the Pilgrim Fathers, and, as the author of two of our most famous Christmas hymns, is immortal. He was graduated from Harvard and became a Unitarian minister in Massachusetts. Doctrinal views with regard to the person of Christ were more in accordance with orthodox Christianity than is usually ascribed to Unitarians. His authorship of volumes, "The Fourth Gospel," "The Heart of Christ," is evidence of his faith and is appreciated by both Unitarians and Trinitarians.

When only ten years old, working in the field, he composed verses of poetry and wrote them with chalk on his hat. When he showed these to friends at home they would not believe they were his unless he would write more, and he wrote another verse at once before their eyes. He was an able writer of prose, but his lasting fame is dependent upon his poetic work, and his poetical style was of unusual merit.

Mr. Sears was just out of college when he contributed to the "Boston Observer" his first Christmas song. It was recognized at once as superior to the mass of sacred verse which was now being produced in America. It begins

Calm on the list'ning ear of night
Came heaven's melodious strains,
Where wild Judea stretches far
Her silver-mantled plains.

His contemporary, Oliver Wendell Holmes, in a lecture at Lowell Institute, Boston, pronounced this "one of the finest and most beautiful hymns ever written." But a few years later he wrote another Christmas hymn which has become even more widely used than the former. It was first sent to the editor of the "Christian Register," Doctor Morrison, who was "very much delighted with it." It seldom is overlooked at any Christmas season, and is too well known to repeat except to call attention to its opening lines,

It came upon the midnight clear,
That glorious song of old;
From angels bending near the earth
To touch their harps of gold.
Peace on the earth, good-will to men
From heaven's all-gracious King;
The world in solemn stillness lay
To hear the angels sing.

Samuel Wolcott (1813-1886)—Doctor Wolcott was a Congregationalist, who was graduated from Yale and from Andover Theological Seminary. Later in life he was pastor of the Plymouth Congregational Church in Cleveland. He tells that he never wrote a line of poetry until he was fifty years old when he tried to write a hymn. At that time the Young Men's Christian Association of Ohio met in Cleveland. Over the platform were placed the words, "Christ for the World, and the World for Christ." He was deeply impressed by the words, the more so because he had been in his earlier days a foreign missionary. He made his second effort to write a hymn. How well he succeeded the hymnals of the Church now testify in the following noble missionary hymn,

Christ for the world we sing,
The world to Christ we bring
With loving zeal;
The poor and them that mourn,
The faint and overborne,
Sin-sick and sorrow-worn,
Whom Christ doth heal.

It may be noticed that this lyric is as well adapted for home as well as for foreign missions. The author rightly refused to make any distinction, as they are the same missions except in geographic terms.

Henry Harbaugh (1807-1867)—Doctor Harbaugh must not be overlooked, because of his work and lasting influence. He was born on a farm near Waynesboro, Pennsylvania, and according to Doctor Julian was of Swiss descent and not of so-called Pennsylvania Dutch stock. He was one of a family of ten children, and being eager to learn did not want to yield to the pressure to farm, as it was common in those days for the farmers in that part of the state of Pennsylvania to hold their sons on the farm. Being eager for knowledge, he could study upstairs, used candle lights and avoided his father's sight, as he was determined not to be kept long on the farm. He was graduated from Franklin and Marshall College and became pastor at Lancaster and Lebanon, Pennsylvania; later was professor of theology at Mercersburg College of the Reformed Church. He published books on various subjects including a poetic book, both in Pennsylvania German and English, and also "Hymns and Chants for Sunday Schools" in which are included his own hymns. His grandchildren, well-known to the author, told him they never knew of wide usage of their grandfather's hymns till one Sunday walking by a Presbyterian church in Scranton, Pennsylvania, they heard his most famous hymn being sung by the congregation. It is a lovely poem, seemingly kept from still wider usage because of lack of a more adequate or impressive tune,

Jesus, I live to Thee,
The loveliest and best,
My life in Thee, Thy life in me,
In Thy blest love I rest.

Other hymns of his are not in common use to-day. But the above-mentioned is known as the "official hymn" of what is now Mercersburg Academy, where it is known and sung by all the boys of that well-known academy. Young Calvin Coolidge, Jr., sang and "knew by heart" this hymn while a student at this institution, preceding his tragic death at the White House during his father's presidency. From Mrs. Calvin Coolidge the author has this information, that in the beautiful Gothic Chapel of Mercersburg Academy, "this hymn is cut into one of the stones in a transept of the Academy chapel."

George Duffield (1818-1888)—Doctor Duffield was a minister of the Presbyterian Church in Philadelphia at the time he wrote his most famous poem, although his identity has often been confused with that of his father and also his son. But he has tersely checked the confusion in the following words, "The author is not his father, Rev. George Duffield, D.D., the Patriarch of Michigan, born 1796. . . . Neither is he his son, Rev. Samuel W. Duffield, born in 1843. . . . His father has not yet lost his identity, and claims to be his own individual self, namely, Rev. George Duffield, A.M., pastor in Brooklyn, . . . in Bloomfield, New Jersey, . . . in Philadelphia, ten years, leaving there in 1861; and the rest of his life an active pastor in the West."

It should be noted that the son, Dr. Samuel Duffield, is the American hymnologist who wrote the able book "English Hymns," and his other able work, "Latin Hymns." The occasion of his writing this hymn, "Stand up, stand up for Jesus," was the tragic death of his friend and neighbour, the Rev. Dudley Tyng, an Episcopal clergyman, and is related in an earlier chapter. During its history occasionally a compiler of hymns, as is so often done, has changed a word or line, but always against the wishes of the author. He once said, "Since the night it was written it has never been altered by the author, in a single verse, a single line, or a single word, and it is his earnest wish that it shall continue unaltered until the Soldiers of the Cross shall replace it by something better." It originally consisted of six verses, but the hymnals to-day usually give four verses with the second and fifth omitted.

Arthur Cleveland Coxe (1818-1896)—Coxe was the Protestant Episcopal Bishop of Western New York. He was the son of a prominent Presbyterian minister who could well be proud of his son, his high character, lofty motives and Christian humility. He had no eagerness for distinction and no inclination to seek promotion. His master passion was love for the advancement of the Kingdom of God, with zeal for service in his own Church. Bishop Coxe was a brilliant scholar and gifted poet. He also wrote prose, notably his "Thoughts on the Services," being an exposition of the days of the Christian Year and their significance. It is still in use in its revision by his friend, the late Bishop Cortlandt Whitehead of Pittsburgh. His volume of "Christian Ballads" contained some splendid selections. He also wrote various hymns of much merit. His lovely missionary hymn begins,

Saviour, sprinkle many nations,
Fruitful let Thy sorrows be,

written in 1850 at Magdalen College, Oxford. It gained a place in most English and American hymn books, except in the official hymnal of his own Church, because of "his too scrupulous modesty." Being a member of the Hymnal Commission of 1871 he refused to permit the insertion of his own hymns. But later editions of the Episcopal hymnal justly contain this and other hymns of his.

Another hymn of Coxe's written earlier than the above and classed as a hymn for the Epiphany season, so splendidly written, is

How beauteous were the marks divine,
That in Thy meekness used to shine;
That lit Thy lonely pathway, trod
In wondrous love, O Son of God!

Another famous poem of his is taken from "Christian Ballads," and was first printed in 1839 in the New York "Churchman," which seemed more prophetic then, and now more truly fulfilled,

O where are kings and empires now
Of old that went and came?
But, Lord, Thy Church is praying yet,
A thousand years the same.

Still another lyric of his, included in certain new hymn books, which is a truly majestic poem and might be effectively recited as well as sung, is

We are living, we are dwelling
In a grand and awful time,
In an age on ages telling;
To be living is sublime.
Hark! the waking up of nations,
Hosts advancing to the fray;
Hark! what soundeth is creation's
Groaning for the latter day.

Edward Hopper (1818-1888)—Doctor Hopper was born in New York City, was graduated from Union Theological Seminary and entered the Presbyterian ministry. After serving various churches he returned to New York as pastor of the Church of the Sea and Land, where he spent the rest of his days. He did a noble work among the seafarers and many sailors attended his services. He received his doctorate degree from Lafayette College. He wrote many poems and they were published anonymously. The end of his life came suddenly. He was found dead sitting in his study chair and on the sheet of paper before him were found new lines about "heaven" which were unfinished on earth. His one lasting hymn so well expresses the faith that he had preached to sailors,

Jesus, Saviour, pilot me
Over life's tempestuous sea;
Unknown waves before me roll,
Hiding rock and treacherous shoal;
Chart and compass come from Thee,
Jesus, Saviour, pilot me.

The hymn originally had six verses, of which the first, fifth and sixth remain in common use.

Julia Ward Howe (1818-1910)—Mrs. Howe was born in New York City and had distinguished lineage on both sides. Her ancestors were famous in Revolutionary history. She was brought up in a strict religious atmosphere of evangelical Episcopalians. Her father was an ardent Calvinist in belief, but the daughter's mind could not accept the old rigid Calvinistic doctrines. After her marriage to Dr. Samuel Howe and removal to Boston she entered the circles of the "Liberal Faith" and later became a member of the church of which James Freeman Clarke was pastor. She belonged to the Radical Club and often listened to speakers of anti-Christian type. But instead of being led away from her strong Christian beliefs, she said, "Nothing of what I heard or read has shaken my faith in the leadership of Christ in the religion which makes each man the brother of all, and God the beneficent Father of each and all." She believed in the presence of God, in his over-ruling power among men, as appears in her immortal "Battle Hymn." During her girlhood the question of slavery was becoming widespread, and after she and her husband came into contact with William Lloyd Garrison and Wendell Phillips, they began to take active interest in the abolitionist cause, and on the day of the execution of John Brown, who once had called on the Howes, they attended a service in the Church of the Disciples and heard an appropriate sermon by Doctor Clarke.

During the Civil War, Howe, then an officer of the Sanitary Commission, Mrs. Howe, Doctor Clarke of Boston and Governor Andrews of Massachusetts, visited the Army of the Potomac. One day they rode out from Washington to witness a review of troops. The review had been halted by a sudden movement of the enemy. As they returned to Washington their road was filled with infantry and they heard the soldiers singing the then popular song, "John Brown's Body." Doctor Clarke remarked to Mrs. Howe, already recognized for her poetic ability, "Mrs. Howe, why do you not write some good words to that stirring tune?" Mrs. Howe went to bed that night as usual, but she tells us, "I awoke in the grey of the morning, and as I lay waiting for dawn, the long lines of the desired poem began to entwine themselves in my mind, and I said to myself I must get up and write these verses down, lest I fall asleep and forget them! So I sprang out of bed and in the dimness found an old stump of a pen, which I remembered using the day before. I scrawled the verses almost without looking at the paper." This poem was published in "The Atlantic Monthly" in 1862. The editor paid her five dollars for it. As it had no name, the editor suggested "The Battle Hymn of the Republic"; but neither editor nor author dreamed of its future. Chaplain McCabe of an Ohio Volunteer Infantry did much to give it fame, especially at a large meeting in Washington. The chaplain was asked to sing it to the great audience which included President Lincoln. When he finished amid tumultuous applause, the President, with tears in his eyes, cried out, "Sing it again"; and it was sung again. Henceforth it became a national hymn, and Chaplain McCabe did more than any other to bring it to public favour. It found its way into

American hymnals, and even into some of the hymnals abroad. It should be known by all Americans, and its lines are quickly recognized,

Mine eyes have seen the glory of the coming
of the Lord;
He is trampling out the vintage where the grapes
of wrath are stored,
He hath loosed the fateful lightning of His
terrible swift sword:
His truth is marching on!

This hymn well illustrates her "crusading" character, which continued after the Civil War by her advocacy of Woman's Suffrage, and later of World Peace, for which she gave a lecture in England urging arbitration as the ideal means for settling international disputes. She lived to be over ninety years old, and only twelve days before her death in 1910, she visited Smith College and received the honorary degree of LL.D.

Samuel Longfellow (1819-1892)—Samuel was the youngest brother of the eminent American poet, Henry W. Longfellow, and was born in Portland, Maine. He was graduated from Harvard and later completed his course in divinity. While a theological student he, in conjunction with his class-mate, Samuel Johnson, prepared a new hymn book for Unitarians. He was highly recognized for his literary gifts. The young men searched widely for their poems. So hymns by Whittier, Sears, Mrs. Stowe, Emerson and Lowell, as well as others then unknown in public worship, were included in this hymn book. Later the two men published another collection called "Hymns of the Spirit." When Samuel was ordained, his brother Henry wrote the ordination hymn, "Christ to the young man said," the only hymn except one other the distinguished poet ever wrote.

Samuel became pastor of the Second Unitarian Church in Brooklyn, and was a pioneer in starting vesper services which later became popular. His best known hymn is called "Prayer for Inspiration," beginning,

Holy Spirit, Truth Divine,
Dawn upon this soul of mine;
Word of God, and inward Light,
Wake my spirit, clear my sight.

Another hymn of Longfellow's is

I look to Thee in every need
And never look in vain;
I feel Thy strong and tender love
And all is well again.

Another hymn of special merit, with appreciation of the Church as an institution, is

One holy Church of God appears
Through every age and race,
Unwasted by the lapse of years,
Unchanged by changing place.

It is surprising how many hymns of Longfellow's are included in new hymnals. The "New Pilgrim Hymnal" has in it as many as thirteen of his hymns. The volume, "Hymns for the Living Age," contains fifteen of Longfellow's lyrics. Some of these are particularly appropriate for Seasons and Holy Days, with poetic description from earthly scenes. His verse, appropriate for offertory, is

Bless Thou the gifts our hands have brought,
Bless Thou the work our hearts have plan'd;
Ours is the faith, the will, the thought;
The rest, O God, is in Thy hand.

Samuel Johnson (1822-1882)—Doctor Johnson was a man of strong opinions, and often referred to as a Unitarian. But in truth he never united with any denomination, as he desired the widest freedom possible, and was once called "the apostle of individualism." A friend said of him, "He would not belong to any Church, or subscribe to any creed, or connect himself with any sect, be a member of any congregation, regardless of the fact that he sympathized with its aims." But the Church was more charitable and kindly to him by recognizing the man's religious vision and with appreciation admitted his sacred lyrics into the hymnals.

As already seen he was a class-mate and co-worker with Samuel Longfellow, and together they published hymnals, although older in years. After his graduation from Harvard and the Divinity School, he established an independent church at Lynn, Massachusetts, which he served till 1870. He then went to Salem, where he devoted himself to literary work during his remaining days. While his hymn books were radical in theology, they possessed poetic merit. Poems of his own appeared in both collections he and Longfellow compiled. Probably his best hymn, which most communions appropriated, was the "City of God." Its vision suggests the glories of the future of the Kingdom, with its uncommon appeal,

City of God, how broad and far
Outspread thy walls sublime:
The true thy chartered freemen are
Of every age and clime.

Another favourite hymn by Johnson is

Father, in Thy mysterious presence kneeling,
Fain would our souls feel all Thy kindling love;
For we are weak and need some deep revealing
Of trust and strength, and calmness from above.

And another good hymn is

Life of ages, richly poured,
Love of God, unspent and free,
Flowing in the prophet's word
And the people's liberty.

Phoebe Cary (1824-1871)—Miss Cary was a younger sister of Miss Alice Cary, born in the country on a farm near Cincinnati, in a home struggling with poverty. The two sisters had ambition, and their stepmother had little sympathy with the girls' desire to learn, even denying them candles for evening study; and their "night reading" had to be done by the light of a tallow dip.[2] They soon began to write poems which were accepted by various papers and magazines. This brought them letters of encouragement from the outside world, one being from Whittier. Being encouraged and helped by a New York publisher, the sisters left their country home to make their venture in the metropolis. Their first years in New York were a continuation of their struggle for a livelihood, as they were entirely dependent upon their writing for an income. But after a few years of strict economy their income was increased and their reputation established, so they could live in comfort.

The older sister wrote more poetry, but it was given the younger sister, Phoebe, to write the one outstanding hymn, "One sweetly solemn thought." The sisters attended the church of which Doctor Deems was pastor; and one Sunday morning his sermon on the

[2] *The Story of the American Hymn,* by Edward S. Ninde, The Abingdon Press, 1921

shortness of earthly life so impressed Miss Cary that it suggested the theme of a hymn, which kept weighing on her mind all the way home, and as soon as she was alone she began to write and soon finished the lines which expressed the thoughts of the sermon,

One sweetly solemn thought
Comes to me o'er and o'er,
I am nearer to my home to-day
Than I ever have been before.

When it was included in a hymn book, the author exclaimed, "Oh, that was not written for a hymn." But soon its usage was widespread. The truth of the theme was illustrated in the life of the author some years later when her sister Alice died around fifty, having been broken in health, partly at least, as a result of her earlier hardships. The loss of this sister, from whom all her life's struggle and work was inseparable, so grieved Phoebe that in a few months later within the same year she too had fulfilled in her life the thought of her hymn,

Nearer the bound of life,
Where we lay our burdens down,
Nearer leaving the cross,
Nearer gaining the crown.

Mary Ann Thomson (1834-1923)—Mrs. Thomson was born in London, and after she came to America was married to John Thomson who later was librarian of the Philadelphia Free Library. Both were members of the Church of the Annunciation (Episcopal). Several of her hymns were in the old Episcopal hymnal, but only one is found in the later hymnal of that Church and in other recent hymnals. "O Zion, haste" is a noble missionary hymn, possessing beauty and force with prophetic character. When she wrote the hymn she put it in the metre of the tune for "Hark, hark, my soul"; but it did not become popular until united with its present tune, "Tidings." Since then it has become a great favourite and is much used to-day in services of missionary character.

She as a mother, watching at the bedside of a sick son, was brought to think of widespread sickness in the world, and also of the sustaining power of Jesus. She then gave voice to the "high mission" of Christianity and a world in need of consolation, when she sang,

O Zion, haste, thy mission high fulfilling,
To tell to all the world that God is light,
That He who made all nations is not willing
One soul should perish, lost in shades of night.

Refrain: *Publish glad tidings, tidings of peace,*
Tiding of Jesus, redemption and release.

Joseph Henry Gilmore (1834-1918)—The Rev. Dr. Joseph H. Gilmore was the son of a New Hampshire governor, born in Boston, and was graduated from Brown University at head of his class, and later from Newton Theological Seminary. He served briefly in Baptist churches and in 1868 became professor of English Literature in Rochester University, where he remained till his death in 1918. He wrote several hymns, but only one became very famous, "He leadeth me, O blessed thought," sung the world over. To-day in the business centre of Philadelphia is a large office building on the corner of Broad and Arch Streets owned by the United Gas Improvement Company. Officers of this company, with reverence for spiritual things, placed a bronze tablet in memory of Gilmore, because of their appreciation of the famous hymn. On the tablet is inscribed all of the first verse.

Doctor Gilmore tells his own story of its writing: "I was supplying for a couple of Sundays in the First Baptist Church in Philadelphia in 1862. At the mid-week service I set out to give the people an exposition of the Twenty-third Psalm, which I had given on former occasions. But this time I did not get any further than the words, 'He leadeth me.' Those words took hold of me as never before. I saw in them a significance and beauty of which I had never dreamed. It was the darkest hour of the Civil War. I did not refer to that fact, that is, I don't think I did, but it may subconsciously have led me to realize that God's leadership is the one significant fact in human experience, that it makes no difference how we are led or whither we are led, just so we are sure God is leading us. At the close of the meeting a few of us in the parlour of my host, good Deacon Watson, who resided next door to the church (on the ground now occupied by the above-mentioned building), kept talking about the thought I had emphasized. Then and there on a blank page I pencilled the hymn, handed it to my wife and thought no more about it. It occurred to her afterward to send the hymn to a paper published in Boston where it was first printed. It attracted the attention of William B. Bradbury who slightly modified the refrain and set the hymn to music which has done so much to promote its popularity. I did not know until 1865 that my hymn had been set to music. I went to Rochester to preach as a candidate before the Second Baptist Church. Going into their chapel I took up a hymnal to see what they sang and opened it at my own hymn. I accepted it as an indication of divine guidance and I have no doubt I was right."

The author of the hymn said he received many testimonials of the help and comfort it has rendered God's children. A former student wrote him that it was the favourite hymn of the Japanese Christians. The hymn was once sung by a Chinaman in a court of justice to show the presiding justice what a Christian hymn was like. The Chinaman, being on trial for renting a building to Christians who had opened an opium refuge, told the judge the Christians prayed and sang hymns, and when asked for a specimen he sang "He leadeth me, O blessed thought."

Phillips Brooks (1835-1893)—Bishop Brooks was born in Boston, and attended Harvard, where he was influenced by the writings of Emerson and Theodore Parker. After graduation he taught in the Boston Latin School, but was said to be "a conspicuous failure." He then studied at Cambridge Theological Seminary and in Alexandria, Virginia. After graduation he became rector of the Church of the Advent, Philadelphia, and later rector of Holy Trinity Church in that city. While still a young man he was called to the famous Trinity Church, Boston, where his largest work was done. In 1891, after having declined the office of preacher at Harvard, professorships, and the assistant bishopric of Pennsylvania, he was elected Bishop of Massachusetts. Brooks was more distinguished as a preacher than as a poet, for he is regarded as one of the ablest preachers America has produced. He was referred to as a giant in body—six feet, four inches—a giant in mind and in heart. He had wide fertility and elevation of thought, rare gifts of eloquent speech, and powers of inspiration. He appealed to people of all classes and phases of religious thought. He came to Trinity Church, Boston, at a time when the Unitarian movement was in the ascendency and the evangelicals were over-shadowed by the leading preachers, and a majority of the literary lights who were now of the Unitarian belief had turned away from the austere Puritan type of religion. But the influential preaching of Brooks once more gave the evangelical faith a secure status in Boston. He preached a Christ of love and sympathy, as the Eternal Son of God who came to teach that God is our Father and all men His children.

Bishop Brooks was widely recognized overseas as well as throughout America. Lord Bryce said of him, "Few men have possessed in equal measure the power of touching what is best in men and lifting them suddenly by sympathetic words to the elevation of high-strung feeling and purpose which they cannot reach of themselves, save under some wave of emotion due to some personal crisis in life."

When Brooks was a boy, the children in his home were in the habit of learning hymns and reciting them before the family on Sunday evenings. By the time he went to college he had committed to memory as many as two hundred hymns. The household always knew when Phillips was up in the morning because he would begin to sing hymns. When older it was natural for him to write hymns. He wrote both Easter and Christmas carols. One of his Christmas carols has become very famous and is now sung throughout the English speaking world:

O little town of Bethlehem,
How still we see thee lie!

It was not till after he had returned home from a trip to Palestine where he had attended the Christmas Eve service in the old Church of the Nativity at Bethlehem that he wrote this hymn and had his organist, Mr. Redner, on a Saturday night write an appropriate tune for use on Sunday morning. Singularly enough it was twenty years before this song received general recognition. It is worthy of remembrance that Brooks wrote another beautiful Christmas hymn, not generally included in hymnals, the first verse of which follows,

The earth has grown cold, with its burden of care,
But at Christmas it always is young;
The heart of the jewel burns lustrous and fair,
And its soul full of music breaks forth on the air,
When the song of the angels is sung.

Washington Gladden (1836-1918)—Contemporaneous with Doctor Gilmore was another American clergyman, Dr. Washington Gladden, who was born two years later, but died the same year as the former. Doctor Gladden was a distinguished Congregationalist. He was graduated from Williams College in the class of '59 and accepted a pastorate in Brooklyn. Shortly after he became pastor of the North Congregational Church in Springfield, Massachusetts, where he began literary work by contributing to the "Springfield Republican," which was much appreciated. Later he wrote for the New York "Independent" and the "Outlook." He differed with the policy of the "Outlook" because he thought it was over-zealous in upholding capitalism and its methods. In 1882 he began a pastorate of thirty-eight years in Columbus, Ohio, "which proved to be a notable career, not only in that, but far beyond. He was concerned with all phases of modern life, social and political as well as religious." [3]

He became interested in the improvements of city government in Columbus. He was elected to the City Council where he found out much of the inside political workings of government and used the opportunity to fight evils he thought wrong. He opposed the franchise of the City Railway Company and the increase of fares, and was always keen for the public welfare. Although pastor here of a congregation of many rich people, he was ever mindful of the poor, and spoke out courageously against ill-gotten wealth. He was a man ahead of his time on questions of social justice and was frequently much criticized. He wrote many books, among them various volumes on social problems, and not only with pen, but also on the lecture platform, he sought to bring employers and employees to a mutual understanding of industrial relations.

While in Springfield he edited a weekly paper, "Sunday Afternoon," in which there was a column named, "The Still Hour," devoted to religious topics; and in this column in 1879, he wrote "O Master, let me walk with Thee." His comment, years later, was that he had no thought of making a hymn when he wrote these verses. Those who knew his family realized how courageously he bore "the strain of toil, the fret of care," during the long years of his wife's distressing malady and helplessness. Moreover, it is a sublime prayer for walking with God, his service in full surrender to the Master's purpose despite hardships and whatever cost of sacrifice because of misunderstanding and taunts of the worldly and the self-righteous criticisms of those who would not dare to face the real truth. It is well adapted to times of quiet dedication when groups of Christians are hushed with reverent mood and prepared in heart to sing:

O Master, let me walk with Thee
In lowly paths of service free;
Tell me Thy secret, help me bear
The strain of toil, the fret of care.

[3] *The Story of the American Hymn,* Edward S. Ninde, The Abingdon Press.

Help me the slow of heart to move
By some clear, winning word of love;
Teach me the wayward feet to stay,
And guide them in the homeward way.

Frederick Lucien Hosmer (1840-1928)—Doctor Hosmer, a Unitarian minister, was born in Framingham, Massachusetts, and was descended from James Hosmer of Kent, who was one of the first settlers in Concord in 1635. He was educated at Harvard, and had charges at Northboro, Massachusetts, Quincy, Illinois, Cleveland, St. Louis and Berkeley, California. He was the lecturer on hymnody in 1908. He, like others, had talent for poetry, but unlike others he wrote very few hymns before forty years of age. His compositions appeared in "The Thoughts of God in Hymns and Poems," which he and his associate, Dr. W. C. Gannett, published in 1885, and a later series in 1894. Hardly any of his hymns were generally recognized until recent years. The first hymn to gain recognition, written after he had reached fifty years, was his Advent hymn,

Thy Kingdom come on bended knee,
The passing ages pray.

Another hymn of similar thought as applied to world peace and righteousness is

Thy Kingdom come, O Lord,
Wide circling as the sun:
Fulfil of old Thy Word
And make the nations one.

Another of Hosmer's hymns, teaching the living presence of our God, which was written earlier than others, is

O Thou, in all Thy might so far,
In all Thy love so near,
Beyond the range of sun and star
And yet beside us here.

One more of his hymns is now recognized which was written when he was older in years, during the first of the twentieth century,

When shadows gather on our way,
Fast deepening as the night,
Be Thou, O God, the spirit's stay,
Our inward Light.

Mary A. Lathbury (1841-1913)—Miss Lathbury was born in a devout Christian home in Manchester, New Hampshire. Her father was a "local preacher" in the Methodist Episcopal Church, and two of her brothers were ordained ministers in that communion. As a child she showed talent for both composing verses and drawing. As she grew up she became known as a contributor to periodicals for young people. In 1874 she became assistant to Dr. John Vincent, then secretary of the Methodist Sunday School Union, and later head of the movement at Chautauqua, New York. There she became well known as the Laureate of Chautauqua, and her hymns were frequently sung at this assembly year after year. One of her hymns has the record usage as the opening hymn for Sunday evening service there for over fifty years. She was called upon to write hymns for special occasions at Chautauqua. There were five poems. Her two most famous hymns were written for use at this famous assembly by request of Bishop Vincent. One of these, so appropriate as a vesper hymn, has been most popular and very widely used ever since, not only at Chautauqua, but throughout the whole nation,

Day is dying in the west,
Heaven is touching earth with rest.

Her second best known hymn, as used there by the beautiful Chautauqua Lake, very appropriately alludes to the breaking and blessing of the loaves "beside the Sea" of Galilee, and has been used both in America and abroad, and begins,

Break Thou the Bread of life,
  Dear Lord, to me;
As Thou didst break the loaves
  Beside the sea;
Beyond the sacred page
  I seek Thee, Lord,
My spirit pants for Thee,
  O Living Word!

Maltbie Davenport Babcock (1858-1901)—Doctor Babcock, the able Presbyterian divine, was born in Syracuse, New York, and as a boy showed those qualities of leadership and independence, which helped to make him a man of strong influence among men. He was large in stature, and a noble specimen of physical strength—an athlete who was a very able baseball player and swimmer, and leader in athletic events. Naturally young men and boys idolized him. The story is told of him that while full of fun he would not tolerate the wrong type of action. One day when an older fellow was trying to bully one younger than himself and was indulging in some unsavoury language, Babcock quickly seized him by the neck and seat of the trousers and with a word of forceful warning pitched him over the fence.[4]

The same strong virility marked his preaching also. He was pastor in Baltimore, and while there exerted large influence, so much so that the authorities of Johns Hopkins University set aside a special room for his use. Later in New York City his forceful character and influence made itself felt. He preached a manly religion and was himself such a manful example that he influenced many other young men to resolve to be true men also. Knowing the man, it would only be expected, when he wrote poetry, he would pen such lines as

Be strong!
We are not here to play, to dream, to drift,
We have had work to do, and loads to lift,
Shun not the struggle, face it, 'tis God's gift.

As a great lover of nature, who admired the works of his Creator, he eloquently spoke,

This is my Father's world;
And to my listening ears
All nature sings, and round me rings
The music of the spheres.
This is my Father's world;
I rest me in the thought
Of rocks, and trees, of skies, and seas—
His hand the wonders wrought.

From his "Thoughts for Every Day Living," written not long before his early tragic death in 1901, he wrote,

When the great sun sinks to his rest,
His golden glories thrilling me,
And voiceless longings stir my breast,
Then teach me, Lord, to worship Thee.[5]

[4] *The Story of the American Hymn*, by Edward S. Ninde, The Abingdon Press.

[5] These hymns of Babcock's are copyrighted by Charles Scribner's Sons, 1901.

Ernest Warburton Shurtleff (1862-1917)—Shurtleff was born in Boston and entered the Congregational ministry. He was graduated from Andover Theological Seminary in 1887, and his class-mates recognized the poetic ability he possessed. He already had written two volumes of poetry. His class-mates asked him to write a hymn which they might all sing together before separated from the seminary. He thus produced the hymn which is the best he ever wrote. Appropriately it expressed the Church Militant spirit for the young ministers starting out on their life's career. The first verse follows:

Lead on, O King Eternal,
The day of march has come;
Henceforth in fields of conquest
Thy tents shall be our home.
Through days of preparation
Thy grace has made us strong,
And now, O King Eternal,
We lift our battle song.

Ernest Shurtleff continued to write other poems but none to excel his one famous hymn. He held several pastorates in this country until he went to Paris in 1906 where he continued his labours, having charge of the Students' Atelier Reunions until his death in 1917.

Other American writers who have produced at least one outstanding hymn are as follows:

Adams, John Quincy—Send forth, O God, Thy light and truth.
Bacon, Leonard—O God, beneath Thy guiding hand.
Bethune, George W.—It is not death to die.
Blaisdell, James A.—Christians, lo, the star appeareth.
Brown, Phoebe H.—I love to steal awhile away.
Burleigh, William H.—Lead us, O Father, in the paths of peace.
Doane, William C.—Ancient of days who sittest.
Gannett, William C.—Bring, O morn, thy music.
Hopkins, John Henry—We three kings of Orient are.
Key, Francis S.—Lord, with glowing heart I'd praise Thee.
Lanier, Sidney—Into the woods my Master went.
Leland, John—The day is past and gone.
Longfellow, Henry W.—I heard the bells on Christmas Day.
Lowell, James Russell—Once to every man and nation.

March, Daniel—Hark, the voice of Jesus calling.
Parker, Edwin Pond—Master, no offering, costly and sweet.
Parker, Theodore—O Thou great Friend to all.
Prentiss, Elizabeth P.—More love to Thee, O Christ.
Roberts, Daniel—God of our fathers, whose almiglity hand.
Sigourney, Lydia H.—Blest Comforter divine.
Stowe, Harriet Beecher—Still, still with Thee.
Tappan, William Bingham—'Tis midnight and on Olive's brow.
Warner, Anna B.—We would see Jesus for the shadows lengthen.
Williams, Theodore Chickering—When Thy heart with joy o'erflowing.
Willis, Love M.—Father, hear the prayer we offer.

GOSPEL SONGS

The Gospel Song came into vogue during the last quarter of the nineteenth century and is of American origin and development, although it first gained its distinctive impetus in England under the patronage and usage of D. L. Moody and his singing co-partner, Ira D. Sankey. These men began conducting their evangelistic campaign in Newcastle in 1873. They made use of a book previously compiled by Philip Phillips, entitled "Hallowed Songs," and supplemented by Mr. Sankey's own compositions. The following year, in this country, Major D. W. Whittle conducted similar evangelistic meetings and followed Mr. Moody's example by having associated with him a singing evangelist, named P. P. Bliss, who, like Sankey, was much admired by his hearers.

These two Americans compiled a book similar to that which had been prepared for the English but called it "Gospel Songs," a name thereafter applied to this type of lyric. When Moody and Sankey returned to America in 1875, the four men decided to combine their compositions in one book, the title page of which read, "Gospel Hymns and Sacred Songs, by P. P. Bliss and Ira D. Sankey, as used by them in Gospel Meetings." The book became popular and six editions were published. Many and varied have been the subsequent publications of books of this character by self-appointed compilers and committees whose lack of good judgment and of literary and musical training have often weakened rather than enhanced this movement in religious song. We should keep in mind that the Gospel Song first gained attention by its introduction on special occasions amid the glamour and enthusiasm of large crowds, with large choruses and often loud musical instruments; when extra time was given to singing and an ingenious leader was able to work people's feelings up to higher state. This movement came at a time in the nineteenth century following a tendency to lose sight of the individual, while the new Gospel Song tended to bring back the importance of the individual, and thus gained favour and appeal with the common throng.

There has been much discussion of the merits of this movement, and much disagreement concerning its place and value in religious worship. This much is certain that such lyrics are ephemeral and only a few of the best among the many thousands will have permanent value. Their melodies are of the street-song variety and can quickly be learned by the average person without much effort. Prof. Waldo S. Pratt says, "They tend to embody more sentiment than thought, and to express it rather crudely, even melodramatically. . . . Some of them shade off into the more sentimental of true hymns containing both valuable feeling and felicitous expression. But the mass of them being produced in a more or less commercial way and with merely jingling dexterity are commonplace, sometimes vulgar." [6] Professor Pratt tells us further that it is probably true that some of the modern dislike of church services found among some people is doubtless caused by their impressions of Christianity derived from such songs. On the other hand, Professor Pratt, as well as other writers on the subject, recognize that some of their songs have served a purpose. They have been used with much effect in evangelistic meetings and mission services of the Church and are adaptable to pioneer conditions; are useful for children's services, and in rural districts, where there is lack of means, they afford a cheap book for temporary use. But surely in the regular stated worship of the church, only the dignified and reverent usage of hymns, with possibly the very best of Gospel Songs approaching hymnic character, are appropriately adapted for regular use.

Such critics as Humphreys in his book "The Evolution of Church Music," Curwen in his "Studies in Worship Music," and Dickinson in his "Music in the History of the Western Church," give a place to the Gospel Songs, but at the same time utter true warnings against their great limitations and faults. Professor Dickinson says, "Those churches which rely mainly upon Gospel Songs should soberly consider if it is profitable in the long run to maintain a standard of religious melody and verse far below that

[6] *Musical Ministries,* G. Schirmer, Inc., 1914.

which prevails in secular music and literature. The Church cannot afford to keep its spiritual culture out of harmony with the higher intellectual movements of the age." The value of this advice is even more important to-day than when Dickinson's words were written. Doctor Breed well says, "Many a worshipper has been misled with regard to the qualities of a true hymn and the nature of sacred music. Reverence degenerates into familiarity, and solemn worship is displaced by musical harangue." [7]

There have been continuously found in almost every Gospel Song publication at least a few widely sung lyrics of an appealing nature. Among the earlier ones were, "Almost persuaded," both words and music by P. P. Bliss; "Jesus loves even me"; Dr. Robert Lowry's melody, "Shall we gather at the river" and Sankey's melody to "The Ninety and Nine."

Many others have been widely sung for a time during succeeding years down to the present time when we have such newer popular songs as "The old rugged Cross" (words and music by George Bennard), and "When I have gone the last mile of the way," by Johnson Oatman, Jr., with its pleasing melody by William Edie Marks.

There are some which are hymns in form and can be accepted as hymns, and are in truth odes of praise to Almighty God and not merely exhortation to fellowman, or morbid introspection, or subjective resolutions of better living. For example, Mrs. Annie S. Hawks's "I need Thee every hour" is a worthy hymn. Some of Fanny Crosby's songs are likewise of hymnic character, such as "Jesus, keep me near the Cross" and "Safe in the arms of Jesus." Fanny Crosby, who was blind and married a blind man, taught in New York City many years in a school for the blind. She frequently helped with mission work on the east side, and wrote over eight thousand lyrics, more than any other American. Several became very popular Gospel Songs, and perhaps none have been more useful than her famous "Rescue the Perishing," and also her "Throw out the life-line." But such songs as "Hold the fort" and "When the roll is called up yonder" are not hymns in the proper sense of the word. According to the definition and essential qualities of a hymn as enunciated in Chapter 3, most Gospel Songs cannot be ranked as hymns.

In Doctor Breed's book his chapter, "Gospel Songs and Singers," ably sets forth the difference between this type of song

[7] *The History and Use of Hymns and Hymn-Tunes,* David R. Breed, Fleming H. Revell Co., 1903.

and the standard hymn, and rightly claims it was a mistake to change the title of "Gospel Songs" to "Gospel Hymns" when in truth they are not hymns, and their music is not generally claimed to be up to the standard of the best hymn tunes. The solo and chorus of many of these are objectionable for congregational music. Nor is their imitation of the old fugue tune which the church has abolished as unsuitable for modern standards of worship desirable. The structure of the tunes, even without these objectionable features, is lacking in the stately strength and dignified harmony of the hymn tune, especially when the harmony notes change but once or twice in a measure, and the harmony parts are the merest accompaniment to the melody.

Particularly objectionable is the music with exaggerated rhythm when it sounds like the music of the dance hall and is more suitable for dancing than for devout worship.

One more important point to be remembered is the fact that exclusive use of Gospel Songs means the neglect of growth in Christian grace, as they deal almost exclusively with the first stage of the Christian life, which is conversion, and with the last stage which is going to heaven. Simply dealing with the beginning and ending of earthly life is leaving out a large part of what pertains to Christian life and its spiritual development.

When it is desired to make use of Gospel Songs there are several writers of these melodies who are among the leading composers of this type of music, such as Ira D. Sankey, William B. Bradbury, P. P. Bliss, Robert Lowry, James McGranahan, George C. Stebbins, William H. Doane, C. C. Converse, Charles H. Gabriel and others.

While the words of these songs, of which there are many authors, present approaches to conversion and life after death, there are some which stand out prominently and have been much sung. A few of them, which are addressed directly to Almighty God instead of to man, approach the hymn form of lyric. When they "shade off" into a hymn it is difficult at times to make a clear distinction wherein it is a Gospel Song, just as it is difficult at times to say whether a lyric is a carol or hymn, or when stained window glass shades off from green to blue, or vice versa. This particularly applies to some of Fanny Crosby's lyrics which might be classed as either hymns or Gospel Songs, or even fittingly called "Gospel Hymns."

The main consideration in the use of Gospel Songs is that the humble people who are least able to appreciate both the words and music of dignified hymns are more surely reached by this type of song. Jesus himself often used the common things of life to impress his humble hearers. These songs do not represent art or music *per se*. They are the initiation or beginning of religion in the minds and hearts of some people, and as such do they not deserve a place in the evolution of the Gospel? But it shall ever be borne in mind that this type of song is only the beginning and not the end of achievement in worship or praise, and this beginning should be followed by further advance. The great pity is that so many religious folk are content to remain merely singers of these lyrics both in the church and in the home and do not try to progress in their sphere of praise. It seems that the scriptural injunction fitly applies here, "But grow in grace and in the knowledge of our Lord and Saviour, Jesus Christ."

Horace F. Erwin, the well known evangelistic singer of wide experience and travel, has found certain Gospel Songs and hymns are great favourites among the crowds of the south and middle west, and are valuable as "contact songs" with new audiences and the unchurched throng that have never learned to love the old hymns of the Church. He uses the Gospel Songs as means to an end, combining the best of these songs with the old hymns in the services, with a majority of Gospel Songs of a Sunday evening, climaxing the singing with an old hymn, such as "Come, Thou Almighty King," and Wesley's "Love divine, all loves excelling" and "Jesus, Lover of my soul." He makes the further practical suggestion: "A hymn without a good medium of expression in melody would be better quoted in a sermon or address than sung poorly by a congregation or used with a poor tune."

Among the songs Mr. Erwin has found most useful either as "contact" selections or selections, calculated to enlist the interest and singing of the most people in a religious gathering because of their general appeal, are the following:

Maltbie D. Babcock's This is my Father's world; P. P. Bilhorn's Sweet peace the gift of God's love; Fanny Crosby's Blessed assurance, Jesus is mine; and, I am Thine, O Lord; P. P. Bliss's Wonderful words of life; Charles H. Gabriel's O that will be glory for me; J. H. Gilmore's He leadeth me, O blessed thought; Katherine Hankey's I love to tell the story; W. D. Longstaff's Take time to be holy; C. A. Mile's' I come to the garden alone; A. A. Pollard's Have Thine own way, Lord; F. H. Rowley's I will sing the wondrous story; J. H. Sammis's When we walk with the Lord; Joseph Scriven's What a Friend we have in Jesus; H. G. Spofford's When peace like a river.

SUMMARY

In this chapter we have considered with special paragraphs the following: Thomas Hastings; William Cullen Bryant; William Augustus Muhlenberg; George Washington Doane; John Greenleaf Whittier; Ray Palmer; Samuel Francis Smith; Oliver Wendell Holmes; Edmund Hamilton Sears; Samuel Wolcott; Henry Harbaugh; George Duffield, Jr.; Arthur Cleveland Coxe; Edward Hopper; Julia Ward Howe; Samuel Longfellow; Samuel Johnson; Phoebe Cary; Mary Ann Thomson; Joseph Henry Gilmore; Phillips Brooks; Washington Gladden; Frederick Lucien Hosmer; Mary A. Lathbury; Maltbie D. Babcock; Ernest W. Shurtleff; Gospel Songs.

For Further Reading

The Story of the American Hymn, Edward S. Ninde.
Lyric Religion, H. Augustine Smith.
The Hymns You Ought to Know, Philo Adams Otis.
The Hymns and Hymn Writers of the Church, C. S. Nutter, W. F. Tillett.
One Hundred and One Hymn Stories, Carl F. Price.
More Hymn Stories, Carl F. Price.
Some Hymns and Hymn Writers, William B. Bodine.
The Music and Hymnody of the Methodist Hymnal, Carl F. Price.
The History and Use of Hymns and Hymn-Tunes, David R. Breed.
Annotations on Popular Hymns, Charles S. Robinson.
Musical Ministries in the Church, Waldo S. Pratt.

PART THREE

XIII

SOME TWENTIETH CENTURY HYMNS

IN SELECTING the best hymns among the more recent productions we deal with hymns of short existence and cannot fully appreciate their lasting worth. Especially is this true of hymns written within a period of less than twenty years, for it takes an average of about twenty years for a hymn to win general recognition and usage. It is true also that some hymns attain general favour quickly because of unusual helpful circumstances. Again, it is true that other hymns are much longer than twenty years gaining recognition because of circumstances which have tended to hold back their progress toward deserved fame. The background of twentieth century hymns has included such national and world events as the World War, which gave impetus to much poetry, most of which was merely ephemeral. But the extenuating influences coming out of the war led to human aspirations for peace. Besides, the industrial developments and material forces led to opposing aspirations for social justice and social welfare, and deeper concern for the well-being of the common man. Hence came a further growth than later nineteenth century hymns in the production of "social service" hymns.

Moreover, there has come forth in the present century a widening tendency in the form and substance of lyric praise. How much this tendency will enrich our books of praise yet remains to be seen and tested by the succeeding generation of worshippers. We have already seen that the hymn became well established in form and character in the eighteenth century, both the objective character of Watts's hymns and the subjective character of the evangelical hymns of Charles Wesley and others. The Evangelical Movement of the eighteenth century established the homiletic or preaching hymn, i.e., the hymns as used to reaffirm and reinforce the message of the sermon.

The Oxford Movement of the nineteenth century brought forward the liturgical and devotional type of hymn. Added to this the literary movement modified and extended the character of lyrics used for worship. In the twentieth century there have been at least two prominent forces in the development of hymnody: First, the liturgical influence which has extended and modified the usage among non-Episcopal churches in observance of the feasts and fasts of the Church Year which heretofore was largely confined to the Anglican Church. Now these hymns for the Church Year are in other hymnals. Secondly, the literary motive which was even more pronounced than in the latter part of the nineteenth century. The concern for literary style and expression has widened the area of hymn poetry. Thus we have a freer and wider variety of hymns chosen from the field of religious poetry.

The definition of the hymn has been made more elastic. While the standard type of hymns of the eighteenth and nineteenth centuries still reigns supreme, and likely will in the future as in the past, yet the larger literary field of religious lyrics has become more general. The present tendency of some hymnologists to adapt the religious writings of literary poets, both past and present, is seemingly stretching the definition of the hymn as taught during the past two hundred years. How much gain this is for effective hymn worship remains to be seen and determined in the future.

During the early part of this century a few hymnals seemed to go out of their way to include such literary writings as Tennyson's "Sunset and Evening Star," Sidney Lainer's "Into the woods my Master went," and Dr. Josiah Holland's "There's a song in the air, there's a star in the sky."

There are also more recently such subjective types of poetry as Christina Rossetti's hymns and Dr. Allen Eastman Cross's poems which have commanded attention and been used as hymns. The new "Songs of Praise" [1] (in England) has gone far in its attempt to adapt literary poets as hymn writers to include several lyrics of Tennyson, when previously only one or two poems of his were found in hymnals; poems of William Wordsworth not previously found in hymnals except one in Anglican books; several poems of George Herbert, and three from Robert Browning, including his familiar poem,

The year's at the spring,[2]
And day's at the morn,
Morning's at seven,
The hillside's dew-pearled,

[1] *Songs of Praise,* Oxford University Press. Used by permission of the Macmillan Company.
[2] *Ibid.*

The lark's on the wing,
The snail's on the thorn,
God's in His heaven—
All's right with the world.

The above does not seem to have the character of a hymn of spiritual praise. While God is in His heaven, we cannot believe "all's right with the world" in these days of such chaotic conditions.

The poem by John Masefield, the present Poet Laureate, in this same hymnal above-mentioned seems a little more adaptable for hymnic praise:

O Christ who holds the open gate,[3]
O Christ who drives the furrow straight,
O Christ the plough, O Christ the laughter
Of holy white birds flying after.

Even this poem we could not conceive of Watts or Wesley or even Heber including in a hymn book if they were living in the twentieth century.

However we may regard with favour or disfavour this recent influence of literary poetry, there has been at least one distinctive gain in twentieth century usage, that is, the more unifying influence of hymn singing among the different communions. Each denomination's hymnody has gradually lessened, and the body of hymns which all alike sing has slowly enlarged, so that to-day the new hymnals give striking testimony of the spiritual unity of the churches. This growth in the catholic spirit of our hymnals has tended to widen and enrich our common praise.

It is obvious from what has already been said that there is no great certainty about the lasting character of what we have to offer for twentieth century worship. In fact, James King of London gives in "Anglican Hymnology," before the end of the nineteenth century, a list of the then new hymns which might become a permanent addition to the hymnal. About one-half of them are now generally used. The same is true of a short list of hymns suggested some years later by Prof. Waldo S. Pratt in his "Musical Ministeries." About one-half of the hymns in this list are now being used. We can therefore only hope that at least one-half of the hymns we shall mention in this chapter may have any real permanent usage.

[3] *Ibid.*

Katharine Lee Bates (1859-1929)—Miss Bates was born on Cape Cod at Falmouth, the daughter of William Bates, a Congregational minister, who died when Katharine was but a few weeks old. Her grandfather was the Rev. Joshua Bates, once president of Middlebury College, Vermont. Her oldest brother, Arthur Lee Bates, through his labours and self-sacrifice was able to help his youngest sister to obtain an education. From the village school she entered the Wellesley High School, and after graduation entered Wellesley College from which she was graduated in 1880. During her college years she wrote a few stories and poems which were published in papers and magazines. After graduation she began her teaching of the classics and other branches. She soon became a teacher in Dana Hall and later accepted the professorship in English in her alma mater, and continued her profession till she became professor emeritus in 1925, when her college conferred upon her the degree of LL.D. She published various volumes of poetry and prose, including travels in Spain and England; also writing for children, of whom she was very fond. It was her custom to entertain royally the neighbourhood children every Christmas afternoon at her home. The author is indebted to one of her fellow-members of the faculty for an estimate of her appearance and character. She was "very fat, with broad face and flat nose; but her countenance once lightened, her face showed a winning personality."

Miss Bates was a woman of strong friendships and her kindly interest and sympathy toward all made her much beloved by both pupils and friends. It is said she entertained her students in classroom more than she stimulated them to work. Her fame as a teacher and writer was more local till she wrote her one outstanding hymn, written in 1893, when this New Englander made her first extensive trip to the west and the Chicago World's Fair, that same year, which inspired her patriotic song.

After a day spent on Pike's Peak with some fellow teachers, looking over the great Rocky Mountains, she sat down in the evening in Colorado Springs and wrote her

O beautiful for spacious skies,
For amber waves of grain,
For purple mountain majesties
Above the fruited plain.

This lyric has now taken its place alongside of "My Country, 'tis of thee," and "The Star-Spangled Banner," as leading national songs, which are found in all books of popular songs.

It is a true hymn and well emphasizes the fact that our vast country alone without God's help cannot attain its purpose and glory but by fulfilment of its closing words of prayer,

God shed His grace on thee,
And crown thy good with brotherhood
From sea to shining sea.

Louis Fitzgerald Benson (1855-1930)—Benson was born in Philadelphia, where he also died, In truth he belongs to both the nineteenth and twentieth centuries, but his greatest service was in the twentieth century during which he lived for thirty years. He was graduated from the University of Pennsylvania in 1874, was admitted to the bar in 1877 and practiced law until 1884. He was graduated from Princeton Theological Seminary in 1887, and received his doctor's degree from the University of Pennsylvania, nearly ten years later. In 1886 he became pastor of the Presbyterian Church of the Redeemer which position he resigned in a few years to give his time to hymnological work and lecturing on liturgies and hymnology at Auburn Seminary and thrice at Princeton Seminary.

He was the author of various books on hymnody and editor of different Presbyterian hymnals. He was the author of "The Best Church Hymns," and a handbook for the same, and of "Studies in Familiar Hymns, first and second series." His monumental work was his "The English Hymn, its Development and Use in Worship," second only to Julian's "Dictionary of Hymnology." He contributed to the second edition of Julian's stupendous work and published works in church worship also. His last able work was his "Hymnody of the Christian Church" in 1927. In short, he has been America's greatest student and scholar in hymnology. For this reason he deserves a high place for his untiring efforts, rather than for his own original hymns, which may yet become more recognized as the years go by. His wide knowledge and grasp of his favourite study are almost equalled by his unassuming character and beautiful Christian spirit, as testified to by one well qualified to know, the nurse in the Benson family for a time. At his death his extensive library of hymnology (about 9,000 volumes) was left to Princeton Theological Seminary. It contained many ancient Latin tomes, German chorales and many liturgies; some of the books are the only copies now in existence.

Among his own original hymns, perhaps the one now gaining most recognition is

O Thou whose feet have climbed life's hill
And trod the path of youth.

This was written in 1891, but his other hymns of note were written later, as his

The light of God is falling
Upon life's common way.

Another one begins,

Our feet have wandered far away,
Our wilful hearts have gone astray,

also

O Thou, whose gracious presence blest
The home of Bethany,

a hymn in carol style,

O sing a song of Bethlehem
Of shepherds watching there,

and a translation of an old hymn ascribed to Ambrose of Milan, beginning,

O splendour of God's glory bright
From light eternal bringing light.

Walter Russell Bowie (1882-)—Doctor Bowie was born in Richmond, Virginia. His father was Walter Russell Bowie, and his mother, Elizabeth (Branch) Bowie. He took his A.B. at Harvard, and the following year, 1905, his A.M. Richmond College bestowed upon him the doctorate degree. He was made a deacon in 1908 by Bishop Peterkin and ordained to the priesthood the next year by Bishop Gibson. He married Jean Loverack of Buffalo in 1909. His first work was in Greenwood Parish, Virginia. In 1911 he was called to the large St. Paul's Episcopal Church in Richmond, in the city of his birth. He has held many positions on commissions of one kind and another in the Episcopal Church. He was chaplain of a base hospital in France during the war. He was also editor of "The Southern Churchman" in 1920-24. He next became rector of Grace Episcopal Church, New York, succeeding the late Bishop Charles L. Slattery of Boston. He has written valuable books, both for children and adults. One of his best books is "The Master," a life of Christ, 1928. Doctor Bowie has been an outspoken clergyman on social justice and political issues. He has written poems of merit which are finding sure space in new hymnals.

Among his present recognized hymns are:

God of the nations, who from dawn of day[4]
Hast led Thy people in their widening way,
Thro' whose deep purpose stranger thousands stand
Here in the borders of our promised land.

Another begins,

O Holy City seen of John,[5]
Where Christ, the Lamb, doth reign,
Within whose four-square walls shall come
No night, nor need, nor pain,
And where the tears are wiped from eyes
That shall not weep again,

while his hymn of our Lord's passion is

Lovely to the outward eye[6]
Seemed Jerusalem to lie;
Yet 'twas there Thou cam'st to die,
Jesus, Son of Mary.

John Brownlie (1859-1925)—Doctor Brownlie was educated in Glasgow at the University and the Free Church College. In 1885 he became junior minister of the Free Church, Portpatrick, Wigtownshire, to the full charge of which he succeeded in 1890. He took keen interest in education in his county, and for sometime was chairman of the governors of Stranraer High School.

His interest in hymnology bore fruit in "Hymns and Hymnwriters of the Church Hymnary" (1890), and his many original hymns in "Hymns of our Pilgrimage Zionward," "Hymns of the Pilgrim Life" and "Pilgrim Songs." He cultivated the field of Latin and Greek hymnody; "Hymns of the Early Church," "Hymns from East and West," and "Hymns of the Greek Church," attested to his learning in this field and his ability as a translator. A number of these translations have passed into use in modern hymn books.

His original hymn is "O Light, that knew no dawn," and his translation based on the Greek is "The King shall come when morning dawns, and light triumphant breaks."

[4] Used by permission of the author.
[5] *Ibid.* [6] *Ibid.*

Thomas Curtis Clark (1877-)—Author, born in Vincennes, Indiana, son of Thomas Jefferson Clark and Emma Rose Jennings Clark, he was graduated at the University of Indiana in 1899; later studying at the University of Chicago; still later becoming member of the editorial staff of "The Christian Century," Chicago, continuing since 1912. He has been also editor of "Twentieth Century Quarterly" since 1919. He is a member of the publishing firm of Willett, Clark and Colby; also of the Poetic Society of America and of the Disciples of Christ Communion.

He is the author of "Poems and Songs" (1909), "Love Off to the War" and other poems (1918), "New Poems of Faith" (1929). He wrote other books, and has been a syndicate writer. His home is in Chicago.

His hymn of love and gratitude is

I sought His love in sun and stars,
And where the wild seas roll,
I found it not, as mute I stood,
Fear overwhelmed my soul;
But when I gave to one in need
I found the Lord of Love indeed.

Another hymnic poem dealing with world peace is

Who goes there in the night
Across the storm-swept plain?
We are the ghosts of a valiant war,
A million murdered men.

Allen Eastman Cross (1864-)—Doctor Cross was born in the chief city of New Hampshire, Manchester. He attended Phillips Andover Academy, Amherst College and Andover Theological Seminary. For a decade he was associate pastor of the Old South Church, with Dr. George A. Gordon. In 1914 he became pastor of the First Congregational Church of Milford, Massachusetts, where he served until 1925, when he resigned to give his time to writing, and returned to his old home in Manchester.

What Doctor Gordon, with whom he was long associated, says of him is significant, "Doctor Cross had a distinctive literary gift much appreciated by many of our people. He was and is a gifted poet as well as a preacher."

He has written a volume of religious poems, "The Torch," at least some of which contributed to twentieth century hymnody. The rather unusual thing is that new hymnals have selected from this volume different poems, instead of the same ones. The one based on the boyhood of Jesus at Nazareth should be of special interest in "Praise and Service":

The hidden years at Nazareth![7]
How deep and still they seem,
Like rivers flowing in the dark,
Or waters in a dream!
Like waters under Syrian stars,
Reflecting lights above,
Repeating in their silent depths
The wonders of God's love.

The hidden years at Nazereth;
How clear and true they lie,
As open to the smile of God
As to the Syrian sky!
As open to the heart of man
As to the genial sun!
With dreams of vast adventuring,
And deeds of kindness done!

The hidden years at Nazereth!
How radiant they rise,
With life and death in balance laid
Before a lad's clear eyes!
O Soul of Youth, forever choose,
Forgetting fate or fear,
To live for truth or die with God,
Who stands beside thee here!

Another hymn selected by the "Pilgrim Hymnal" is

America, America, the shouts of war shall cease,
The glory dawns! the day is come of victory and peace,
And now upon a larger plan we'll build the common good
The temple of the love of man, the house of brotherhood.

The new Presbyterian Hymnal and new Methodist Hymnal contain

Jesus kneel beside me, in the dawn of day;
Thine is prayer eternal, teach me how to pray.

[7] The hymns of Allen Eastman Cross, used by permission of the author.

The "Hymns for the Living Age" has another,

More Light shall break from out Thy word
For pilgrim followers of the gleam,
Till, led by Thy free spirit, Lord,
We see and share the pilgrim dream.

Ozora Stearns Davis (1866-1931)—Davis was born in Wheelock, Vermont, the son of Alexander Warner Davis. He was graduated at Dartmouth in 1889, and from Hartford Theological Seminary in 1894. He received the degree of Ph.D. from the University of Leipsig, and D.D. from Dartmouth. He married Grace Emeline Tinker of White River Junction, Vermont. He was ordained to the Congregational ministry in 1896. He was principal of White River Junction High School a short time. Later he held pastorates at Springfield, Vermont, Newtonville, Massachusetts, and New Britain, Connecticut. He became president of Chicago Theological Seminary in 1909. Doctor Davis wrote several books on a variety of subjects; biographical, religious, and theological, such as "International Aspects of Christianity," "The Gospel in Light of the Great War," "Using the Bible in Public Address."

A hymn which seems already to be a favourite, teaching needed courage for to-day, is

We bear the strain of earthly care,
But bear it not alone;
Beside us walks our brother Christ,
And makes our task His own.

A second hymn of recognition begins,

At length there dawns the glorious day[8]
By prophets long foretold;
At length the chorus clearer grows
That shepherds heard of old,
The Day of dawning brotherhood
Breaks on our eager eyes,
And human hatreds flee before
The radiant eastern skies.

Percy Dearmer (1867-1936)—Doctor Dearmer was born in London, educated at Westminster School abroad and at Christ Church, Oxford. He served as curate in St. Anne's, Lambeth,

[8] Used by permission of Mrs. Ozara Stearns Davis.

and at other churches. Then from 1901 to 1915 he was vicar of St. Mary the Virgin, Primrose Hill. He was secretary of the London branch of the Christian Social Union, and chairman of the League of Arts. After much service abroad during the war, he became (1919) Professor of Ecclesiastical Art in King's College, London, and Canon of Westminster. Many books have come from his pen, i.e., "The Parson's Hand Book," "The Sanctuary," "Body and Soul," "Highways and By-ways in Normandy," "The English Carol Book" (with Martin Shaw), "The Art of Public Worship," "The Power of the Spirit," "The Church at Prayer and the World Outside." He was secretary of the committee that prepared the "English Hymnal," and acted as editor of that epoch-making book. He edited also "Songs of Praise" (1925-1931) with the co-operation, in the music, of Dr. R. Vaughan-Williams and Martin Shaw.

Among his hymns the leading one at present is his needed and timely temperance hymn:

Father, who on man dost shower
Gifts of plenty from Thy dower,
To Thy people give the power
All Thy gifts to use aright.

The second verse is particularly applicable,

Give pure happiness in leisure,
Temperance in every pleasure,
Holy use of earthly treasure,
Body clear and spirits bright.

Another, the morning hymn, which is a translation from Gregory the Great, is well recognized:

Father, we praise Thee, now the night is over,
Active and watchful, stand we all before Thee.

"Praise and Service" has additional hymns of Doctor Dearmer's, among which is his

Lord of Health, through life within us
Strength of all that lives and grows,
Love that meets our hearts to win us,
Beauty that around us glows.

Harry Webb Farrington (1880-1931)—A clergyman of the Methodist Communion, born in Nassau, British West Indies, a son of William Gilliland and Emma Russell Farrington, whose mother died during his infancy, he was thrown on his own resources when a boy, but was able to work his way through schools. He received part of his education at Darlington Academy and later was graduated from Dickinson Seminary in 1903. He obtained his S.T.B. degree at Boston University Theological School and his A.M. from Harvard.

He has been a teacher successively in Syracuse University and Harvard University. He inaugurated in the Methodist Episcopal Church the Week Day Church School at Gary, Indiana, and in New York City; and was also lecturer on Religious Education at Chautauqua, New York.

Farrington is the author of "Poems from France" and other poems: a writer of prose, as biographical sketches of Franklin, Washington, Lincoln and Theodore Roosevelt attest. He is also author of modern hymns.

Among his hymns, the one that has now attained most attention is his hymn written in 1910 which was the Harvard prize hymn:

I know not how that Bethlehem's Babe
Could in the God-head be;
I only know the Manger child
Has brought God's life to me.

Another hymn of his begins,

Dear Lord, who sought at dawn of day
The solitary woods to pray,
In quietness we come to ask
Thy guidance for the daily task.

Harry Emerson Fosdick (1878-)—This distinguished New York clergyman was born in Buffalo, the son of Frank and Amy (Weaver) Fosdick, and the brother of the distinguished lawyer, Raymond B. Fosdick. Doctor Fosdick was graduated from Colgate in 1900, and the Union Theological Seminary in 1904. He received the degree of A.M. from Columbia in 1908, and later the degree of D.D. from New York University, Brown, Yale, Glasgow (Scotland), Princeton, Boston University; and the degree of LL.D. from other well-known institutions. Doctor Fosdick was ordained to the Baptist ministry in 1903 and the next year became pastor of the First Church of Montclair, New Jersey. He is a trustee in various colleges, but is well known in the threefold capacity of professor in Union Theological Seminary, pastor of the new Riverside Church, and distinguished preacher. He is the author of a number of famous books, almost all on important phases of Christianity. Like Doctor Van Dyke, he wrote one book dealing with his travels in the Holy Land, "A Pilgrimage to Palestine."

His hymnological writings are found in a few new hymnals, as his timely hymn for world peace:

The Prince of Peace His banner spread [9]
His wayward folk to lead
From war's embattled hates and dreads,
Its bulwarked ire and greed.
O marshal us the sons of sires
Who braved the cannon's roar,
To venture all that peace requires
As they dared death for war.

Another hymn praying for light and guidance is

O God, in restless living
We lose our spirit's peace.
Calm our unwise confusion,
But Thou our clamour cease.
Let anxious hearts grow quiet,
Like pools at evening still,
Fill Thy reflected heavens
And all our spirits fill.

Another hymn of special worth in the new Methodist Hymnal is

God of Grace and God of glory.

William Hiram Foulkes (1877-)—Doctor Foulkes was born in Quincy, Michigan, the son of Reverend William and Harriet (Johnson) Foulkes. He was graduated at the College of Emporia, Kansas, from which school he received the A.B. and A. M. degrees, and a few years later the doctorate degree. After his graduation from McCormick Theological Seminary (Presbyterian) in Chicago, he took post-graduate work at New College, Edinburgh, following his ordination to the Presbyterian ministry

[9] Used by permission of the author.

in 1901. He, as a classmate of the author, was known for his ability as student and able speaker from seminary days. He first was settled as pastor at Elmira, Illinois, and subsequently had pastorates at Clinton, Iowa, Portland, Oregon, and at Rutgers Church, New York City. He became secretary of the Ministerial Relief and Sustentation of the Presbyterian Church; later was called to the Old Stone Church, Cleveland, and later pastor of the Old First Church, Newark, New Jersey. He has been a member of numerous philanthropic organizations both national and international; special radio preacher; contributing editor to the "Christian Herald" and "Christian Endeavour World."

He has also written hymn poems well worth singing and including in different modern hymnals, as

Take Thou our minds, dear Lord, we humbly pray,[10]
Give us the mind of Christ each passing day;
Teach us to know the truth that sets us free,
Grant us in all our thoughts to honour Thee.

Another hymn of courage and discipleship is

Gird us, O God, with humble might
To serve the souls who tire;
Give us stout hearts ablaze with right
To kindle far its fire.

Robert Freeman (1878-)—Doctor Freeman was born in Edinburgh, Scotland, and came to America in 1896. He later entered Allegheny College, Meadville, Pennsylvania, from which school he was graduated in 1904, and was a class-mate of the author's wife. A few years later he received the degree of D.D. from the same institution. He helped make his way while in college and seminary by supplying the pulpit of various churches, including one of the Presbyterian churches in Erie, and the Lafayette Avenue Presbyterian Church in Buffalo. He was first ordained in the Baptist Church, but later joined the Presbyterian Church and went to Pasadena, California, as pastor of the Presbyterian Church in 1911, where he has remained many years.

Doctor Freeman was an able student in college and from the first was recognized as a very promising preacher. During the war he was director of the Expeditionary Division of the Y. M. C. A. He has written "The Land I live in," (verse) and

[10] Used by permission of the author.

also works of prose. His hymn poetry has been already included in the new Presbyterian hymnal, and in "Praise and Service" by Prof. Augustine Smith. One begins,

Braving the wilds all unexplored,
Dreamers of dreams and pioneers,
Wielding the sickle, goad and sword,
They marched with the sun to the last frontiers.

But his "Hymn of Gratitude" is more of a favourite with Doctor Freeman himself, and presents a topic on which there is need of more good hymns:

Backward we look, O God of all our days,[11]
Guard of our youth, and Guide o'er all our ways,
For life, for love, for health, for work, for food,
Lord of our lives, we sing our gratitude.

Inward we look and marvel at Thy power,
Christ of our souls, who savest hour by hour;
For joyful hearts, for every righteous mood,
Lord of our lives, we sing our gratitude.

The third and fourth verses logically follow with first lines, opening, "Forward we look"; and "Upward we look." Also his hymn of praise is carefully written:

For Thy mercy ay pursuing[12]
Through the winding ways of years;
For Thy grace our souls enduring
'Gainst the tumult of our fears;
For Thy patience with our crudeness,
Thy forgiveness toward our ways;
Hear, O hear us, God of Goodness,
Hear in heaven Thy children praise.

For the order of creation,
Law in earth, in air, and sea;
For the ever sure foundation,
Universal verity;
For the tides that ne'er betray Thee,
Dawns that never fail the days,
Hear, O God of Truth, we pray Thee,
Dear in heaven Thy children praise.

[11] Used by permission of the author. [12] *Ibid.*

Marion Franklin Ham (1867-)—Born at Herveysburg, Ohio, son of George Wilson Ham, educated in the common schools, he married Louise Jenkins of Lexington, Kentucky, in 1902. He entered the Unitarian ministry in 1897; was pastor of All Souls' Church, Chattanooga, Tennessee, from 1897-1905, and later was at First Church, Dallas, Texas. He next became pastor of the Christian Union Church, Reading, Massachusetts, in 1909.

He is the author of "The Golden Shuttle," a book of poems, "The Mountebank in the Pulpit," kitchen stories in Negro dialect for public reading. He contributed hymns for "The Standard Hymnal and Songs of the Spirit," including hymns and poems of religious nature. His hymn of discipleship is

O Lord of life, Thy Kingdom is at hand,
Blest reign of love and liberty and light,
Time long foretold by seers of every land,
The cherished dream of watchers through the night.

Another one is

I hear Thy voice, within the silence speaking
Above earth's din it rises, calm and clear,
Whatever goal my wayward will is seeking,
Its whispered message tells me Thou art near.

John Haynes Holmes (1879-)—Born in Philadelphia, graduated from Harvard in 1902, he received his S.T.B. in 1904. Later he was given the degree of D.D. in 1930 from the Jewish Institute of Religion. He was ordained in 1904 by the Third Religious Society (Unitarian), Dorchester, Massachusetts. He became pastor of the Church of the Messiah in New York in 1907. He has been president of the Unitarian Fellowship for Social Justice. He was a director of American Civil Liberties Union. It was in 1919, just following the World War, that he left the Unitarian fellowship and became an independent, and his church with him also left the Unitarian fold. This action followed his travels in Russia, as one of the first observers of the Soviet régime.

Doctor Holmes is the author of various publications on problems of the day and on religious topics. But he will be better known for his acceptable religious poetry. His best hymn probably is

O God, whose love is over all[13]
The children of Thy grace,
Whose rich and tender blessings fall
On every age and place;
Hear Thou the songs and prayers we raise
In eager joy to Thee,
And teach us as we sound Thy praise
In all things Thee to see:

To see Thee in the sun by day,
And in the stars by night,
In waving grass and ocean spray,
And leaves and flowers bright;
To hear Thy voice, like spoken word
In every breeze that blows,
In every song of every bird
And every brook that flows:

To see Thee in each quiet home,
Where faith and love abide,
In school and church where all may come
To seek Thee side by side:
To see Thee in each human life,
Each struggling human heart,
Each path by which in eager strife
Men seek the better part.

Another almost or equally worthy hymn which should be regularly sung throughout, but of which space only permits mention, is

The voice of God is calling
Its summons unto men,
As once He spoke in Zion
So now He speaks again.

Shephard Knapp (1873-)—Doctor Knapp is a clergyman, the son of Shephard Knapp, and was graduated from Columbia University in 1894. He received his B.D. at Yale in 1897. Later he received the degree of D.D. from New York University. In 1897 he was ordained to the ministry in the Congregational Church and became pastor of the Congregational Church in Southington, Connecticut. Four years later he became assistant pastor of the Brick Presbyterian Church in New York City. Later he accepted

[13] Used by permission of the author.

the call to the Central Congregational Church in Worcester, Massachusetts, where he has continued to reside. He has been elected trustee of the Worcester Polytechnical Institute, Memorial Hospital and Worcester Public Library. Doctor Knapp served as Y. M. C. A. secretary in France during the World War. He is the author of a history of the Brick Presbyterian Church, and "On the Edge of the Storm," and has written stories in verse.

Among his hymns found in some new hymnals, his chief one is

Lord God of Hosts, whose purpose never swerving
Leads toward the day of Jesus Christ Thy Son,
Grant us to march among Thy faithful legions,
Armed with Thy courage till the world is won.

Doctor Knapp also arranged a poem by Robert Louis Stevenson for hymn use:

Thy people, Lord of many lands and nations,
In evening praise are met to wait Thy will.
Weak men and women, living by Thy patience:
Be very patient still.

Milton Smith Littlefield (1864-1934)—The son of Milton Smith Littlefield, he was a clergyman in New York City. He was in John Hopkins University 1888-89, and in Union Theological Seminary 1889 to 1892. He received the degree of D.D. from Washburn College, Topeka, Kansas, in 1915. He was assistant at Central Presbyterian Church, New York City, 1892-96; later pastor of the First Union Presbyterian Church, New York City. Then he went to Bay Ridge Presbyterian Church in Brooklyn. Some years later, in 1921, he became pastor of the Union Evangelical Church, Corona, Long Island. He held membership in the American Geographic Society and The Hymn Society of America. He was the compiler of "The School Hymnal" and other hymn books; also a lecturer on hymnology.

The first two verses of his hymn of conflict and discipleship follow:

O Son of Man, Thou madest known,
Thro' quiet work in shop and home,
The sacredness of common things,
The chance of life that each day brings.

O Workman true, may we fulfil
In daily life our Father's will,
In duty's call Thy call we hear
To fuller life, thro' work sincere.

His morning hymn has also special merit:

Come, O Lord, like morning sunlight,
Making all life new and free,
For the daily task and challenge,
May we rise renewed in Thee.

Earl Bowman Marlatt (1892-)—A teacher of philosophy, born in Columbus, Indiana, son of the Rev. Abram Newton Marlatt, he received his A.B. degree from DePauw University, Greencastle, Indiana, in 1912, S.T.B., Boston University, 1922, and Ph.D. from the same institution in 1929. He took postgraduate work at the University of Berlin and Oxford University, and is unmarried. He has been professor in Boston University since 1925.

Doctor Marlatt was the winner of the Golden Flower May Day Poetry Tournament in Boston in 1925. He is a member of the American Philosophic Association and of the New England Poetry Association and various other societies. He is a member of the Indiana Conference of the Methodist Episcopal Church. He is author of "Chapel Windows" (poems) and "Protestant Saints." He was associate editor with Prof. H. Augustine Smith of the "American Student Hymnal." One of his hymns begins,

Spirit of Life, in this new dawn
Give us the faith that follows on,
Letting Thine all-pervading pow'r
Fulfil the dream of this high hour.

Another of his, challenging our loyalty and courage, is

"Are ye able," said the Master,
"To be crucified with me?"
"Yea," the sturdy dreamers answered,
"To the death we follow Thee."

Refrain

"Lord, we are able." Our spirits are Thine.
Remould them, make us, like Thee, divine.
Thy guiding radiance above us shall be
A beacon to God, to love and loyalty.

John Masefield (1874-)—Doctor Masefield is the present Poet Laureate of England. In his youth he worked at various humble positions. He came to America as a young man, almost penniless, and secured menial jobs in New York. At the same time he read and studied, till at last his writings became recognized, and he climbed up the ladder from poverty and humility to distinction both as novelist and poet.

His varied publications include "Salt Water Ballads," "Captain Margaret," "Multitude and Solitude," "The Everlasting Mercy," "Sard Harker," "The Coming of Christ," novels, plays and poems.

Probably his best known hymn is the one already mentioned, taken from "The Everlasting Mercy":

O Christ who holds the open gate,
O Christ who drives the furrow straight.

Another poem, which has been adapted as a hymn, is

Sing, men and angels, sing; [14]
For God, our life and King,
Has given us light and spring
And morning breaking.

William Pierson Merrill (1867-)—Doctor Merrill was born in Orange, New Jersey; studied at Rutgers College and at the Union Theological Seminary. From both these foundations he received later the D.D. degree. He was ordained to the Presbyterian ministry in 1890; held charges at Philadelphia; Sixth Church, Chicago; and since 1911, the Brick Church, New York. A preacher of note, he has published several books that have wide acceptance: "Faith Building," "Faith and Sight," "Footings for Faith," "Christian Internationalism," "The Common Creed of Christians," "The Freedom of the Preacher," "Liberal Christianity."

Doctor Merrill's outstanding hymn is [15]

Rise up, O men of God!
  Have done with lesser things;
Give heart and soul and mind and strength,
  To serve the King of kings.

[14] Used by permission of the Macmillan Company.
[15] Used by permission of the author.

Rise up, O men of God!
His kingdom tarries long:
Bring in the day of brotherhood,
And end the night of wrong.

Rise up, O men of God!
The Church for you doth wait,
Her strength unequal to her task;
Rise up and make her great!

Lift up the cross of Christ!
Tread where His feet have trod:
As brothers of the Son of Man,
Rise up, O men of God.

Another fine hymn of Doctor Merrill's is

Not alone for mighty empire,
Stretching far o'er land and sea,
Not alone for bounteous harvests,
Lift we up our hearts to Thee.

Doctor Merrill has also arranged hymns from earlier sonnets, as his

Lord, what a change within us one short hour
Spent in Thy presence will prevail to make.
What heavy burdens from our bosoms take,
What parchèd grounds refresh as with a shower!

Frank Mason North (1850-1935)—A New York clergyman, born in that city, eighty-seven years ago, the son of Charles Carter and Elizabeth Mason-North, he received his A.B. from Wesleyan University, his A.M. in 1875, his D.D. in 1894 and his LL.D. in 1918. He was ordained a Methodist Episcopal minister, and was pastor at Florida, New York, and other rural New York parishes. Later he served Calvary Methodist Episcopal Church, New York City, which was erected during his pastorate, and still later was pastor at Middletown, Connecticut, until 1892.

Doctor North became Corresponding Secretary of the New York City Church Extension and Missionary Society, and later Corresponding Secretary of the Board of Foreign Missions of the Methodist Episcopal Church, and held other responsible positions in his Communion.

Probably his most conspicuous labour was his doing more than any other man to found the Federal Council of Churches of Christ in America, over a quarter of a century ago, when it was a difficult task at that time to bring together such different bodies of conflicting beliefs, and persuade them to adopt high ground and unite on a social service platform. He wrote the first social creed for the Federal Council which called for advanced teachings on social justice, which are now beginning to be more realized. He was president of the Council for four years.

On the twenty-fifth anniversary of its founding, when Doctor North was eighty-three years old, he was unable to attend the anniversary celebration in Washington, but listened by radio to the proceedings, to President Roosevelt's speech, heard his name honoured, and heard the singing of his most famous poem on Christian social service:

Where cross the crowded ways of life,
Where sound the cries of race and clan,
Above the noise of selfish strife,
We hear Thy voice, O Son of Man.

Written in 1903 in New York City, it has become one of our greatest social service hymns. Another one is in the new Methodist Hymnal:

O Master of the waking world
Who hast the nations in Thy heart.

John Oxenham—We do not know the date of Oxenham's birth in England, but his leading religious lyric was written in 1908, "In Christ there is no east or west." This spiritual idea is somewhat in contrast to another modern English poet's familiar lines:

Oh, East is West, and West is East, and never
the twain shall meet,
Till earth and sky stand presently
at God's great judgment seat.

Oxenham's hymn mentioned above,[16] Prof. H. Augustine Smith tells us, is taken from the "Pageant of Darkness and Light," which was widely produced throughout England and America. He wrote the whole text which contains also noble lines, as the "Livingstone Lament," the Hindu prayers, and the "Processional of Nations," beginning,

[16] *Lyric Religion,* D. Appleton-Century Company, 1931.

Through tribulations and distress
They come,
Through perils great and bitterness,
Through persecutions pitiless
They come.

Oxenham received his university training at Victoria University, Manchester. He entered the business world, travelled much in Europe and America. He went to the south with a view to orange growing and farming. The British "Who's Who" says that "he took up writing as an alleviative and alternative from business and found it much more enjoyable." He has since written many novels and various books in prose on religious subjects, such as "The Hidden Years" (1925); "The Splendour of the Dawn" or "Cross Roads" (1930); "Christ and the Third Wise Man" and "The Man Who Would Save the World." Further writings in verse are his "Selected Poems" in one volume. He wrote a beautiful meditative hymn in 1917,

'Mid all the traffic of the ways,
Turmoils without, within,
Make in my heart a quiet place,
And come and dwell within.

The other three verses are of equal merit, and should be read or sung.

Henry Hallam Tweedy (1868-)—Doctor Tweedy was born at Binghamton, New York, son of Asa Raymond and Sarah Pratt Tweedy. He received a degree from Yale in 1891 and his M.A. degree some years later. He attended the Union Theological Seminary in New York and the University of Berlin. In 1902 he married Grace H. Lanfield of Binghamton. In 1898 he was ordained to the Congregational ministry and held successive pastorates at Plymouth Church, Utica, New York, and South Church, Bridgeport, Connecticut. In 1909 he became professor of practical theology in the Yale School of Religion. He was joint author of "Moral and Religious Training in the School and Home," "Religion and the War," "The King's Highway" series, and other volumes.

His contribution to the hymnal includes his prize hymn, chosen from a list of a thousand hymns submitted to the Hymn Society for the best modern missionary hymn in 1929, and it is set to a new tune, "Sarah," by Rhys Thomas the London organist, which tune won The Hymn Society prize in 1930. The hymn begins,

Eternal God, whose power upholds[17]
Both flower and flaming star,
To whom there is no here nor there,
No time, no near, nor far,
No alien race, no foreign shore,
No child unsought, unknown:
O send us forth, Thy prophets true,
To make all lands Thine own!

Another hymn which has already won somewhat general recognition is

O Gracious Father of mankind,
Our spirits' unseen Friend,
High heaven's Lord, our hearts' dear Guest,
To Thee our prayers ascend.

Doctor Tweedy has written another hymn on the Holy Spirit, the first verse beginning,

O Holy Spirit, making whole[18]
Thy sons in body, mind and soul,
Thou Light of life, Thou Fire Divine,
Inspire Thy Church, and make it Thine;
Till Christ shall rule the hearts of men,
And Pentecost shall come again.

Henry Van Dyke (1852-1933)—This distinguished clergyman was born in Philadelphia, the son of Henry Jackson and Henrietta (Ashmead) Van Dyke. He was graduated from the Polytechnical Institute of Brooklyn and from Princeton University in 1873, and from Princeton Seminary in 1877. The doctorate degree was conferred upon him by Princeton, Harvard and Yale. The degree of LL.D. was conferred by the University of Pennsylvania, and Geneva, Switzerland, and the D.C.L. by Oxford. Doctor Van Dyke was ordained to the Presbyterian ministry. He was made pastor of the United Congregational Church, Newport, Rhode Island, from which post he was called to the Brick Presbyterian Church in New York City, which he served for many years. He became professor of English Literature in

[17] Used by permission of The Hymn Society of America.
[18] *Ibid.*

Princeton University from 1900-23. During this time he was Moderator of the General Assembly of the Presbyterian Church in the United States; minister to Netherlands; president of the National Institute of Arts and Letters, and member of other literary societies.

He wrote a large number of books, many well known, on religion and literature, patriotism, travels and various other topics. So many of his books are known that it is unnecessary to enumerate them, and some have been among the "best sellers" of their day. His hymns are few, compared with the number of his other poems, and prose writings. Probably his most acceptable hymn is one on human service and brotherhood,

Jesus, Thou divine companion,
By Thy lowly human birth
Thou hast come to join the workers,
Burden bearers of the earth;
Thou, the carpenter of Nazareth,
Toiling for Thy daily food,
By Thy patience and Thy courage
Thou hast taught us toil is good.

His hymn of adoration begins,

Joyful, joyful we adore Thee,
God of glory, Lord of love,
Hearts unfold like flowers before Thee,
Hail Thee as the sun above.

Other Writers—There are other writers who are as deserving of recognition as some of those previously named, but only space is here given to list their names with mention of one of the hymns of each:

Robert Bridges, "Gird on thy sword, O man."
George W. Briggs, "Lord of all majesty and might."
Henry Sloan Coffin (arranged), "God himself is present."
Robert Davis, "I Thank Thee, Lord, for strength of arm."
Mary S. Edgar, "God who touchest earth with beauty."
Frank Fletcher, "O Son of man, our Hero."
James Gordon Gilkey, "Outside the Holy City."
Edward Grubb, "Our God, to whom we turn."
S. Ralph Harlow, "O young and fearless prophet."
Calvin W. Laufer, "We thank Thee, Lord, Thy paths."

Charles W. Littlefield, "Move on, O Church triumphant."
Sebastian W. Meyer, "We build our school on Thee, O Lord."
J. Edgar Park, "O Jesus, Thou wast tempted."
Charles H. Richards, "Our Father, Thy dear name doth show."
Athelstan Riley, "Ye watchers, and ye holy ones."
Howard C. Robbins, "Put forth, O God, Thy Spirit's might."
Jay Thomas Stocking, "O Master workman of the race."
Howard Arnold Walter, "I would be true."
Frances W. Wile, "All beautiful the march of days."

There are many others doubtless who have written worthy songs, which have not as yet gained, or may never gain, a place in the Church's public praise; still others who in the future, as in the past, will offer their hymnic work. Public praise is a characteristic feature of the followers of Christ. Christianity is more distinguished by its praise from the worship of other religions than by any other element. John Harrington Edwards says, "Infidelity has no hymnology: Atheism as a rule is musically barren: Unbelief does not praise." But to devout Christians, to whom it is not given to write immortal song, the opportunity is always present to make their daily lives praise God and glorify His holy name:

God make my life a hymn of praise,
Each day a note, each year a phrase,
With tenderness and beauty filled,
Played in the way that Thou hast willed.

Help me to play this tune for Thee,
My part in Thy great symphony,
Until the last "Amen" shall ring
With that new song the angels sing.

XIV

CAROLS — INCLUDING SPIRITUALS

HAVING considered the growth and extension of hymnody, it would seem to be a serious omission to ignore some mention of carols. To the uninformed, carols may be regarded as some later or simpler deduction from the standard type of hymn and hymn tunes. But carols are really the older type of folk song, used by the people long before the modern hymn became known. The pre-Reformation carol was the common expression of song from the mouths of the common people. In the Middle Ages the worship of the Church was in the hands of the monks and priests who produced the music, and the people had little chance to express their feelings in sacred song. Yet the people then, as always, needed the opportunity of self-expression in song. In the age of the beginning and development of the carol, the people who were deprived of this necessary natural expression would sing outside the church, and on other occasions of their activities and social life, such as pilgrimages, festivals and celebrations of various kinds, for community and family life must have music in some way if not in church. Thus there came into existence hundreds of folk songs before the Reformation Period, which were the outlet for the emotional life of the common people. Songs were composed to be sung on such occasions as at the time of washing and beginning work, undressing and house warming. "For lovers separated, for widow or widower delivered from a troublesome yoke fellow, for musicians and for most all common activities of life."

The word "carol" is from "carola" which means a ring dance. When the people began to dance, rude singers from among the people expressed in song feelings of emotion which were affecting them and those around them, or their utterances told stories in a simple and natural manner with no conscious art. How the song began is best expressed by a writer on the subject who says, "The folk song composes itself. It is the song of the people and came into being without the influence of conscious art, marked by certain peculiarities of rhythm, form and melody traceable to racial or national characteristics in subject matter." It is found in Germany, France, Russia and Italy; also in the Scandinavian countries; in Germany among the early shepherds. In England it had the dramatic quality of folk song, as in France. So the folk songs, composed by the people, were everywhere marked by certain qualities. They are frequently vividly pictorial. The words are always simple and concrete. The scenes described and experiences are related. The language is the common dialect of the people, and not the formal language of books, nor the careful diction of the educated. Like the ballad, it is usually made with a refrain, is repeated over and over, and soon memorized. The carol tells the story in much detail and frequently runs into many verses.

As to its music, the rhythm is an important element. The occasions which have called out the largest body of folk song have been the periods of religious revival and the Church Year festivals when touched by the graphic re-telling of Bible stories and the presenting of mystery plays. In the song of the donkey, the child escaped the cruel massacre of the infants, safely with his parents on the donkey upon which he rode. The people anxiously wait to see the donkey and the parents and child. In their emotions, one exclaims, "There comes the donkey." "How beautiful he is," another shouts. While another adds, "How steady and strong, he will get them down to Egypt." So putting the exclamations together we have the story. "Out of the east, the donkey comes, beautiful and very strong, well-fitted for his burden, Hail, Sir Ass, Hail!" Or to illustrate further, the fictitious naming of the Ohio River in America, the writer heard when a boy along the banks of the Ohio. The story says one Indian swam across the river and then exclaimed "O," a second Indian swam across and uttered "Hi," while the third Indian, after swimming the stream, exclaimed "O," and the fourth Indian completed the name after crossing by putting the exclamations all together, exclaiming "O-Hi-O."

The carol, as we recognize it to-day, became prevalent back in the thirteenth, fourteenth and fifteenth centuries. There were, of course, early folk songs about the Annunciation and the Birth of Jesus, and those circumstances surrounding the early life of our Lord. Yet it was twelve centuries later before the great mystic of the middle ages, St. Francis of Assisi, that we have the beginning of the carol, or at least the germ of the carol, as we understand it, also the germ of the mystery play. In the time of Francis, and preceding his birth, there was prevalent the Manichean heresy which was antagonistic to the church doctrine of the Incarnation. In order to combat this opposing influence to Christianity, St. Francis found a plan to popularize in the minds of the people a knowledge and understanding of the teaching of the Incarnation.

When in 1223 he went to Grecia to spend his Christmas-tide, he first obtained permission to have made a little manger or crib, with an ass and all the ordinary trappings of a stable, and placed these in the church to make very realistic the representation of the events of the first Christmas at Bethlehem. His followers sang on this occasion Christmas songs, describing the events of the Nativity. The whole community responded to the call of St. Francis, and the crowds poured out their hearts in praise to God and his world gift of a Son. This manger, or creche, as it is commonly called to-day, and the singing around it, was the giving of the Christmas carol, and this little tableau of St. Francis was the beginning of the mystery play.

The mystery play and miracle play also were used by the Church to teach people in an age when few people could read, by putting into play Bible stories before them. At first those plays were performed by the clergy themselves and given in Latin, when women were not permitted to play on the stage, the female parts being taken also by priests. Later when the mystery play and miracle play passed into the hands of the people, comedy scenes and buffoonery of the vulgar sort were introduced, and such amusement became popular. Sometimes the most important was the devil who acted the part of a clown. For a long time the "Feast of Fools" was performed on the Feast of the Circumcision, New Year's Day, but as it became more vulgar, Bishop Grosseteste in the thirteenth century condemned it, and by the end of the fourteenth century it had died out, and justly so.

But we should not forget the thirteenth century which has been called "the keystone of the superstructure of mediæval history" and brings in a better establishment of both language and music. In the song in praise of the cuckoo we get a glimpse of the English verse striving to make definite assertion, and the melody of its music was a distinctive advance over the music of the Latin prose. Of the carols which have come from this period we have the still popular carol, "Corde natus," used at Christmas, as translated by Doctor Neale, beginning, "Of the Father's love begotten"; also the "Tempest Adest Floridum" is a good example of the spring carol. The words of another carol, which music was in the Dorian mode, read as follows:

Gabriel's message does away
Satan's curse and evil sway;
This was wrought by Christmas day,
Therefore, sing, "Glory to the Infant King."

With the coming of the fourteenth century the carols were marked with an advance in melody, being more rhythmically perfected, and thus became more of a conscious vehicle of self-expression. At first the carols were sung as the intermezzo between scenes of the mysteries, just as the orchestra plays between acts of the modern drama. In the course of time these carol interludes became favourites of the audience. This resulted in rivalry between the actors and carol singers. However, the difficulty was soon overcome, and the players and singers were both included in the play, during the thirteenth and fourteenth centuries, by having the music produced on the stage as part of the play itself. Thus the singers came to lead the players. The age was notable for men able to assist the progress of music, counterpoint was further developed, wide impetus was given to the composition of music, and the Church shared in this development, although papal authority suppressed certain types of composition. But church musicians did not hesitate to borrow from secular melody. Yet vulgar music of this period was scarce. The age did not favour its preservation. Would that the same could be said of the miserable jazz of the 1920's and 30's! There is preserved a good cradle song melody, but set to crude words. In the country districts were found such carols as "Lullay my child" and "Slepe no more," "Lullay, lullow, lullay, my barne, slepe softly now," and others of similar type.

It was in the fifteenth century that the more authentic type of carol arose with the ballad, because people wanted to sing something less staid than the old Latin office hymn, and something more vivacious than the older plain song melodies. The carol, like the mystery play, was the freeing of the people's song from the older Puritanism which had long opposed the dance and the drama, denounced communal singing, and tried to suppress the tendency of the people to disport themselves on the occasion of festivals in the church.

This fifteenth century was the beginning of the modern era, and the period of Chaucer's influence and the spread of humanism in England. In Italy this century began with the full tide of the Renaissance, and when the famous artist Leonardo was approaching his prime. Before the century closed printed books became common, and the New World was being discovered. The early written carols were taken from the manuscripts of that century, and from the collection which Richard Hill made at the beginning of the sixteenth century which contained the "Boar's Head" carol. The earliest printed collection which has survived (and only a small part, at that) was issued in 1521 by Wynkyn de Worde, the successor of the first English printer, William Caxton, who learned the art abroad and set up the first wooden press in England about 1476.

The story-telling carol now comes to the front. Among the most famous carols of this era is the poem:

I sing of a maiden
That is mateless,
King of all Kings,
To her she chose.

Another is the famous cherry tree carol. The story of it is found in the Coventry mystery plays of the fifteenth century, although the poem as we have it to-day was probably a later work. This carol is in two parts. The first part is in the form of a dialogue between Joseph and Mary. When on their way to Bethlehem, preceding the birth of Jesus, they passed a tree loaded with cherries. Mary wished for some of the fruit and requested Joseph to pluck some cherries. Joseph bluntly refused, whereupon the tree bowed down and offered its fruit to Mary. The third, fourth and fifth stanzas are as follows:

Joseph and Mary walked
Through an orchard green,
Where were berries and cherries
As thick as might be seen.

"Oh," then bespoke Mary,
So meek and so mild,
"Pluck me one cherry, Joseph,
For I am with child."

"Oh," then bespoke Joseph
With words most unkind,
"Let him pluck the cherry
That brought thee with child."

The dialogue is continued for several more short verses, the second part being better and more solemn, and proceeds:

As Joseph was a-walking,
He heard an angel sing,
"This night shall be born
Our Heavenly King.

"He neither shall be born
In house nor in hall,
Nor in the place of Paradise,
But in an ox's stall."

The carol continued to flourish throughout the fifteenth and sixteenth centuries. In the sixteenth century, during the Elizabethan Era, poetry reached its peak, at least in quantity, if not in quality. It was a time when it was popular or customary to write almost everything in rhyme. Even the acts of Parliament were written, or written about, in poetic form. But this heyday of every-day rhymes was effectively checked when Puritanism in revised form suppressed it by the middle of the seventeenth century.

In 1624 the people of England had to keep Christmas Day as a fast because it happened to fall on the last Wednesday of the month, the day the Long Parliament had ordered to be kept as a monthly fast. Three years later the Puritan Parliament abolished Christmas and other festivals altogether. So most of the old narrative or story-telling carols were written during two and a half centuries between the death of Chaucer in 1400 and the ejection of the Rev. Robert Herrick from his parish by Oliver Cromwell's soldiers in 1647. During the remainder of the seventeenth century, and also throughout the eighteenth century, there was little recognition or knowledge of carols. Even the preservation of the former carols was mostly neglected, and about all there was produced was Tate's Christmas carol, "While shepherds watched their flocks," and Wesley's "Hark, the herald angels sing," and still later, John Byrom's "Christians, awake, salute the happy morn," written as a Christmas poem for his little daughter, which is more of a hymn than a simple carol.

The forgotten treasury of carols was not restored at the beginning of the Romantic revival, not even by Charles Dickens, the author of "A Christmas Carol," which was not in truth a carol. But the last half of the nineteenth century did bring forth a revival of carols.

The first really useful effort was by Doctor Neale and the Rev. Thomas Helmore who published a collection of twelve carols in 1853. Neale had translated some carols and hymns from a Swedish book, and Helmore adopted the tunes from the sixteenth century. To this work the following year they added twelve Easter carols, the first recognition since olden times of the carol for use at other feasts than Christmas. Thus some of the best carols were given back to the Church, both in words and music.

The next most worth-while effort to form a useful collection of carols was in 1871 when forty-two Christmas carols, new and old were given us by Rev. H. R. Bramley of Magdalen College, Oxford, and Dr. John Stainer, then organist of that college. This book came into general use, and brought into use some traditional carols with suitable music as well as modern compositions. Later they included a total of seventy carols with twenty-seven traditional ones and forty-three modern ones. While some of the poems were not the equal of Neale's collection, yet we owe to Bramley and Stainer the restoration of the carols to the Christian Church. Other efforts of production of this type of song during the last quarter of the nineteenth century were many, but did not attain to the standard of Bramley and Stainer which continued as the standard of usage.

At the first part of the twentieth century, Dr. R. G. Woodward published the "Cowley Carol Book" which contained twenty-one of Neale's carols, and this reopened the little treasury of foreign music which Neale and his assistant, Helmore, had discovered a half century before.

But after the first quarter of the twentieth century had passed, or in 1928, a more extensive and thorough treatment of the subject was published, the "Oxford Book of Carols" by Percy Dearmer of England and his two chief assistants, Vaughan-Williams and Martin Shaw. This able work contains more than two hundred carols collected from various sources, old and new, from the various countries which have produced worthwhile carols, and with music from many traditional sources; many English from different centuries, Dutch, French, German, Flemish, Spanish, Russian and other sources. Thus there has come a revival of carols in recent times but with more or less indifferent attention to this kind of praise, except to some of the nineteenth century's Christian carols. But these now most used Nativity songs of the Church are really carol hymns, or possibly better called hymn-carols. We need only look at these universally sung hymn-carols to see that they are both carol and hymnic in character, as the very familiar songs, "It came upon the midnight clear," "O little town of Bethlehem," "Silent night, holy night," "We three kings of Orient." All possess the characteristics of the carol and with hymnic element combined, especially in the closing verses they lift up their ode of praise to Almighty God. The latter mentioned came from a Pennsylvania clergyman, the Rev. J. H. Hopkins, which we, receiving by way of England, have come to regard as of English origin. Then, too, such carols as the "First Nowell" and "All my heart this night rejoices" are typical, yet even these lift up their song in the closing verses in aspiration to Christ or God. The Epiphany hymn, "Brightest and best of the sons of the morning," and the Easter hymn, "O Filii et Filiae," "O sons and daughters let us sing, the King of heaven the glorious king," are characteristically hymn-carols. The Epiphany hymn, "From the eastern mountains, pressing on they come," and "As with gladness men of old, Did the guiding star behold," begin as carols but soon turn to hymnic poetry, thus having more of the nature of hymns than of carols.

It is worthy of notice that many of the German hymns with their modern English translations in our hymnals had much of the element of the carol in their verses. The hymns of the German source mentioned in Chapter 6 have much in them which pertains to the character of the carol, as may readily be observed in reading them.

SPIRITUALS

We should not close the chapter without including brief mention of the folk song of the Negro, which in its original simplicity of character is at least closely related to the carol. Like the early carol of the thirteenth and fourteenth centuries, the origin of the spiritual among the Southerners is found when women sing as their backs bend up and down over wash tubs, or as their hoes chop out the weeds from the growing corn; and when the strong men cut the timber in the river swamps, keeping time when they swing their axes or with the separate motions of their crosscut saws. Even prisoners in the chain gang sing to the clink of their shackles when swinging their picks into the ditches along the roadside. These Negroes are ever ready to thus express their emotions, and the folk songs are conceived without conscious art, and the songs are marked by racial peculiarities in rhythm, form and harmony.

They are usually expressed in the style of simple words and narrative phrases and scriptural story references, expressing the common emotions of the Negro race. More often, however, they are produced in the sad and pathetic strain, rather than in the cheerful utterance of the older carols. Their lives have more of hardship and discouragement and struggle, which naturally produced the emotions of longing and pathos. The more fruitful periods of their composition have been those of the religious revival and the camp-meetings. They live more in the hope of the joys of the world to come, rather than of the joys of the past or of the present world. A large proportion of their songs are the "Spirituals." After their conversion it was regarded as their duty to sing religious songs, and they lived close to the thoughts of death and heaven. It was only natural for them when they saw a child upon a fruit tree to think of a scriptural parable and sing, "My brother sittin' in the tree of life." We may call their conception childish, otherwise their ideas could not be so simple and vivid.

Mr. Moton, the successor of Booker T. Washington as president of Tuskegee, has spoken of the spiritual as being "the life of the soul, manifesting itself in rude words, wild strains, and curious but beautiful harmonies." These were based on any vivid and dramatic Bible story to which they were keenly alive, as "Didn't old Pharaoh get lost in the Red Sea," or "Didn't my Lord deliver Daniel." The very words called up whole scenes before the eyes of their vivid imagination. The scene of Noah and the ark was expressed in the spiritual, "Oh, it rained forty days, forty nights 'out stoppin'; Noah wasn't busy 'bout de rain stop drippin', till he hear de angels moanin', didn't it rain, tell me, my Lord, didn't it rain."

Almost every situation in life and story interested these humble people and inspired their folk song. But the thoughts of death took strong hold on their imaginations, and so we have many spirituals which we may call the "Dying Songs," among which are some of the most impressive folk songs in all the world. Examples are "Swing Low, sweet chariot, Comin' for to carry me home," or

Dig my grave narrow and long;
Make my coffin long and strong,
Bright angels to my feet, bright angels to my head,
Bright angels to carry me when I'm dead.

A better known spiritual with its beautiful melody (not to be confused with "Old Man River") is

O deep river, my home is over Jordan,
Lord, I want to cross over into camp ground,
Oh, don't you want to go to that gospel feast,
That promised land where all is peace?
O deep river.

Almost every civilized country is credited with having its own folk song. But America's most characteristic folk song has been chosen from the class of the Negro spirituals. Some of these are great favourites with all classes of people to-day. Many people have heard with much pleasure such favourite songs with their sweet melodies as "Trouble here," "A Union Band," "Nobody knows the trouble I've seen"; also

I want to be ready, I want to be ready,
I want to be ready, to walk in Jerusalem,
Just like John.

Others are "Couldn't hear nobody pray," "I've got a robe, you've got a robe," "I ain't gwine study war no more," "I want to be ready," "Little David," and various spirituals which are used, among which is the popular one,

Roll, Jordan roll, roll Jordan, roll,
I want to go to heaven when I die
To hear Jordan roll.
O brothers, you ought t'have been there,
Yes, yes, my Lord, a-sittin' in the kingdom,
To hear Jordan, Jordan roll.[1]

Moreover, it should be kept in mind that the music of these spirituals is as unusual as the words. The spiritual has distinctive rhythm and harmony as well as melody. The Negro was endowed with a great musical gift. The spiritual stems from African music and the rhythm is fundamental in African songs. Yet the American spiritual is more developed in melody, and especially in harmony.

The spirituals today are regarded by some as representing the true folk song of America, together with other Southern songs by Stephen C. Foster, such as "My Old Kentucky Home" and "Old Black Joe."

And "Were you there when they crucified my Lord?"

Not only have the spirituals their pleasing melodies but also their soft harmonies which arrest the attention. The Rev. Dr. Earle Cochran of Los Angeles says, "Part of the miracle of their birth lies in the ability of the Negro to improvise. He has an unusual sense of harmony." In the South the Negroes during leisure hours practised their music together and thereby instinctively discovered and developed close harmony.

It is also to be continually borne in mind in the rendition of these songs that it is very important to catch "the swing" of the spiritual in the peculiar rhythm of the melody, else much of the effect is lost. It is often difficult for capable musicians to succeed in rendering such rhythms. The very distinctive rhythm, melody and harmony—all three basic elements—are well illustrated in the music of spirituals, such as,

Steal away, steal away,
Steal away to Jesus.
Steal away, steal away home,
I ain't got long to stay here.

For Further Reading

a) on Carols

The Story of the Carol, Edmonstoune Duncan.

Carols; their Origin, Music, and *Connection with Mystery Plays,* William J. Phillips.

Excursions in Musical History, Helena A. Dickinson.

"Introduction" to *Oxford Book of Carols,* Percy Dearmer.

Christmas and New Year's Songs from *Folk Songs of Many Peoples* (Womens Press, Y. W. C. A.).

Christmas Carols from Various Countries, C. and H. Dickinson.

Christmas Carols, New and Old, Music edited by Sir John Stainer.

b) on Spirituals

"Negro Music and Negro Minstrelsy" in *American History and Encyclopoedia of Music.*

Folk Songs of the American Negro, John Wesley Work.

On the Trail of the Negro Folk Song, Dorothy Scarborough.

Spirituals, Doctor Dett, Hampton Institute, Hampton, Va.

American Negro Spirituals, James W. Johnson.

XV

THE MUSICAL SETTING OF THE HYMNS

WE NOW take up the musical aspect, or the second half of hymnology. But the scope of this book will not permit going into the historical development of church music through the centuries as we have traced the growth of sacred poetry. (There are many good books on the musical aspects of church music. Those wishing to pursue the musical side should read one or more of such volumes.) We must now confine our efforts to the consideration of some general principles and illustrations.

It is more difficult to write about hymn tunes than about the hymns themselves; at any rate, it is more technical. Then, too, people's taste for music seems to differ more than that for religious poetry. There is less agreement on the character and quality of sacred music.

Adverse opinions of musicians seem to complicate the proper estimate of music. Certainly one, travelling from place to place, may hear all grades of sacred music by all kinds of singers and players. The rendition of singers and organists may mar a good tune, or make a rather poor tune sound sweet and beautiful. A good musical composition set to a mediocre hymn may raise it to fame and widespread usage, while on the other hand many a good hymn has been unable to survive because of the lack of a helpful tune. The tune therefore becomes of vital importance. It is the channel through which collectively we offer our praise to God in sacred worship. It is not enough that the music appeal to mere human ears, but it should be worthy of presentation to God, possessing that dignity and reverential tone which belongs to the worship of the Christian Church. Doctor Lutkin says, "Fundamental worth, artistic merit, historic associations, fitness as to time and place, practicability, are all factors which should be given due consideration in the selection of tunes." This should be done because of the usefulness and help of hymn-singing to the propagation of the Christian religion over the world. We should not overlook the fact that singing is one of the best grounds of both unity and uniformity among Christian bodies.

The music, therefore, becomes a very important part of hymnody. It is not too much to say that the use of a good hymn depends fully one-half upon the tune. But we should not expect the music to carry the burden of inadequate words of praise, yet we should not over-emphasize the music to the exclusion of the substance of the teaching contained in the words. As in a previous chapter we gave warning against thinking only of the music, as so many people mistakenly do, while giving little consideration to what words are united with the music. Some composers and singers are too ready to set music to any text without sufficient regard to the words, and in so doing they only handicap themselves. Walter Kramer, editor of "Musical America," says, "A fine song can only result from a fine poem, for the music stems from the poem in the composing of art-songs. Thus the composer (or singer) cannot rise above his poem."

The late Dr. Peter C. Lutkin said, "In the practical consideration of hymn-singing, the text is of first importance. If a hymn is sung for the mere pleasure that the tune gives as music, the whole object of hymn-singing is frustrated."

Years ago there was a paucity of good hymn tunes; consequently, one tune was often used for several hymns or psalms of the same metre, as in the days of exclusive psalm singing and early English hymn-singing. But now with an increased quantity of original tunes and many adaptations from older and classical sources, we expect a tune for nearly every hymn.

The desirable thing is for each hymn to have its own tune with which it is united and the union to be universally recognized. So much so that the mere mention of the first line of the poem calls to mind the melody. On the other hand, the humming of the melody calls to mind the words to which the melody is united in the hymn book. This ideal "marriage" ought to obtain and a divorce should not be conceded unless for very weighty cause. This faculty of a tune in recalling words was one of Luther's arguments in favour of congregational singing.

Sir John Stainer and the late Horatio Parker, among our good composers, would not substitute a new tune for an old one which was suitably "married" to its hymn. It is said that Dykes never wrote a new tune for a hymn already suitably provided for. Such should be the moral relationship of one to the other. On the other hand, we should not fail to make exceptions to this general principle. Sometimes a good old hymn may fall into disuse because its tune has become worn out or has ceased to have its former appeal, in which case a new and more fitting tune should be supplied to give the sacred lyric continued usefulness. Sometimes very worthy hymns are too little used only because their music is inadequate. Sometimes also copyright restriction interferes with obtaining the most suitable musical setting.

One of the best American hymns failed of recognition for a time, or until it was finally set to Calkins's "Waltham," then "Fling out the banner, let it float" came into its own. Not until set to "The Church's one Foundation," did "Aurelia" help to make the hymn famous. On the contrary, one of the most frequently sung hymns to-day, Newman's "Lead, kindly Light," would never have gained its fame had it not been for Dykes's favoured tune, which fact Newman himself was fair enough to recognize (as stated in a previous chapter) and gave Dykes the greater credit which was rightly deserved.

One of Lyte's best hymns, "Jesus, I my cross have taken," and Harbach's "Jesus, I live to Thee" have not the usage they should have because so many hymn books fail to furnish adequate music, while Lyte's "Abide with me" is most popular to-day, not only because it is a fine lyric, but also because of Monk's splendid tune with which it has long been united. Hopkins's alternate tune "Benediction," although a beautiful tune, is not so suitable to Lyte's hymn, and besides its usage would break the long and happy "marriage" of the former tune to the old hymn of "Abide with me."

Again it should be fully recognized that the music must be appropriate to the character and meaning of the poem. "Onward, Christian soldiers" has its appropriate martial music by Sullivan. The Christian hymn, "All my heart this night rejoices," has its appropriate music by Horatio Parker. The solemn prayerful hymn of Isaac Watts, "O God, our help in ages past," has its fitting tune by William Croft.

The meditative Holy Communion hymn by Osler, "O God, unseen but ever near," is beautifully expressed in the music of Gower's "Meditation," which some hymn book compilers have apparently not yet discovered, although the tune "St. Flavian" from Day's "Psalter" is also a suitable tune to the foregoing words.

Thus when due consideration of the words is properly taken into account, the music suitable to express the text becomes obvious to the composer or compiler of hymn tunes, unless judgment and taste are found wanting. Moreover, the statement, made years ago by the late Peter C. Lutkin, also applies here, when he was expressing a reason for the poor quality of church music at that time, "that then men who composed the music were not inspired by the words, and without the religious feeling one could not expect music for the Church."

Furthermore, if the tune does not respond to the inner meaning of the hymn, it is a misfit and a failure. When we begin to fit music and words together we are at once concerned with our available sources of supply. It is interesting to note that just as the classic poets have given us few hymnic poems for our hymnals, so the classic composers have in the past not written much music for our hymnals, although we have more help from the latter class. The majority of the great composers were either not church musicians at all or were Roman Catholic. Bach is the outstanding exception. Many of our composers of fine hymn tunes have not been distinguished in other works of composition. Among the classic composers of the eighteenth and nineteenth centuries only a few wrote expressly for sacred words. From the works of Handel and Haydn arrangements for hymns were made by later musicians, and Bach did much by harmonizations and arrangements of the chorales. Some well-known composer said, "With these few exceptions none of the great composers have written hymn tunes," for the reason they have not been acquainted with this kind of composition. Lightfoot tells us that Mendelssohn was once appealed to by an enterprising compiler for a new "long metre tune." The famous composer courteously replied, "I am sorry I cannot write exactly what you desire, but I do not know what a long measure psalm tune means, and there is no one to whom I can apply for explanation."

In more recent times we have put to use more than a few arrangements and adaptations from the famous composers, not only the above-mentioned composers, but also such as Beethoven, Mozart, Schumann, Mendelssohn or others.

When we begin the subject of sacred music which is sacred only when based on sacred association of words, or set to sacred words (otherwise the music may be called secular), we find that sacred music has come through various developments during centuries of time. Our modern music system roots in Greek musical theory; and some of our modern hymns have come from that source, as we have seen.

Sacred music passed through certain changes and developments under St. Ambrose of Milan and Gregory the Great. Other changes and developments came in successive periods down through the centuries, until Palestrina and Bach, when modern hymn tunes were started.

We cannot take up English tune composers without first acknowledging our debt to preceding sources, as the plain song, folk song and German chorales.

To have an outline of the kinds of hymn tunes in use to-day, here is presented an outline division (slightly modified) by Dr. Charles N. Boyd, instructor in Church music at the Western Theological Seminary, Pittsburgh.

I. Plain Song, or Gregorian Tunes.
II. German Chorales.
III. Psalm Tunes.
IV. Early English Hymn Tunes.
V. Nineteenth Century Hymn Tunes.
VI. American Tunes.
VII. Recent Tunes and Folk-song Arrangements.

Taking up the first or earliest type, we now consider plain song.

PLAIN SONG

The earliest type of music which concerns the Christian Church is the plain song, or Gregorian melodies. Not until the tenth century was there any stable system of musical notation. The Gregorian is regarded by many musical authorities as based on the Greek scales, probably influenced to a small extent by the earlier Hebrew and Roman music. The early or true form of plain song has no bars or measures. The time and accent is not in set form but verbal, depending on natural inflection and recitative speaking voice. Eventually it was written in a notation of square notes on a four line clef; but modern influence, with constant observance of rhythm, has modified the old music and given it accent and time, and some of it in use has been harmonized also. But it was first written long before the art of harmony came into use, and its singing was in unison without accompying instruments.

At first plain song had several notes to each syllable; later two or more notes were slurred to one syllable, and this principle has become a characteristic of plain song. For a long time this style of music was largely confined to the Roman Catholic Church and to a smaller extent in Anglican churches, but is now being sung in Protestant churches. These melodies have often been regarded as awkward and representative of the beginning of modern music. This is untrue and their variety and highly developed art of melody have gained the attention of various musical groups. To-day modern hymnals have a number of such tunes, and they are often written without measures of fixed time, and the time is determined by the utterance of the words. They are well-suited to solemn and reverent worship. These old melodies have lasting qualities and some have come down to us and are in general use.

For example, the "Veni Emmanuel" to "O come, O come, Emmanuel" is a general favourite for singing. It is usually ascribed to the French Missal of the thirteenth century, but is not a pure specimen of plain song melody. A more authentic song is "Veni, Creator Spiritus," ("Come, Holy Ghost, our souls inspire"), and is an early Sarum plain song. Other interesting melodies of this kind are "Jam Lucis," to "Before the ending of the day," and "Orientis Partibus," a mediæval French plain song. "O Filii et Filiae" to "O Sons and daughters, let us sing" is a fifteenth century French tune of wide recognition. "O Quanta Qualia" to "O what their joy and their glory must be" is another example which is arranged in measure and four-four time. Other examples are "Corde Natus" and "A Solis Ortus." Many plain song melodies in modern use are barred, which is a modern addition.

THE GERMAN CHORALE

This type of music came into existence about the time our present system of harmony was getting well started. Martin Luther, a noted hymn writer, tune composer and arranger, was the promotor of this type of tune, which ranks high in the Protestant world, and in later simplified form is well-adapted to congregational music. It is singable, expressive and melodious, and is gradually increasing in present-day usage. At the time of the Reformation it was the custom to develop a rather long composition from a theme which was often either a plain song or folk song melody. These themes were often developed according to set formulas. At first stiff and mechanical, they soon became less stiff and lesser in range for the average voice, and finally evolved into masterly harmony by the famous John Sebastian

Bach, and so became the foundation of modern hymn music. Bach usually put the melody in the soprano. But the earlier custom in part music was to put the melody in the tenor. Ravenscroft's Psalter shows the tenor as the melody.

The chorale conforms more nearly to our modern scales and method of harmony, and so is easily learned and appreciated more than the old plain song music, and as also the latter, is well suited to unison singing.

Luther and his contemporaries arranged the chorales in their day from folk song and from the Roman Catholic liturgy, and Luther and his contemporaries added many original melodies. As the emotional element in music was not far developed at that time, the song was an austere and weighty matter.

The most famous of these melodies of Luther's time is "Ein' Feste Burg," ("A mighty Fortress is our God"). The tune is also ascribed to Luther, but may have been a composite adaptation and arrangement of his own and used by Meyerbeer in his opera, "Les Huguenots."

Many other chorales come down to us which are all of a stately and dignified character, possessing vigorous strength and far removed from a weak or sentimental melody.

"Nun Danket Alle Gott" ("Now thank we all our God") was composed by Johann Crüger about 1648, or a century after Luther's time, and was used by Mendelssohn in his cantata, "Hymn of Praise."

The "Passion Chorale" ("O sacred head, now wounded" or "surrounded") was composed originally by Hans Leo Hassler, and adapted and harmonized by Bach and used by him in his great "Passion According to St. Matthew." An earlier chorale of the sixteenth century is "Allein Gott in der Höh sei Ehr," the metrical version of *Gloria in Excelsis,* was written both text and music by the Rev. Nicolaus Decius.

"Wachet Auf" ("Wake, awake, for night is flying") was written by Rev. Philipp Nicolai, and also adapted and arranged by Bach.

"Vigili et Sancti" ("Ye watchers and ye holy ones"), called "Cologne" from "Geistleiche Kirchengesang," is readily appreciated by nearly everyone, and should always be sung in unison, and impressiveness is added if the Alleluia refrain is sung antiphonally.

"St. Theodulph" ("All glory, laud and honour") was originally written in five-part harmony and composed by Melchior Teschner, first published in 1615. It is well-known and a general favourite.

"Worgan" ("Jesus Christ is risen to-day"), written about the same time as the last-named above, is a favourite Easter melody, of unknown origin, often ascribed, probably incorrectly, to one named Worgan.

Other valuable tunes of German chorale type are "Salzburg" by Rosenmuller; "Henlein" ("Forty days and forty nights"), one of the few tunes in minor key taken over in American books, and other later tunes, as "Winchester New," "Munich," "Stuttgart." The "Austrian National Hymn" by Haydn, so much sung to-day to "Glorious things of thee are spoken," is not a chorale but is of folk song origin.

PSALM TUNES

Psalm tunes may be generally characterized as the tunes which were used in the psalters promoted by the followers of Calvin in Switzerland, England, Scotland and Holland. These books date from 1539 to approximately 1700. Calvin's theory was that the singing should be unisonal, not harmonized, and that one note only should be given to each syllable of the text. The melodies came from the countries involved, sometimes from plain song or even secular originals, and there was a considerable interchange of melodies between the countries, perhaps more marked in England than elsewhere. For example, Ravenscroft's Psalter of 1621 classifies a group of tunes as follows: English, 22; Scotch, 7; Welsh, 5; French and German. From the purely melodic originals harmonized versions were presently provided, the melody at first assigned to the tenor, but the Calvinistic theory of one note to a syllable persisted.

From the Geneva Psalter, 1552, we have such tunes as the "Old 100th," the "Old 107th," the "Old 124th" and the "Old 22nd." The "Old 100th" is ascribed to Louis Bourgeois and is widely known. The "Old 107th" is from the Scottish Psalter but is based on the Geneva Psalter. The "Old 124th" has its melody taken from the Geneva Psalter written about 1552. The "Old 22nd," written shortly after the former tune, is from the Anglo-Genevan Psalter.

Among other old psalter tunes is the "120th" taken from the Este Psalter, written near the close of the sixteenth century. Another good tune from Este's Psalter is "Winchester Old" in 1592, and now often sung to Nahum Tate's hymn, "While shepherds watched their flocks by night"; also the Cheshire tune, set to words taken from Day's Psalter, has much of the minor strain.

"Song 67" by the English composer, Orlando Gibbons, and arranged by Henry Smart, is sung to the 96th Psalm in the Scottish Psalter.

"Dundee" is a very well-known tune taken from the Scottish Psalter, composed in 1615 and set to various metrical psalms and hymns.

"Wigtown" is also from the Scottish Psalter, a few years later in origin, and is in the new Presbyterian Hymnal, but much less known than "Dundee."

"Southwell" from Damon's Psalter, 1579, is commonly known, but is an easy melody with limited range and easy progressions, and is a "short" tune for four lines in contradistinction to the eight-line tunes which were then in use.

EARLY ENGLISH TUNES

The first of the early English tunes were much like the psalm tunes of the same period, but were different from the early chorales in that they were not so "picturesque" in outline, and were not so extended in range, and not so varied in character. Like the psalm tunes, they were syllabic in form, i.e., one note to each and every syllable, and regular in rhythm, each note having the same value in time. They not only were simple in structure, but also had rugged and lasting qualities, which have kept the better ones in use till the present time. They did not have the florid suavity of the later English tunes. They were suited to the character of their texts and thus fittingly interpreted words of their setting.

The oldest English tune in common use to-day is "Tallis' Canon," 1567, to the evening hymn, "All praise to Thee, my God, this night." It is a canon which means that the melody starts with a given voice, and after a few notes another voice begins the same melody and follows the first one, the whole harmonizing together. In Tallis's tune the tenor is the follower and not the leader in modern editions. Later we have such English tunes as "St. Anne's" by William Croft ("O God, our help in ages past") which is one of the best examples of a good hymn tune. It is regular in time and syllabic, and has also the character of the post-Reformation chorales.

Another tune by the same composer is "Hanover" ("Ye servants of God, your Master proclaim"). It is of like character to "St. Anne's." From the same period we have a tune from the "Lyra Davidica" to the Easter hymn, "Jesus Christ is risen to-day."

"Wareham" by William Knapp ("Great God, we sing Thy mighty hand") is from this period, as also "Amsterdam" ("Rise, my soul, and stretch thy wings") by James Nares from the "Foundery Collection" of 1742. A little later, during the latter part of the eighteenth century, a special type of tune was produced. These retained the vigour and strength of the preceding tunes and yet added the greater freedom in melody and larger variety of rhythm. Among these were such representative tunes as "St. Thomas" ("I love Thy Kingdom, Lord") from Aaron Williams Collection, or Darwall's 148th ("Shall hymns of grateful love") by John Darwall in 1770.

The tune "Melcombe" by Samuel Webbe in 1782 ("New every morning is the love") is one of the finest constructed tunes and is set to other hymns besides Keble's "Morning Hymn." "Truro" is a favourite old tune set to different hymns in different hymnals, and probably best suited to "Lift up your heads, ye mighty gates" by Charles Burney, 1789, and taken from "Psalmodia Evangelica." Another very worthy tune, "Yorkshire," which should be called "Stockport," by John Wainright set to a hymn, "Christians, awake, salute the happy morn," should be used with some other newer and more vital text and not be lost to the hymnal because its words are often omitted from the newer hymnals.

"Adeste Fideles," or the "Portuguese Hymn," was published or republished the latter part of the eighteenth century. Its origin is unknown and it was in use in Roman Catholic churches before that time. This is a great favourite and was "ahead of its time" in its flowing melody and slurred notes.

"Miles Lane" ("All hail the power of Jesus' name"), used alternately with "Coronation," and regarded as a superior tune to the latter, was composed by William Shrubsole in 1779.

NINETEENTH CENTURY TUNES

The earlier tunes of the nineteenth century began to show evidences of the more modern type of composing, and were more florid in melody than those of the preceding period, using more of the slurred notes. Still wider variety of melody and rhythm is found in this period. More modern tunes include those compositions since 1800. The fuller development of the more modern tune did not come until after 1830, and the leader of such music in America was Lowell Mason.

The tunes of the nineteenth century began to lose some of the ruggedness of the earlier compositions and take on more sinuous melody and softer harmonic chords. Between 1800 and 1830 we find tunes of this character, as "Belmont" from "Sacred Melodies," 1812, by William Gardiner, a florid tune with less virile melody than earlier tunes.

"Mendon," arranged by Samuel Dyer, 1828, is from a German melody and set to different hymns by different hymn book compilers, and its use repeated in the same book so that it does not seem to be wedded, especially to any one hymn.

"Greenland," taken from B. Jacob's "Psalmody," 1819, and arranged from J. Michael Haydn, is sometimes set to an Easter hymn, "The day of resurrection, earth tell it out abroad," and is rich in melody and harmony.

"Monoah" from the Greatorex Collection is another fine melody with pleasing harmony.

The very original compositions follow in the tunes of other men as:

"St. Albinus" by Henry J. Gauntlett in 1852 ("Jesus lives, thy terrors now") is full of vigour. "St. Alphege" and "St. George" by the same composer are characteristic tunes of Gauntlett's.

"Ewing" by Alexander C. Ewing in 1853, written for the words, "For thee, O dear, dear country," is now used as a satisfactory tune to "Jerusalem the golden."

"Aurelia" ("The Church's one foundation") by S. S. Wesley, a grandson of Charles Wesley, and one of the best musicians of his day, gives us a specially fine tune.

We come now to the more widely developed type of tune by the versatile writers of the Victorian Period, or the last half of the nineteenth century. Here are a large number of tunes, common to all hymnals by such well-known writers as Henry Smart, George J. Elvey, Edward J. Hopkins, William Henry Monk, John B. Dykes, Joseph Barnby, and the two later composers, John Stainer and Arthur S. Sullivan.

Smart and Elvey show some degree of the robust character of the earlier English tunes. But the change from the singing of psalm versions to more general use of hymns of the more intimate and personal type was reflected in the tunes to be sung to them. Smart, the prominent London organist, wrote "Regent Square" ("Christ is made the sure Foundation"), a vigorous and singable tune. So also his tune "Pilgrims" ("Hark, hark my soul, angelic songs are swelling") is a beautiful and more quiet type of music. "Lancashire" is also a favourite, being set to various hymns in the hymnals.

Sir George Elvey's "Windsor" ("Come, ye thankful people, come") and his "Diademata" ("Crown Him with many crowns") are both strong tunes, well-suited to their texts.

Dr. Edward J. Hopkins's tune, called either "Ellers" or "Benediction" ("Saviour, again to Thy dear name we raise"), is a general favourite of a quiet and graceful type. "Athanasius" ("Sing, O sing this blessed morn") is a typical nineteenth century tune by Hopkins.

Among these composers who did most to set the style of the modern hymn tune are Monk, Dykes and Barnby. Monk was musical editor of "Hymns Ancient and Modern," which was and is the most widely used hymn book in the world.

Monk's tunes are graceful, tuneful, and reflect intimately the spirit of the text. There are few greater favourites than his "Eventide" to "Abide with me." Doctor Monk wrote this tune at a time of great sorrow, which further shows its appropriate union with Lyte's solemn words. His wife writes that when the fading rays of an evening sun ended, he took a piece of paper and pencilled the tune which has gone over all the earth. It is claimed to be an almost perfect hymn tune, not only in its adaptation to its words but its high quality of melody and splendid harmony. The above-mentioned tune, together with Monk's "Coronae" ("Look, ye saints, the sight is glorious") and his "Unde et Memores" ("And now, O Father, mindful of the love") show a varied musical style, deservedly popular.

Rev. John B. Dykes and Sir Joseph Barnby are leaders in the modern style of lines which sympathetically interpret their texts. Although now frequently criticized as being over-sentimental, some of these tunes have sinuous melody and softer harmonies with a chromatic tendency. The tunes of these two musicians have had extensive popularity on both sides of the Atlantic; yet recent hymn books in England are using fewer of their tunes than formerly.

Dykes, precentor at Durham Cathedral, produced his "Nicæa" ("Holy, holy, holy"); "Lux Benigna" ("Lead, kindly Light"); "St. Cuthbert" ("Our blest Redeemer, ere He breathed"); and "Melita" ("Eternal Father, strong to save"), all general favourites. His "Vox Dilecti" ("I heard the voice of Jesus say") and

"St. Andrew of Crete" ("Christian, dost thou see them"), both have dramatic contrasts between the opening part in a minor key, followed by the major key. Barnby succeeded Gounod as conductor of the Royal Albert Hall Choral Society. We must be more discriminating with him than with Dykes, as some of Barnby's tunes are beautiful and have general popularity, yet a goodly portion of his are not so suitable for congregational praise, and belong to what is called "choir tunes," better suited to choir singing because of their complex or chromatic harmonies.

His "Merrial" ("Now the day is over") has been very popular; also "Laudes Domini" ("When morning gilds the skies"). One of the last tunes Barnby wrote, "Crossing the Bar" ("Sunset and evening star"), is a very unusual and extended tune, requiring all four verses of its hymn to sing it through and is a majestic and beautiful piece of music, of greatly varied melody and beautiful harmony, but suited only for choir singing.

His "Cloisters" ("Lord of our life, and God of our salvation") is a fine tune. "Paradise" is a strong yet easily singable tune and has become a widely popular melody, especially for burial services.

Sir John Stainer and Sir Arthur S. Sullivan were the youngest of these leading Victorian church musicians, both of whom lived to the end of the nineteenth century. Stainer succeeded Sir John Goss as organist at St. Paul's, London, and there improved the music of that historic cathedral. His music has been more used in England than in America. His tune "Crucifixion" is from his famous oratorio, "Crucifixion," and is well fitted to "In the cross of Christ I glory," and is more of the older type of music; while "Blessed Home" ("There is a blessed home") follows the later type, more characteristic of Barnby's music.

"Charity" has more strength and lasting qualities than the preceding, and is sung to "Gracious Spirit, Holy Ghost." His "Beati," sometimes called "All Saints" or "Rest" ("The saints of God their conflict past"), is a fine tune possessing both splendid melody and harmony. Stainer has also arranged good tunes from earlier musical sources which are valuable for use.

Sullivan wrote a variety of music, both sacred and secular, including symphonic overtures and light opera. In a close music contest, when a young man, he finally won over the older musician and nearest rival, Joseph Barnby. He was a master of melody and was hardly excelled in orchestration. Some of his tunes excel, while others are close to the ordinary, but most are popular because so tuneful. "Lux Eoi" to the Easter hymn, "Alleluia, hearts and voices heavenward raise," is one of his best tunes and deserving of high recognition.

Two more are popular Easter hymn tunes: "St. Kelvin" ("Come, ye faithful, raise the strain") and "Fortunatus" ("Welcome, happy morning"). "St. Edmund" to "Nearer, my God, to Thee" is superior to Mason's tune which has long been wed to this old hymn, but Sullivan's may some day lead in usage. "Hanford" ("Jesus, my Saviour, look on me") is a pathetic and ultra-expressive type of tune. "St. Gertrude" to "Onward, Christian soldiers" is very popular and its hymn is widely used, but it is a very ordinary melody and its rhythm is not the best type for hymn tunes. A better tune for this hymn is the Welsh melody, "Rachie."

There are other splendid tunes written during the latter half of the nineteenth century, and a search through the new hymnals will reveal them.

St. Christopher ("O Lamb of God, still keep me") and "Rest" ("Dear Lord and Father of mankind"), both by Frederick C. Maker, are much beloved by the average worshipper.

"Waltham" ("Fling out the banner"), "Nox Præcessit" ("Spirit divine, attend our prayers") and "Sefton," less known, are worthy tunes by J. Baptiste Calkin. Notable among these tunes are "St. Asaph" ("Through the night of doubt and sorrow") by W. S. Bainbridge, "St. Margaret" ("O Love that wilt not let me go") by A. L. Peace, "Watermouth" ("O Saviour, precious Saviour") by A. H. Mann, "Marion" ("Rejoice, ye pure in heart") by A. H. Messiter, "Maryton" ("O Master, let me walk with Thee") by H. Percy Smith, "Festal Song" ("Rise up, O men of God") by William H. Walter, "Petra" ("Go to dark Gethsemane") by Richard Redhead and many other worthy nineteenth century tunes which are left unnamed here.

AMERICAN TUNES

When taking up American tunes we do not find an extensive list of important tunes, nor do we have such able contributors to hymn music as to American hymn poetry. The most famous composer is Lowell Mason, and next to him is the late Horatio Parker, although his fame as a tune writer is not nearly so wide. The compositions of other Americans are for the most part very ordinary in quality. The first attempts worthy of mention were made in New England where not content to depend entirely on imported tunes, original composition was begun. Among the first was William Billings, born in Boston in 1746, an uneducated tanner by trade, who was more interested in music. Self taught only, he began to train choirs, and his tunes became popular in those days of the Revolutionary War. His best known tune was "Chester," a patriotic type of song, often played by fifers in the army. His chief contemporary was Oliver Holden whose tune, "Coronation," ("All hail the power of Jesus' name") is the oldest American tune in common use to-day.

The first worthy attempts of composition in our country were those of Thomas Hastings and Lowell Mason, who together prepared the first American hymn and tune book of lasting worth. Hastings wrote hymns as seen in a preceding chapter, but his musical work was that of elevating the church music of his day. He wrote many hymn tunes, some of them under a *nom-de-plume*. A few of his tunes are often sung to-day, as his "Toplady" ("Rock of Ages"), "Ortonville" ("Majestic sweetness sits enthroned") and "Retreat" ("From every stormy wind that blows").

But more than the good work of Hastings in his day is the superior work of Lowell Mason. His first conspicuous musical work was the "Handel and Haydn Collection of Sacred Music," published by the famous Handel and Haydn Society without the use of his modest name, many thousand copies being sold. Later, other pretentious musical works of his were published with very wide circulation. Mason has done more than any other American to elevate sacred song and was the most outstanding tune composer in America. He wrote many suitable tunes of his own composition, and gave us many arrangements from classic sources. The hymn books since his day have contained many of his tunes, although the new hymnals have fewer of them.

Among his best are "Hamburg" ("When I survey the wondrous cross") and "Olmutz" ("And let our bodies part"), arrangements from Gregorian tones.

His original "Missionary Hymn" ("From Greenland's icy mountains"), "Bethany" ("Nearer, my God, to Thee") and "Olivet" ("My faith looks up to Thee") have been very widely sung. They are good examples of simple construction, and well adapted for ordinary usage.

Next after Mason we have William B. Bradbury who has been a prolific composer and his music has appealed much to the popular ear: "Aughton" ("He leadeth me"), "Woodworth" ("Just as I am"), "Bradbury" ("Saviour, like a Shepherd lead us") and his arrangement of an English folk song are all acceptable to the average church-goer, and are widely sung, doubtless partly because of the popularity of the hymns to which they are set.

A little later we have few American compositions, except arrangements and adaptations of music from earlier sources.

William F. Sherwin wrote some very acceptable tunes. His "Chautauqua" ("Day is dying in the west") is a deservedly popular song and much used. "Bread of Life" by him as set to another of Mary Lathbury's hymns, "Break Thou the bread of life, Dear Lord," is a tune very appropriate to the words of its hymn.

Richard S. Willis has given us a very popular tune, "Carol," which will long be remembered, as it is set to one of our favourite Christmas carols, "It came upon the midnight clear."

There are two others, who were English born, but whose life and work were completed in America. First, Rev. J. S. B. Hodges of Baltimore, whose "Eucharistic Hymn" ("Bread of the world in mercy broken") and "Hodges" ("O day of rest and gladness") are favourite tunes of many people. Second, Dr. Arthur H. Messiter, organist and choir-master of old Trinity Church, New York City, has given us a much beloved processional tune, "Marion" ("Rejoice, ye pure in heart").

Among more recent composers there is another outstanding name, Horatio W. Parker of Yale, regarded as second only to Lowell Mason, as one giving most serious efforts to writing hymn tunes. He chose imposing and vigorous hymns for which to write his tunes. His melodies are virile, with rather wide vocal range, and his harmonies are strong and effective. Among his typical tunes are: "Stella" ("All my heart this night rejoices"), a growing favourite carol; "Jubilate," to Wesley's "Rejoice the Lord is King," is another vigorous tune and interesting melody; "Courage," set to "Fight the good fight," is another strong tune but of difficult vocal range; "Garden City," in contrast to most of his tunes ("Our day of praise is done"), is a beautiful Sunday vesper hymn of subdued spirit; "Pro Patria" ("God of our fathers, whose almighty hand") is well adapted to this patriotic hymn; "Mount Zion," set to Tate and Brady's version of the 122nd Psalm, is another vigorous tune with unusual melody and harmony.

The late Dr. Peter C. Lutkin of Northwestern University, Evanston, has many tunes in the 1905 Methodist Episcopal Hymnal, but to-day the two outstanding tunes are "Lanier" ("Into the woods my Master went"), which is an unusual melody in the minor key, and his "Carman," set to "Come, my soul, thou must be waking," which is a fine tune in free rhythm. His "Benediction," set to the benediction hymn, "The Lord bless you and keep you," is necessarily irregular, but a beautiful piece of music, and especially impressive as interpreted by the Boston University Choral Art Society.

RECENT TUNES AND ARRANGEMENTS

When we come to recent compositions and tendencies in hymn tunes we note there is a partial return to the older type of music, the chorale and plain song, and especially to adaptations of folk songs of different periods and of different countries. The present trend in hymn tunes may be summed up as follows:

I. The revival of English and other folk songs and their adaptations to hymns. For example: "Forest Green," an English traditional melody ("Thy word is like a garden, Lord"), which is now much recognized and set to different hymns in different hymnals; "Terra Beata" ("This is my Father's world") is an old English melody arranged by F. L. Sheppard and is a tuneful and joyful melody; "Prince Rupert" ("Onward, Christian soldiers") is an old English march arranged by Gustav Holst.

II. The revival of German and other chorales with special featuring of the Bach harmonizations, as "Innsbruck," a traditional German melody, ascribed to Heinrich Isaak with harmonies by Bach; "Sleepers Wake" ("Wake, awake, for night is flying") is an old German melody by Philipp Nicolai, harmonized by Bach; "Salzburg" is another German melody from Jacob Hintze, harmonized by Bach, and set to "At the Lamb's high feast we sing."

III. The increasing use of plain song and chant, or unmetrical singing by congregations, as: "Veni Sancte Spiritus" ("Come, Holy Spirit, come") is an old plain song of the eleventh century; "Ecce Jam Noctis" ("Ah, holy Jesus, how hast Thou offended") is an old Sarum plain song and has been ably harmonized by Winfred Douglas.

IV. The introduction of discant and faux-bourdon into hymn tunes and chorales. For example: "O God, our help in ages past," the old tune of "St. Anne," arranged with faux-bourdon by Martin Shaw with melody in the tenor as in the old chorales; "Old Hundredth" ("All people that on earth do dwell"), also arranged with faux-bourdon by J. Dowland in "Ravenscroft Psalter" (1621) and now restored to use in the English book, "Songs of

Praise"; the "Austrian Hymn" ("Glorious things of thee are spoken") has an alternate version in discant by F. H. Ingram.

V. The active interest of contemporary composers in writing new hymn tunes of high musical quality; although it should not be forgotten that it is difficult to write new tunes, considering the large number of tunes of the various types contributed in the past centuries.

Among the able compositions of recent tunes, first note: "Sine Nomine" ("For all the saints who from their labours rest") by R. Vaughan-Williams, which is regarded as one of the best of twentieth century tunes. It is a vigourous tune, and a fine example of a useful tune.

"Miles Animosus" ("Stand up, stand up, for Jesus") by Geoffrey Shaw is another example of a vigourous tune of lasting worth. But Webb's very familiar tune has a strong hold on people from long usage.

"Comavon" ("The lone, wild fowl in lofty flight") is a new tune to a new hymn. The tune was written by Philip James, and is another type to be sung with less vigour in the minor key, but with true feeling.

"Ora Labora" ("Come, labour on, who dares stand idle") by T. Tertius Noble, is becoming recognized as a worthy tune and, like others of its kind, is better for unison singing. It is more tuneful than many other tunes to the untrained ear.

"St. Dunstan's" ("He who would valiant be") by Canon Winfred Douglas, is a fine example of a fine tune and very singable. It has become a great favourite with many people.

TESTS OF SUITABLE TUNES

The tests of a good tune, suitable for congregational praise, rest upon different elements therein. As the fact of long continued usage helps to determine the worth of a hymn, so does continued usage for several decades help to determine the value of a tune, although usage may not be regarded as an infallible test. Such poor types of popular songs as " 'Taint go'nta rain no more," "The Isle of Capri" and "The music goes 'round and 'round" will have their little day, but will soon die, or should die quickly and never be resurrected. But Schumann's "Traumerei" and Dvorak's "Largo" will surely live long.

The author's own experience will illustrate the point in question. When a theological student he heard a fellow-student in a parlour, near his room, play on a small reed organ a fine hymn tune, five or six days a week, for several months. At the end of the school year, instead of being tired of hearing the constant repetition of the same tune, he only loved and appreciated the tune more than when he first heard it. On the other hand, not long afterward, the author was attending a summer conference in the middle west, when a new Gospel Song was used several times a day for a few days. This at first seemed to be an appealing and catchy melody, but before the end of a week, when he was standing outside the large auditorium, this same oft-repeated song was started again, and it drove him up over the nearby hill to get away from its sound.

So the good tune will bear frequent repetition, while the cheap tune, even though at first somewhat pleasing, will soon fail to appeal if often repeated. But there are other more definite tests.

II. The tune must be tuneful. It should have a distinctive melody, readily recognized by the ear, and not supplanted by rhythm, such as the present-day cheap jazz, which has excessive rhythm and little or no recognizable melody. A tune which looks like a vocal exercise running up and down the scale is not tuneful.

III. The tune should have moderate range for congregational singing. If the tune has too low-pitched or too high-pitched notes for the average voice, it is not suitable for church services. Nor should the tune have sustained notes in the higher range. A tune running at or near the top of the staff for several successive phrases will induce flatting.

IV. Extreme intervals, especially if frequently used between successive notes, are not practical, as octaves, sevenths, augmented fourths; and even sixths in certain relations are not easy for congregations to sing.

V. Tunes should be adapted to the hymns. In other words the accents of the hymn and the tune need to coincide to a reasonable degree at least. Having the same metre for a hymn and tune is no assurance that they will fit in accent. When the beat of the time comes on the wrong accent of the poem, the tune is not adaptable. This is why the good tune to one hymn is often unsuitable to some other hymn of the same metre.

VI. Tunes with too florid counterpoint are unsuitable for congregational singing because they demand independent reading and a balance of parts beyond the capacity of the ordinary singer. There is also a consciousness of notation rather than a freedom from musical form as such, and the words are almost necessarily obscured.

Finally, a word should be said about the rate in which tunes should be sung. Some congregations have the regular habit of dragging the tune, and *sometimes organists encourage* such by holding too long the last note of each line. This interferes with good singing. On the other hand, it is equally bad, or even worse, to sing speedily through the song, as if it should have so-called "pep" to hold the interest of the young. Such undue speed in sacred song is poor praise, if not actually irreverent.

Some hymnals indicate the metronome rate at beginning of the music at which the tune should be sung, and these indicative figures are helpful. Also the character of the text helps to determine the speed (as mentioned in first of this chapter). The meditative or prayerful hymn should not be speedily sung, neither should the joyful or processional hymn be dragged, or too slowly rendered. The too common tendency of singing most hymns at almost the same rate is to be much deprecated, for there should be variety in tempo of hymn tunes, as we expect variety, and not monotony, in almost every other human endeavour.

In concluding we should utter a word of encouragement to able musicians and composers to give serious effort to the production of new tunes, even though the task is not easy. Especially should they endeavour to furnish new tunes for new hymns, and not force new hymns to seek tunes from among the old familiar music long associated with old favourite hymns.

For Further Reading on Church Music and Hymn Tunes

Music in the Church, Peter C. Lutkin.

Church Music and Worship, Earl E. Harper.

Musical Ministries in the Church, Waldo S. Pratt.

The Music and Hymnody of the Methodist Hymnal, Carl F. Price.

American Writers and Compilers of Sacred Music, Frank J. Metcalf.

Excursions in Musical History, Helena A. Dickinson.

Music in the History of the Western Church, Edward Dickinson.

Oxford History of Music, "Evolution of the Art of Music," C. Hubert Parry.

Studies in Worship Music, J. Spencer Curwen.

Hymn-Tunes and Their Story, James T. Lightwood.

Practical Church Music, Edmund S. Lorenz.

Manual of English Church Music, George Gardner, Sydney H. Nicholson.

The Hymns of the Breviary and Missal, Matthew Britt.

Catholic Church Worship, R. R. Terry.

Northwestern University Bulletins on Church Music (Northwestern University Press).

The History of Music, Waldo S. Pratt.

Grove's Dictionary of Music and Musicians.

Stories of Hymn Tunes, Frank J. Metcalf.

Hand Book to the Hymnal (Presbyterian Board of Christian Education).

Handbook to the Church Hymnary, James Moffatt.

Music and Worship, Davies and Grace.

Church Music in History and Practicc, Winfred Douglas.

SUBJECT INDEX

INDEX OF AUTHORS

INDEX TO FIRST LINES

Printed in the United States of America

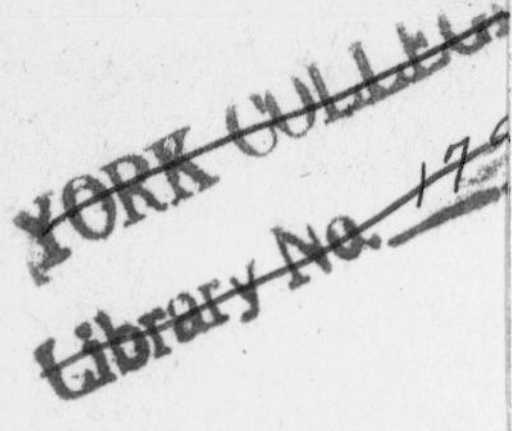

THE RISE AND GROWTH OF ENGLISH HYMNODY

By HARVEY B. MARKS, M.A.

Prof. H. Augustine Smith says:

"Rev. Harvey B. Marks has achieved a most timely book, admirable for fire-side reading, rich in values for the pulpit, balanced and accurate for the class-room. Every page has a certain livingness, growing out of the author's preaching and pastoral duties, out of travel and wide acquaintanceship, out of a genuine love for music and poetry, out of a persistent charm in winning folks to the church and to religion.

"These pages, first of all, are balanced; the ancient, mediaeval, near-modern, and present day lyrics each receiving simple and forceful treatment without undue emphasis anywhere. Again and again practical hymnody and liturgics come to the fore in timely suggestions to clergy and choir on what to do with hymns.

"His intriguing instructions found throughout the book are timely and delightful."

FOURTH EDITION